Defining Jamaican Fiction

DEFINING JAMAICAN FICTION

Marronage and the

Discourse of Survival

Barbara Lalla

The University of Alabama Press

Tuscaloosa and London

Library of Congress Cataloging-in-Publication Data.

Lalla, Barbara, 1949–
    Defining Jamaican fiction :   marronage and the discourse of
survival / Barbara Lalla.
        p.   cm.
    Includes bibliographical references (p.   ) and index.
    ISBN 0-8173-0782-6 (alk. paper)
    1. Jamaican fiction—History and criticism.   2. English fiction—
Jamaica—History and criticism.   3. Literature and society—
Jamaica.   4. Social isolation in literature.   5. Fugitive slaves in
literature.   6. Maroons in literature.   7. Jamaica—In literature.
8. Blacks in literature.   I. Title.
PR9265.4.L35   1996
813.009ŋ97292—dc20   95-31869
                                                            CIP

British Library Cataloguing-in-Publication Data available

For Jean D'Costa

They were tantalized by the conviction that immediately beyond the walls of opaque blue—on the horizon's edge, if only they could get there—they would find waves running before the wind, curling at their crests with a hiss of spray, and a sky loud with swooping birds that shrieked beautiful and reassuring discords.

—John Hearne, *The Sure Salvation*

Contents

Acknowledgments

I N PREPARING THIS book I have relied heavily on materials in the University of the West Indies libraries at St. Augustine and at Mona and in the National Library of Jamaica. I am also indebted to the British Library and the New York Public Library for substantial material. Several people have assisted me in accessing material, and I am particularly indebted to John Aarons, director of the National Library of Jamaica.

In addition, various scholarly journals permitted me to draw on material from earlier articles. I am grateful to MELUS for the material from "Dungeons of the Soul," in MELUS, copyright © MELUS, The Society for the Study of the Multi-Ethnic Literature of the United States; to JWIL for the material from "Unmasking Deviance: Theme and Language," Journal of West Indian Literature, Vol. 7, No. 1, copyright © 1994 by JWIL; and to CARIB for material from "Intercultural Communication," CARIB (Journal of the Association for Commonwealth Literature and Language Studies), No. 6, copyright © WIACLALS. I also am thankful for permission to quote from the following: *The Lunatic*, by Anthony Winkler, used by permission of Kingston Publishers, copyright © Kingston Publishers, 1987; *The Sure Salvation*, by John Hearne, 1985, used by permission of Faber and Faber Ltd., David Higham Associates, and the Estate of John Hearne; and *Wide Sargasso Sea*, by Jean Rhys, used by permission of Penguin Books Ltd., London, UK, 1968, first published by André Deutsch 1966, copyright © Jean Rhys, 1966.

Finally, I must express my appreciation for the study leave and grants from the University of the West Indies that made the research possible and for useful discussions with Professor Gordon Rohlehr of the University of the West Indies (St. Augustine) and Professor Jean D'Costa of Hamilton College (Clinton, New York). The support, understanding, and encouragement of my family and friends have been more than I can possibly acknowledge.

Defining Jamaican Fiction

1

The Dimensions of
Marronage in Jamaica

Time is one distance; space another; and how you see things, yet another.
—Velma Pollard, *Considering Woman*

DISTANCE. From the earliest appearance of Jamaica and Jamaican characters in English fiction to current creations by Jamaican authors, a sense
of distance has contributed to the definition of characters as Jamaican or to
the experience of setting as Jamaican. Quite apart from spatial references to
the geographical distance of the island world, authors have anchored
fictional discourses in the perspectives of narrators and characters who are
remote from crucial points of reference such as their homes, their communities, or civilization as they perceive it. Temporal distances have been variously conveyed but are pivotal to engagement with the past, a definitive feature of Caribbean writing.

The narrator's authority over the events related and the involvement of
the narrator in these events have varied to facilitate this sense of distance.
Authors have controlled their readers' involvement in events to achieve a
number of effects. Some have conveyed the remoteness of the fictional character or the fictional world from the reader; others have entangled the reader
in the alienation of that fictional character or world. The distances are not
only of space and time but of values and worldview.

A compelling character in the story of Jamaica itself is that of the
Maroon. The story of the Jamaican Maroons has been related from various
points of view, and recent scholarship has documented it so well that it is not
necessary to repeat it in this book. Initially, the perspective on these Maroons
was that of the infuriated plantocracy and frustrated officialdom whose lifestyle the runaway slaves rejected through escape and guerrilla warfare so
that they could embrace an arduous but free existence in the mountainous
interior of the island. Such frustration and hostility characterizes the attitude
of historians such as Bryan Edwards and of novelists such as the anonymous

writer of *Marly; or, the Life of a Planter in Jamaica*. Alternative, less biased, yet still external views survive in early histories such as that of Robert Dallas. Similarly dispassionate in tone, *The Diary of George Ross* records an officer's journey with Jamaican Maroons who were transported to Nova Scotia and later moved to Sierra Leone. Yet the gap between the observer and his subjects remains unbridgeable. Modern studies, such as those of Carey Robinson, H. Orlando Patterson, and Richard Price, have taken different points of departure and varied in emphasis from folkloric celebration to sociological commentary and historical analysis. Mavis Campbell's recent history takes "the mode of narrative and analysis," piecing together minutiae of what she fittingly describes as "the Maroon saga" (12). Carey Robinson terms their audacious resistance "the great Jamaican epic" and claims that "it strongly influenced the character of the Jamaican people" (*Iron Thorn* v).

The story of the Maroons certainly seizes on the Caribbean imagination—nowhere more so than in Jamaica. As fictional personae the Maroons continue to weave in and out of oral and literary tales as central and ancient characters of the Jamaican heritage. Moreover, attributes of the maroon character (lowercased to distinguish it from the historical Maroons) surface in other character types that crowd the island's literary history—resentful strangers, travelers, and fugitives; desperate waifs and strays; traumatized or spaced-out recluses, rejects, women in states of dissociation, wild men, and outcasts; rebels in physical or psychological wildernesses.

The attributes of marronage include withdrawal, displacement, exile, and isolation on the one hand but involve resistance, endurance, and survival on the other. That authors should recurrently draw on these features to create Jamaican characters is unsurprising when one considers that Jamaica's history of resistance to oppression is more relentless and more violent than that of any other Caribbean island. The maroon's definitive action is withdrawal from the mainstream of civilization as defined by others, into the wilderness, to make a last stand for freedom.

In Campbell's view, "that some of the Maroon societies exist today . . . is due to atavistic stubbornness. . . . It is the abstract notion of this history exemplified by their Treaties and lands, sacrosanct to them and inalienable, that has fed this stubbornness. It has given them a perception of themselves that borders on 'the chosen' " (260). Price notes that, since the mid–eighteenth century, the treaties brought the Maroons into increasing contact with the rest of Jamaican society, and he suggests that such interchange fostered creolization of Maroon society (228). Perhaps this interchange also accounts in part for the fact that consciousness of their distinct heritage overflows the actual Maroon communities and is upheld by other Jamaicans, who view this

Maroon heritage with shared pride and who treat their saga of resistance as a national treasure.

The cultural dimensions of marronage include traditions that are both nonfictional, in the sense that they are documented in traditional histories, and fictional, in the sense that they compose episodes in imaginative works. In either case, marronage involves a character in a dialectic of escape and rejection and of violent resistance and violent pursuit. Equally important, if not more so, is the fact that marronage requires deviation from the norm, imposes dislocation, and proposes an alternative community. Thus, it adjusts perspective, switches points of departure, and reevaluates established propositions to reveal additional or alternative truths.

Approaching a Literature of Resistance

This book focuses not on the Maroon as a sociohistorical phenomenon but on the developing persona of the maroon as a character type in creative literature. More specifically, this work concentrates on the perspective of marronage. Where the definitive features of a persona are perspectival, it is useful to discuss this persona in both critical and linguistic terms. It is important to consider literary and linguistic categories that govern directional and conceptual orientation. Thus, the analysis that follows supplements traditional tools of critical analysis by some recourse to linguistics and discourse analysis. However, this recourse is eclectic. Its purpose is integrative and so avoids technical jargon as far as possible. Nevertheless, although this study does not pursue linguistics and discourse analysis for their own sake, it presupposes the view that exploring literary discourse in the anglophone Caribbean extends the scope of Caribbean language study and the applications of Creole linguistics.

Definitive features of literary discourse also assist in defining the literature and assist critical analysis in objectively discussing the conceptual level at which worldviews and value systems exist. In addition, observing a specifically Jamaican point of view draws attention to national as well as regional parameters of literature in the Caribbean and enlarges our current vision of Jamaican culture.

Terry Eagleton takes the position that societies define literature on the basis of value judgments that are themselves historically variable, clearly related as they are to social ideologies and to assumptions by which certain social groups exercise and maintain power over others (12–16). This work also adopts a theory of discourse that is culture based, a theory that resists a trend to divorce literature from other cultural and social practices and especially resists dissociation of literary criticism from language analysis.

Gordon Rohlehr describes the revolution of self-perception in the Caribbean as a resistance to stereotyping, to prefabricated identity imposed on the dominated by the dominant. He defines a Caribbean "self in marronage" in terms of violent resistance and of preservation of African traditions ("Articulating" 2). Among the defining traits of revolutionary self-assertion he includes a literature that involves "constant, complex exploration of the no-longer-submerged inner self; the no-longer marooned personality." As the title of his work proclaims, Rohlehr's concern is one of "articulating a Caribbean aesthetic," defining a regional rather than a national literature. In this book I will attempt to distinguish a national fiction within the Caribbean aesthetic, especially as defined by discourse strategies for conveying perspective.

To analyze Jamaican literature is to approach a discourse provoked by exclusion, a discourse that challenges forces that attempt to control or subordinate. Not surprisingly, this discourse has a substantial feminist presence and a growing body of working-class writing that is strengthened by strong oral traditions and is now reaching the reading public through action groups such as Sistren. Yet the concerns of traditional humanism for the imperishable truths of the human condition and the uniqueness of the individual are by no means irrelevant to all current Jamaican writing. Not all traditional humanism need be written off as suburban moral ideology and thus as "imperial." As Eagleton notes, "Political argument is not an alternative to moral preoccupations; it is these preoccupations taken seriously in their full implications" (208).

Jamaican literature transgresses and defamiliarizes some received codes but confirms and reinscribes others. Literary canons in any society are ideologically fixed, and the value systems of texts in such canons are invariably rooted in the history and in the power interests of that society. So too a growing canon of Caribbean literature (of which Jamaican literature is part) is ideologically fixed, and anticolonialism is no longer avant-garde but is growing received, rooted, and entrenched in the value systems of these emerging societies, even as much British tradition continues deep rooted. Canons to the right and left, Jamaican literature resists the loss of its own identity in the regional literature.

Recent developments in literature as a whole have been essentially revolutionary. Current movements, in Sylvia Wynter's view, constitute an epoch-making departure from epistemes entrenched by rigorous, schoollike modes of thought even as this previous epoch itself (liberal humanism) emerged from the European Middle Ages. Jamaican writers are acutely conscious of the "alterability of our governing codes" (Wynter, "Afterword: Beyond" 365). There is in Jamaican literary resistance to canonism a commitment or impulse to break parameters of thought prescribed by epistemes. Current writers such as Michelle Cliff recognize in the summons of the *abeng* a call to break bonds and boundaries, to rupture epistemes, to elect the Jamaican non-elect, to reject master codes, and to disorder and reorder existing imperatives. At the same time, not all Jamaican writing, either creative or critical, is impelled by anti-imperial rage such as Michelle Cliff expresses: "I enjoyed writing this, playing with rhyme and language—it was like spitting in their cultural soup" (*The Land of Look Behind* 14). A number of Jamaican writers are more quietly engaged in their own indigenous creations.

This book is divided into two parts. The first major section inspects alienation in Jamaica, but most of the personae who experience or observe this alienation perceive Jamaica from the outside in. Moreover, most of the authors of these texts are almost certainly non-Jamaican, although some texts are anonymous, so their provenance remains in doubt. Chapter 2 analyzes nineteenth-century texts written from a Eurocentric authorial view. The third chapter traces what we may regard as a parallel view. An author from elsewhere in the Caribbean, the Dominican Jean Rhys, reconstructs the past of a Jamaican character familiar from the British literary canon. The second major section of this book looks inside out as postcolonial Jamaican authors rewrite various aspects of Caribbean experience or create anew from the vacuum of a history exposed as myth. In many ways, the latter approaches imply a reinterpretation of traditional history (nonfiction) as fiction and offer fiction to reconstruct truth; in this sense, they conform to Caribbean postcolonial vision. However, this work also receives its impetus from a sense of an indigenous and distinct literary discourse of Jamaica. Thus, the fourth chapter traces the theme of marronage, essentially through spatial elements of discourse, in a broad spectrum of texts, with special consideration of Erna Brodber's *Myal* and Olive Senior's "Country of the One-Eye God" (*Summer Lightning*). Although ideological and psychological orientations are implied by these perceptual features, the fifth and sixth chapters take up these conceptual planes of perspective in some detail. Chapter 5 explores the psychological dimensions of marronage in the writing of Anthony Winkler, and chapter 6 interrelates spatiotemporal, psychological, and ideological planes of perspective in John Hearne's *The Sure Salvation*. The final chapter draws together definitive features of the discourse of marronage with a consideration of Brodber's *Jane and Louisa Will Soon Come Home* and weighs the significance of Jamaican language to an indigenous perspective.

The most difficult limit to set and maintain has been the restriction to prose fiction. Outcast and alienated personae occur across genres, but where they appear to vary most in treatment between verse and prose is in the earliest literature. Because the study begins with the first fiction set in Jamaica, it may be as well to distinguish the strategies for conveying selfhood and alienation in local eighteenth- and nineteenth-century verse from those of the prose of this time, fiction that novelists framed in a Jamaican setting.

The genres of prose fiction and poetry have quite separate beginnings in Jamaica.[1] A representative sample of early prose and verse including most of the verse referred to below is available in collection (D'Costa and Lalla, *Voices in Exile*). Rooted in this local verse rather than in the essentially European fiction set in Jamaica are concerns that eventually occupy local writers of Jamaican fiction.

An eighteenth-century Jamaican poet, Francis Williams, finds himself (as a free black, educated at Cambridge University) isolated by combined social, emotional, and intellectual barriers. He distinguishes physical from spiritual confinement and separates human vulnerability (regardless of class or condition) from the limitless potential of the human imagination. This conflict lies at the center of a remarkable double vision, the image of the human condition as a universal prison in which the wisest perceive the eternally receding horizons of the human spirit. Williams's tone, bitter but unchastened, echoes eighteenth-century satire yet heralds romantic vision in his preoccupation with fearless intellectual wondering "beyond the world's strong prison gate." He also reflects the stark reality of the black Jamaican's experience:

> every island's but a prison
> Strongly guarded by the sea.

Within the context of spiritual salvation and by ignoring barriers of class and race, the liberated soul finds eloquent expression in one other literary creation of eighteenth century Jamaica. The first oratorio composed in the Western Hemisphere articulates the cry of Jonah from the belly of the whale. Pamela O'Gorman preserves both verse and musical score by Samuel Felsted, who selected from Christian tradition one of its most poignant symbols of the alienated, submerged soul. Felsted's *Jonah* (1775) expresses physical entrapment and powerlessness, together with emotional turmoil, dispossession, and failure. Yet he reaches "Out of the deep . . . "

Eighteenth-century verse from the slaves' perspective voices complaint from the dislocated soul (Moreton 153) or reveals the predicaments of racial and sexual entrapment (Moreton 155). Nineteenth-century verse begins to convey the urgency of changing one's place in the system. In a song to "me good friend, Mr Wilberforce," revolution erupts through expressions of "will" and innuendos of "force" in implications that there "will be force," all entangled in punning on the name of the champion of emancipation (Matthew G. Lewis 228). Spiritual escape through death and traditional yearnings for afterlife in Guinea no longer suffice. There is cold comfort in graveside reassurance about blissful return to Africa and separation from the forces of oppression (Scott 1:219; Madden 1:39–40).

Current Caribbean verse revisits the point at which impatience reaches its limit and tension ruptures in violence. The birth of this spirit of resistance, blazing in the nineteenth-century "Song of the King of the Eboes" (Lewis 228), forces us to review apparent acceptance or helplessness of tone in other early songs. One such song is the otherwise pathetic cry of the ill or disabled slave whose master dumps him in a gully. Intertextuality sensitizes the reader to an ominous echo behind the pathos in the voice of the thrown-away slave: "Oh! massa, massa! me no deadee yet!" (Lewis 322).

Such resistance may be followed to the present day. Carolyn Cooper presents current Jamaican oral culture as transgressive discourse, as subversion of colonially entrenched literary values and practices. In this sense her survey offers valuable insights into the history of Jamaican discourse. Moreover, Cooper's description of popular reaction as "low theory" challenges the very idea of canonicity, pointing to derisive songs of the eighteenth and nineteenth centuries as a strategy for inverting tragic exploitation and hostility to produce comedy at the expense of the exploiter. Cooper roots a creolizing movement that develops into a national popular culture in this early transformation of loss and oppression by ridicule.

In this pre–twentieth century period of literature in Jamaica, most extant verse is folk song and so preserves the perspective of slaves and a voice that is not only dislocated and alienated but also dissatisfied and often antagonistic, foreshadowing the position that Claude McKay describes as being pressed to the wall and "dying but fighting back" (*Selected Poems* 36). In pre–twentieth century verse, free educated blacks who write in the literary tradition are as isolated as the uneducated and for this reason convey the perspective of the outcast. However, they do not articulate resistance to European domination.

It is thus unsurprising that the mainstream of Jamaican nineteenth-century verse is ideologically distinct from the fiction of the time, and it is only in the present century that popular culture begins to gain acceptance in literary prose.

The earliest fiction set in Jamaica is (with the exception of the folktale) almost exclusively written by the British. Indeed, the nineteenth-century fiction has far more in common with nonfiction than with verse of the same period and demonstrates attributes of travelogues and of memoirs that concentrate on social history and domestic manners. In some novels, dialogue displays features of literary debate more regularly than it mirrors realistic oral conversation. The code is essentially British literary standard rather than Jamaican Creole or a standard influenced by Jamaican language.

Jamaican Fiction

The definition of Caribbean literature is in many ways incomplete. Verse, fiction, or drama that is Caribbean in authorship, in characterization, in topic, and in setting is clearly recognizable as Caribbean, but the identification becomes less certain as any of these parameters blurs. For example, when does the work of a Caribbean writer abroad cease to be Caribbean and become immigrant Canadian or (delightful in its nuances) American "ethnic"? Mike Alleyne notes that black British writing "has long since been considered an intrinsic element of the West Indian literary landscape" (1). If the issue of the "Caribbeanness" of black immigrant writing is a pertinent question, it opens a floodgate of others. When does the work of an expatriate resident in the Caribbean become a part of Caribbean literature? Can the work of a visitor ever be so defined? And what if a native Caribbean author selects a setting outside of the Caribbean, creates characters of other nationalities, and explores themes of universal rather than particularly Caribbean relevance? Is a text Caribbean essentially by virtue of some accident of birth?

Inner as well as outer parameters are blurred. To what extent is a text primarily Caribbean rather than, say, Jamaican? It is generally accepted that shared experiences and interests link the creative writing from the several nations of the Caribbean. In *The Womb of Space*, Wilson Harris describes the Caribbean imagination as replacing temporal linearity with spatial plurality as the essential concept for ordering reality. Postcolonial theory observes that the literature inverts "poles of governor-governed, ruler-ruled" and challenges the concept of dominance as the principal regulator of human societies (Ashcroft, Griffiths, and Tiffin 37). While common experiences link the spatially proximate countries of the Caribbean, however, it is by no means obvious that these experiences are otherwise shared. Works by individual authors from throughout the region deal largely with relationships between individual territories and countries or even continents outside of the Caribbean—interactions with Britain, Africa, Canada, India, and the United States. The Caribbean is fragmented not only by physical space but also through a historical absence of psychological unity. Regionalism is real in the sense of a cumulatively unified vision of comparable experience and reaction, but only recently has regionalism been apparent in terms of significant interaction.

In truth, our interest in each other is recent. Indeed, Caribbean literature is also recent—but how recent? Do temporal and spatial parameters exist for defining Caribbean literature? How does the birth of Caribbean literature relate to the appearance of indigenous literatures in individual territories?

Problems of identity are by no means confined to the Caribbean, and we are not likely to solve them entirely. Still, we must progress by taking into account factors of obvious relevance to the definition of a literature. One such factor is the language that is its medium. Pertinent to the definition of Caribbean literature is the question of whether there is a Caribbean literary discourse. This question is too vast to tackle and definitively answer in a book whose focus lies elsewhere, and an exhaustive answer is not the ambition of this work, which explores issues of discourse largely as a supportive and enabling tool for criticism.

Essentially, this pilot study focuses on fiction associated with Jamaica. This approach is not intended as a denial of Caribbean literature, of its reality and wholeness. However, this focus does limit the corpus according to area as well as genre. Selecting Jamaica as a microcosm of a much larger and more varied area has certain advantages. Indeed, both literary and linguistic analyses are readily available, and material pertinent to both literary and linguistic history is accessible.

The most salient reason for a study of Jamaican fiction is its distinctiveness within the overall patterns of regional literary history. Indeed, Caribbean literature begins with conscious effort, in Jamaica, to build a national rather than a regional literature. The All Jamaica Library was a short-lived but valiant effort to establish Jamaican literature at the beginning of the century. Kenneth Ramchand identifies *Becka's Buckra Baby*, by Thomas MacDermot (under the pseudonym Tom Redcam) (1903), as the earliest known work of West Indian prose fiction, which Ramchand defines as fiction by writers born or raised in the West Indies. Actually, a much earlier fiction (by Cyrus Perkins) appeared in the Jamaican *Daily Telegraph and Guardian* in the mid-nineteenth century and will be discussed later. However, Ramchand is no doubt correct in identifying MacDermot as the first creole who practiced as a literary person (52). Indeed, for the first forty years of this century, few of the twenty-eight novels listed in Ramchand's year-by-year bibliography are by non-Jamaican authors. Within this period appears *Banana Bottom* (1933) by Claude McKay, the first West Indian novelist of African descent and the first to go into exile. Ramchand hails *Banana Bottom* as the first substantial novel about West Indian folk experience and the first novel to contain "an achieved West Indian heroine" (14, 259).

Early Jamaican literature seems preoccupied with women and their "situation"—that is, with the realities of their exploitation and resistance. Herbert G. De Lisser's *Jane's Career* (1914) examines a far more fully conceived heroine than any earlier Caribbean novel and presents the first black protagonist—if one discounts the nineteenth-century "Busha's Mistress," by Cyrus Perkins. However, De Lisser's antinationalistic and anti-working-class perspective produces a somewhat fractured vision of the heroine. C. Rhonda Cobham-Sander points out that Jane's desire for security runs counter to working-class political organization against repression ("Women" 202); to ensure security for himself and Jane, Broglie must break the strike. De Lisser concludes with Jane's white wedding and her future as middle-class mistress with her own "schoolgirl" (the term used to denote a junior domestic) to boss about. His sympathy evaporates into ironic amusement at her antics. McKay's heroine, on the other hand, is a consistent and convincing feminine consciousness.

According to Cobham-Sander, "Jamaican literature between 1900 and 1950 is unique within the English-speaking Caribbean in its close documentation of every step in the changing perception of the West Indian woman by its writers" ("Women" 219). Cobham-Sander notes that by 1950 the male protagonist takes over from the female throughout the region and that not until the 1980s do female subjects and themes again become prominent in works by both male and female authors. However, in 1962 there appears *The Hills of Hebron* by Sylvia Wynter, the first black woman novelist of the anglophone Caribbean.

It is commonplace for critics commenting on the literature of exile to present Caribbean literature as beginning in Britain, as C. L. R. James, Edgar Mittelholzer, Samuel Selvon, George Lamming, and Roger Mais arrived in Britain between 1932 and 1951. By then, according to Ramchand, "the deluge had begun" (74). However, Jamaican literature begins in Jamaica, an assertion that does not divorce it from Caribbean literature but rather deepens understanding of Caribbean literature by sensitivity to its composition. Ramchand distinguishes black Commonwealth literature from that of the white Commonwealth literature by arguing that "the synthetic principle ignores too many social, cultural and political differences between the countries it seeks to hold together" (176). Thus, he contrasts the sense of dissolution and regeneration that marks the black Commonwealth from the settled atmosphere of the "older Dominions" (177). Similarly, restricting attention to Jamaica prepares us to observe distinctions between a national and a regional literature, although this study cannot extend to detailed comparison between Jamaican literature and that of the rest of the Caribbean.

Simon Gikandi states, as his basic premise, "The history of Caribbean literature can be written as the evolution of a discourse striving to establish its identity within the parameters defined by the European language and culture which it strives to disperse. . . . Caribbean writers, in response to their historical marginalization, have evolved a discourse of alterity which is predicated in a deliberate act of self-displacement from the hegemonic culture and its central tenets. The Maroon is the most visible symbol of this gesture of cultural *dédoublement*" (19–20). If this is true, an examination of marronage in Jamaican fiction can only contribute to the definition of both the regional and the national literature. Indeed, this book proposes that perspectival features associated with marronage supply some of the parameters of a literary discourse characteristic of Jamaican fiction.

Literary discourse in Jamaican fiction is not identical to what Caribbean critics currently describe as "nation language." Lloyd King sees Kamau Brathwaite's pursuit of nation language as part of a flight from alienation and identifies the relationship between authenticity and writing as a characteristic object of anxiety in Caribbean literature (22, 25). Increasingly, critical attention turns to stylistic choices in Caribbean narration. Sam Selvon's prose, for example, has attracted much discussion, as in the studies of Clement H. Wyke and Maureen Warner-Lewis. However, to describe the discourse of a regional or national fiction, one must look beyond a writer's choice of alternative registers. It seems possible to describe Jamaican fiction in terms of an interlocking system of discourse constraints. Caribbean literature probably operates within the same constraints, but perhaps these constraints interlock in other Caribbean writings differently from the way in which they do so in Jamaican literature. This volume cannot resolve this issue; a rigorous comparative analysis of literary discourse throughout the region lies well beyond the scope of this project. However, it is possible and useful to outline the discourse constraints likely to define Jamaican fiction. (Cf. Elam's definition of discourse constraints on drama, 57–62.)

First, any fiction is constrained by the conceptual organization of the world shared by writer and reader. This epistemic dimension of discourse regulates cognition and so helps to define the context of fiction from a particular area. This context includes assumptions about shared attitudes, for example to location of the self (as creole consciousness) in relation to events.

Ethical and behavioral constraints on discourse categorize experience by setting norms of presentation and judgment and thus providing codes for stereotyping. That is, having observed prototypical features that allow us to place a character in a broad category (such as madman or exploited woman) we assume the presence of other features.[2]

Intertextual and generic features of discourse reflect continuous reaction to European literary traditions as well as their unceasing influence, which has always been pivotal to educational systems throughout the Caribbean. In other words, the double vision that underlies Caribbean postcolonial discourse entails more than the subversion of imperial monolithic perceptions noted by Ashcroft, Griffiths, and Tiffin (37). On the contrary, even as it rewrites, Caribbean literary discourse allows for the survival of values in the traditional canon—including values that modern metropolitan literature may not necessarily perpetuate. This system of influences increasingly includes American and Afro-American viewpoints, deepens awareness of African traditions, and expands discovery of the non-English Caribbean. Interestingly, the Maroon viewpoint has repeatedly been recognized as "restorationist," distinct from "revolutionary" (Campbell 13). Its motivating, unifying ideology centers on heterogeneous survivals of African culture, especially in the areas of religion and military prowess. Marronage in Jamaica may be isolationist, but it also involves the perpetuation of whatever traditions seem integral to freedom and selfhood.

Literary interaction has been generic as well as textual. In Jamaica disparate cultural typologies have intersected, surprising us with characters who originate outside of literary conventions, like characters who recall the Annancy-type trickster. Oral traditions of Creole folk narrative interweave with traditional literary strategies. Again, Jamaican fiction draws on disparate literary genres, such as travelogues and ships' logs, memoirs, sea stories, and romances, sometimes blurring the line between the aims of fiction and those of nonfiction. The indigenous complex that results defeats expectations. Not surprisingly, narrative types in Jamaican discourse blur as writers embed, one within the other, quite dissimilar types of texts. Thus Brodber's *Myal* constitutes a coherent text but is structurally deviant in comparison with more traditional novels. In its textual structure, as in other dimensions, the discourse is hybrid.

Linguistic distinctions between Caribbean and other literary discourses are manifold. In addition, Jamaica differs from much of the English-speaking Caribbean in the survival of a conservative (basilectal) Creole. This is not only incomprehensible to uninitiated Standard English speakers but also difficult for speakers of decreolized varieties in other Caribbean territories. Jamaican literature is linguistically distinct from other literature in English to the extent that it includes selected features of this Creole. Language variation is also essential to the setting of the Jamaican novel, for the nature of this variation indicates the character's language community. In Jamaica, correlation between code choice and social rank is marked in comparison to communities that lack the conservative basilect (cf. Winford 49) but is less affected by ethnicity than might be expected in more ethnically complex communities. Literary recognition and instrumentalization in serious contexts has increased in the later twentieth century.

Some linguistic features of the discourse have psychological implications, as is particularly true of fiction that expresses the trauma of marronage. The psychological orientation that the discourse conveys may include, for example, hypersensitivity to social rank and interpersonal attitudes among characters that display hostility in a socially upward direction and contempt in a downward direction. The center of consciousness is located in multidimensional space with some definable orientation in relation to other characters, to experiences and events; this orientation has implications for the spatial and temporal relations conveyed by the language of the text. For example, a tendency to brood on the past or reinterpret it proliferates devices for time switching or chronological decomposition as the past lives on in the present. This is especially true where the operation of memory is crucial to textual structure, as in the flashbacks of Elean Thomas's *Last Room* and those of John Hearne's *Sure Salvation*.

The literary discourse of Jamaican fiction is also ideologically loaded. It is to be expected that Jamaican writers might evaluate the distribution of power (local or global) or the power relations between different types of characters differently than writers from metropolitan communities. Perhaps they even do so differently than writers from the broader Caribbean. Jamaican literature, for example, does not reflect attitudes toward power differentials between African and East Indian ethnic groups and does reflect attitudes to power differentials between black and brown. Violence, mutiny, and revolution recur in the corpus, and Jamaican writers tend to portray relationships between the individual and the community that associate marronage with resistance and that highlight hostilities and fragmented loyalties.

Characteristically, Jamaican fiction now displays a historical dimension in an obsession with the past that leads writers to reexamine and reevaluate the order and relationship of events. The earliest fiction in a Jamaican setting conforms to a European construct that records European expansion as success, but current Caribbean literature rewrites European expansion as exploitation. Yet this development has in turn spawned its own stereotypes—for example, of the African as innocent victim, of the creole woman as helpless victim, of the exploiter as expatriate male, of the expatriate male as exploiter. Most recently, Jamaican fiction appears to reflect an evolved worldview that includes a dispassionate sense of pan-exploitation. Writers perceive original characters and situations born of the elemental chaos that results from such exploitation, and they celebrate a survival and resilience possible, in such circumstances, only among an obdurate people.

The driving force of the fiction appears to be a commitment to truth—a claim that may seem less trite if the pursuit of truth is linked to shifts of perspective. To withdraw from a community and view it from a locus that is both remote and off-center may be to perceive added dimensions of truth. Arriving at the truth also depends on our presuppositions. In contemporary Jamaican fiction the logical component of the narrative leads to quite different conclusions than did the logical components of nineteenth-century novels set in Jamaica but conceived in Britain.

The logical dimension of any narrative involves causation, necessity, probability, and possibility, which concern valid connections between elements underlying arguments in the text. At the same time, points of departure constrain inference. An early-nineteenth-century romance set in Jamaica can logically unfold only to particular forms of "happy ending," which may require intraracial marriage, restitution of property, and return to civilization. Current Jamaican literary discourse highlights the relativity of such terms as *civilization*.

More and more, contrasts of meaning tend to operate along sliding scales and hierarchies rather than through simple binarism, so that the polarities generally stressed in postcolonial criticism prove to be of limited use in some contexts. In the creole consciousness of *The Lunatic*, for example, the reliability of the characters' perceptions can only be evaluated on a sliding scale. In this text madness is a scaled feature rather than a matter of binary opposition, of sanity present or absent.[3] Truth relations between propositions are more complex for scaled features than for binary ones, and the logical components of these narratives often conclude in ways that defy closure.

Similarly, by approaching fiction as a recharting of history, writers raise questions about traditional identification of nonfiction as fact. Thus, Jamaican authors tend to reveal the fluidity of truth. Such writers may commit themselves to the truth of their propositions by carefully exploiting modality or by relating the unseen (the matter of speculation) to the seen. Hearne's opening paragraphs of *The Sure Salvation* weigh the spreading evidence of corruption against the limited evidence of existence as the only proofs of his characters' being. Indeed, evidence is all. Experience is measured through or by comparison with previous experience, the unfamiliar measured against the known. Similes proliferate in the narrative, as a seascape or a remembered landscape reflects the topography of the mind. But the perspectival shifts produce facets of truth that contradict each other and lead to alternative conclusions. In fiction, theme is accumulated meaning, the global meaning of the discourse, and writers such as Hearne and Senior who conclude with plurality of meaning may be logically conveying the contradictions built into the themes of their discourse.

The epistemic, ethical and behavioral, intertextual and generic, textual, linguistic, psychological, and logical dimensions of narrative interlock with the systemic components, which traditionally include theme, setting, character, point of view, and plot. Any of these may be explicitly Jamaican. Setting tends to alternate between Jamaica and elsewhere—often but no longer always Britain. In some fiction, Jamaica is the elsewhere, and the imperial setting is home. In other fiction, Jamaica is home, and the elsewhere is foreign. In some writings, there is no identifiable home. Such alternation is crucial to perspective or, as it is traditionally termed, point of view.

Perspective usually orients characters spatially with respect to setting. First, the vision may be from outside into Jamaica. Alternatively, the vision may be from inside out of Jamaica. Finally, the vision may be from inside one area of Jamaican society to another, distinct area. Intersecting variables, such as social class, ethnicity, and gender, define character in literature and contribute to psychological distinctions of perspective. Such variables frequently emerge through dialogue or interior monologue. Thus, the multilingual community is an aspect of Jamaican setting, and language choice varies from one domain to the next—each domain being an institutionalized social situation. Characteristic domains include cricket matches, ships, and rural houses.

Perspectival shifts may complicate the logic of the plot. In addition to highlighting the presence of sliding scales discussed above, perspectival shifts may lead to conclusions that are not fixed and that defeat closure in a rational interpretation. Jamaican writers implicate premises and conclusions like those concerning murders that immediately precede and may follow the action of Senior's "Country of the One-Eye God." The discourse often stops short of explicating the outcome, forcing the reader to draw inferences and to choose between alternative inferences (or to choose not to choose).

The texts selected for analysis in this book share features of discourse familiar in the composite literary traditions of the Caribbean but also especially definitive of Jamaica. Jamaican fiction of the past decade departs not only from traditional literature but also from a number of perceptions now familiar in the wider Caribbean. Some Jamaican authors have conveyed these new perceptions by experimenting with altered perspectives. Indeed, the frequency of alternative worldviews in Jamaican literature is significant. It highlights a tendency for authors to shift perspective and approach reality from an unusual or hitherto unsuspected angle so as to arrive at truth by an unconventional route or to uncover a new truth.

Perspective, Alienation, and Truth

Simon Gikandi recognizes exile as the point of departure that has generated Caribbean discourse (36ff.), and supports Jan Carew (91–114) in viewing displacement as generating a discourse on nationalism and identity. Certainly, the expression of alienation typifies Jamaican discourse and surfaces not only thematically and in characterization (the maroon, the outcast, and so on) but also in perspective.

Perspective refers to "the perceptual or conceptual position in terms of which the narrated situations and events are presented" (Prince, *Dictionary* 73). Perspective is neither expression nor narrative information but that which governs expression and regulates narrative information.

Gerald Prince's narrow definition, which he associates with Gérard Genette, differentiates perspective from voice by distinguishing "who sees" from "who speaks." He defines narrative voice as that set of signs that characterize the narrator and govern the relations between the narration and the narrative text, between the narrating and the narrated. Thus, Prince distinguishes as broader definitions those, such as Percy Lubbock's classification and, more recently, Susan Snider Lanser's, that admit consideration of narrative voice. These categories associate perspective with relationships between narrator and narrated by including such distinctions as person. In analyzing perspective, I shall admit considerations of person and other aspects of narrative voice where relevant. Distinctions in narrative voice such as direct versus indirect style closely relate to internal versus external point of view and involve varying degrees of subjectivity.

It is now common to identify the narrator's position as omniscient (not locatable, independent of perceptual and conceptual restrictions, enabling the narrator to unfold more than any or even all of the characters know) or limited (and either internal or external to characters). The issue of orientation to Jamaican setting is also crucial in considering perspective in literature that is set in Jamaica. Whether the narrated situation and events are presented from a perceptual or conceptual position internal or external to Jamaica is pertinent to analysis and, presumably, to definition of literature as Jamaican.

In admitting consideration of how the narrative is oriented in relation to Jamaica itself, it is impossible to avoid reference to the author. While this real or actual author, unlike the implied author or narrator, may be neither "immanent nor deducible from the narrative" (Prince, *Dictionary* 8), the definition of any text as part of a regional or national literature can hardly ignore the writer's position in relation to that region or nation. To describe a position as Eurocentric or even to ascribe a text to a Caribbean canon implies some position associated with the actual author as distinct from the narrator. Indeed such concepts as that of "writing back" (as discussed by Ashcroft, Griffiths, and Tiffin) imply issues of authorial rather than narrative perspective.

In recognizing perspective as governing expression and regulating narrative information, it is possible to approximate it to discourse as a whole. Indeed, Roger Fowler adopts this position in describing the spatiotemporal and the ideological planes on which perspective manifests itself.[4]

Shifts in perspective enable a writer to offer varying views of reality and so to reveal different facets of truth; consequently, the reader can construct a more holistic vision than was previously available. The fact that perspective in fiction is a function of a speaker's orientation to events means that it is directional, relating the persona to the experience by locating that persona along dimensions like time or space relative to the experience. Thus, perspective points the direction between the consciousness and that of which it is conscious, and in this way it governs perceptions and conceptions of truth.

It is greatly comforting to assume that truth is fixed, and empirical truth is indeed determined by actual phenomena in the world. However, this empirical truth can be articulated only through language, and writers can manipulate linguistic truth (which is determined by semantics) or play with linguistic falsehood. For example, all fiction utilizes declarative sentences, and the nature of the declarative sentence is to assert that certain things are "true." The text too makes propositions, which may imply presuppositions. At least by implication then, the opening of *The Lunatic* asserts that Aloysius is a lunatic. Because abnormality is only conceivable in relation to norms, it is natural for the reader to continue with the assumption that Aloysius will contrast with a sane community. However, the text goes on to demonstrate the relativity of the original "truth" (that Aloysius is mad) by offering evidence that his contacts are no saner than himself and, in some instances, less sane: "The woman threw back her head and bellowed a maniacal frenzied laugh—laughter such as Aloysius had never heard outside of the madhouse" (39). The "truth" pertaining to lunacy in the novel appears to be fluid rather than fixed.

Caribbean texts pursue "truth" in various ways. *Wide Sargasso Sea*, for example, denies in places the most central linguistic property of words, which is that they have meaning. When the two main characters insist on the meaninglessness of each other's words, they not only deny the integrity of each other as speakers but throw their two distinct lines of reasoning into confrontation. The book brings into question the idea that words have intrinsic meaning, as distinct from speaker meaning, and so it makes possible parallel and conflicting truths implied throughout the text.

Some conclusions hang on the importance of quantity to truth. When Ma Bell analyzes Jacko in Olive Senior's "Country of the One-Eye God," Ma Bell knows "that everything they said about him was the truth" (16). However, this knowledge is a fraction of the information really necessary to her. Her limited knowledge also includes irrelevant qualifications regarding kinship that lead her to underrate his alienation. These gaps and irrelevancies in logic are fatal, "for stranger he was" (19).

The semantic drift that distinguishes the meaning of a word in one context from the meaning of the same word in a different context is related to historical change in meaning. This does not only mean that words narrow, broaden, and pejorate in meaning but also that deep epistemic changes in a culture transform the meanings that certain words bring to a text. One essential presupposition of early Eurocentric novels set in Jamaica under British rule is that Britain is home and Jamaica is not home. Such implications are clearly linked to social history. Modern works contain fictional events that transfer Jamaican characters to British settings and induce colonial schizophrenia linked with the character's growing uncertainty about the real meaning of home.

In addition, a growing number of texts, often by reference to vagrancy, highlight feelings of homelessness within the Jamaica that should be home. Jamaican fiction that examines homelessness and "outcastness" departs radically from simple binary polarities, such as black/white, exploited/exploiter, and so on, that have contributed to stereotyping in Caribbean literature. Such binarism is useful for ascribing blame, an easy trap for postcolonial criticism, but some recent texts reinterpret history as an essentially irrational unfolding of events for which no one group is responsible yet for which the patients of the action are the waste products of civilization. When a slave ship docks finally on its unknown shore, the contents of its hold "sure as hell don't have no place else to go" (*Sure Salvation* 224). So much for home.

Both literary and linguistic features orient a character to a community, indicate the distance between the character and the community, and suggest how far the character conforms to group expectations. Both literary and linguistic features also define the character's attitude toward the community and the community's attitude toward the character. Understanding marronage in Jamaican fiction involves evaluating relative values of the individual and the community.

Lines of communication link a community, and gaps in communication often separate those excluded from a community. Because language is a symbol of group membership, members of a community use a shared code in what Robert LePage and Andrée Tabouret-Keller have identified as an act of identity. Members who share a preferred code may also demonstrate linguistic prejudice against the code of a despised group. Use of the shared code reassures the speaker when it confirms that the speaker belongs to a valuable group. Speech in fiction is a clue to nonlinguistic information, and in creating a character's speech an author provides essential information about that character. For example, by selecting a code for dialogue, the author signals social background and social attitudes, and an accumulation of linguistic stereotypes can produce literary stereotypes. The outcast often distinguishes himself or herself by using a "lesser" code. A movement from one code to another is thus a crucial strategy for indicating perspectival shift.

Civilization may well be variously conceived in a multicultural context, and "outcastness" may be correspondingly multidimensional. The meaning of *civilization* may be considered componentially—that is, in terms of semantic features that compose full meaning. A dictionary entry for the lexeme defines it as "a developed or advanced state of human society" (*OED*). The meaning of the word as traditionally used is componential, involving community (presence and involvement in mainstream activities; companionship; shared values, worldview and categorizations; acceptance; sense of identity); propriety (behavioral conformity; good breeding; decency of dress and bearing; approved social rank and social relations; approved class relationships); advancement in the arts (codified and textualized language of education, government, and elite; known and approved forms of fine arts, and so on; systematized education); material value (possessions; wealth, concrete manifestations; food; building construction; trade); activity (traffic; business; numerous persons engaged in routine movement); order (government; organization of power; structured existence; conformity; rationality); permanence (establishment; home; familiarity; history); and security (law and observance of laws; reliability; truth). With these components, usage in early imperial texts includes an additional feature: white-inhabited.

Jamaican fiction abounds with various personae who are in some way off-center and separate from "civilized" community because they lack one or more of the components above. Such characters include the stranger, the vagrant, the bumpkin, the trickster, the savage, the rebel, the lunatic, the zombie, the reject, and the outcast. Many of the components that comprise these personae come together to compose that of the maroon.

Thus, from its earliest literary appearance, the Jamaican setting lends itself to a perspective associated with alienation. The persona that most coherently channels this perspective is that of the maroon. Some recent Jamaican writers have utilized alienated personae to present new or alternative visions that reveal previously hidden facets of society, rechart history, and reevaluate such concepts as civilization and savagery. These changes involve a presentation of content through structured shifts in perspective. How far perspectival shifts enlarge our vision of truth depends on the reliability of the marooned consciousness that is the channel for these alternative perspectives.

PART ONE

Outside In

External Views of Alienation in Jamaica

2

An Assembly of Strangers

Isolation and British Romanticism in Jamaican Settings of the Nineteenth Century

This is at least the abode of man: runaway slave, Maroon, or robber.
—*Hamel, the Obeah Man*

THE IMMEDIATE CONTEXT of nineteenth-century fiction set in Jamaica is a cognitive rather than a physical environment, for the authors of these texts operated from a collective perception of Jamaican society that was constrained by the socioeconomic policies of Britain. These writers also operated through a medium affected by literary movements of their period. Conflicting ideologies perpetuated slavery in the Caribbean and urged liberation in Europe, and this conflict refracted the vision of selfhood against which writers of the time conceived their personae. The same ideological conflicts filtered the vision of Jamaica as a setting for fiction.

The context of the nineteenth-century novel set in Jamaica is compositional. One constituent may be the immediate physical environment in which the author wrote, and this may as easily have been Britain as Jamaica. In either case the Jamaican setting relates to the novel's context essentially through a contrast between the British environment and cultivated British society on the one hand and Jamaican landscape and society on the other. In many senses the Jamaica of the nineteenth-century novel is a fictional island, whether entirely imaginary or described on the basis of experience, because the view is filtered through British experience, mediated by British values, and conveyed through British literary traditions. Another constituent of the context is thus the surrounding literary canon in which the novel finds its place, and the expectations associated with relevant genres, such as romances, journals, and travelogues.

The context involves a subset of beliefs and assumptions about the world that the writer and the reader share—what is termed mutual knowledge. However, when the modern reader encounters a nineteenth-century novel of Jamaican setting, it is questionable whether either linguistic co-presence or community membership ensure mutual knowledge. Crucial areas of this shared belief system have diminished through time, modifying the mutual knowledge between the nineteenth-century writer and the twentieth-century reader. In addition, nineteenth-century writers and readers shared a mutual lack of knowledge, a distancing unfamiliarity.[1]

Not all novels set in Jamaica include as part of their context the author's direct experience of Jamaica, which was inaccessible to most writers. *The Koromantyn Slave* (1823) was based on well-known authorities such as Bryan Edwards rather than on experience of Jamaica itself. Hence, the novel contains a plethora of evaluative terms such as *beauty, grandeur, radiance,* and *magnificence* instead of actual description. The physical setting is imaginary and, in part, the filtered vision of yet another writer.

The social environment of *The Koromantyn Slave* is no more authentic than the physical landscape. Proper names, apparently arbitrarily selected, lend a veneer of unfamiliarity (*Yamousa, Bonafou, Quante*). The dialogue departs from Standard English but is not creole: " 'He was much glad,' he said, 'to read the Gospel of Luke; it was so natural, so easy to be understood by poor Black Man.' " (164). Here, the variation in code choice indicates distance from the norm but does not accurately represent Jamaican speech. Indeed, the incomplete transition to dialogue, the limited transfer from indirect to direct speech that shows in the speaker's third-person reference to himself, combines with the capitalized "Black Man" to deindividualize the character and abstract him to a racial stereotype. The nonstandard features are occasional though recurrent, and they are only token departures from Standard literary syntax to consolidate exotic atmosphere. The language of supposedly Jamaican dialogue is not only uninformed by knowledge of the Creole but constructed on the assumption that any deviation from Standard English will authenticate the remote island setting.

The central consciousness is that of the young philanthropist, Beresford. The slave whose persona provides the title is a supportive character, contributing to the reader's understanding and appreciation of the hero. As a converted slave, doer of good works, docile, and pious, Yamousa concretizes the positive influence of Beresford. Beresford's happy ending requires homecoming to England, and while Yamousa can contribute to it, he cannot logically share it. Conveniently, on the way to England, Yamousa is swallowed by a raging sea. The Jamaican experience is contrived from beginning to end.

Both the physical and cognitive dimensions of this novel's context render the Jamaican setting entirely artificial and exclude it and others like it from further consideration in this study. The novels that appear to merit discussion as Jamaican at least in setting are those that are not only nominally set in Jamaica but that emerge from their authors' direct experience of the island and its society. This experience may well be limited in various ways, but the vision provided, however warped or fractured, follows some direct contact.

The novels that fall into this group are securely framed in British literary tradition, and so fiction from and about Jamaica at this time shares some values of British romanticism. The preemancipation temper urges the artist toward themes of freedom and individuality, but prevailing social attitudes entrenched in Eurocentric traditions constrain romantic vision of individual liberty, producing curious effects on theme and character in a Jamaican setting. The limited corpus that survives includes enough literary prose fiction to express collectively attitudes to freedom substantially different from those of local verse acknowledged in the previous chapter.

The ordered universe of augustan literature in Europe had accommodated little questioning of the established social strata that Caribbean society exaggerated. However, creative writing of a place and time torn by the racial and social struggles of emancipation might be expected to share European romantic aspirations to individual freedom and to elevate such aspirations above societal values. European literary traditions neither permeated nor assimilated folk expression, yet nineteenth-century literary developments included growing interest in folk experience and in other points of view hitherto ignored. So it might be expected that fiction genuinely set in Jamaica would enlarge those insights (glimpsed through local verse) into a spiritual struggle for freedom. However, as C. Rhonda Cobham-Sander points out, until relatively recently even the Caribbean writer "was not expected to upset the *status quo* within the society" ("Creative Writer" 304) and this prohibition served to "inhibit creative response to social issues" (305).

Virgil Nemoianu distinguishes the later romantic period in Europe from the earlier by its "disappointed musings in the face of disintegration of revolutionary and high romantic ideals" (2). The Biedermeier model has drawn objections, such as the suspicion that it multiplies, in a sterile way, periodizations and definitions of "the spirit of the age." Early fiction set in Jamaica offers a corpus too small, too underwritten to preserve developments that can accommodate subperiodization. All emerge from European tradition and reflect their time in a general way, but the Jamaican setting both accommodates and resists European romanticism and its aftermath. Even where it facilitates dreams of universal harmony and utopian schemes it falters in articulating the dialectic of the individual in society. Nemoianu supports the Biedermeier model yet notes that the later phases of romanticism in Europe celebrate "human personality in all its privacy, idiosyncrasy, and melancholy specialization (rebellious, hypochondriac, introspective) at least as prominently as in the comprehensive subjectivity of the [earlier] romantic writers" (16). But neither the eighteenth- nor nineteenth-century writers on Jamaica fully reflect this, any more than they can be expected to lament absence of revolution in an outpost of Britain.

To observe, even briefly, the language of fiction at this time is to underline the degree to which the native Jamaican voice is constrained. Whereas Jamaican verse is largely the expression of a peasant voice—black, poor, and untutored—literary fiction in the Jamaican setting is essentially the work of the white, relatively affluent, and educated. The earliest Jamaican verse does not echo simultaneous attempts in European poetry to come to terms with the universe. Yet the fact that the peasant voice claims enough attention to survive in record is itself a romantic development and a stroke for freedom. So indeed is the fact that fiction seriously explores the Jamaican setting. However, in fiction there is limited expression of the folk voice in its own language.

In a sense this is curious because romanticism involves expansion to new and preferably exotic settings, times, and viewpoints. In this sense, fascination with Caribbean proverbs and folktales makes romantic developments of such works as J. A. Udal's "Obeah in the West Indies" (1827), Pamela Milne-Holme's *Mamma's Black Nurse Stories* (1890), and Ada Wilson Trowbridge's "Negro Customs and Folk Stories of Jamaica" (1896). In fact, writings on Jamaica at this time enrich the canon of literature in English as a whole by increasing its dimensions of social interest and by enlarging its range of content. Thus, the Creole and oral literature form part of the total literary context that includes those texts that take the form of actual novels.

However, the reader accesses limited areas of this total literary context for interpretation. The novels in Jamaican setting stimulate access to some areas of contextual information rather than to others. One such area is the span of interests associated with British romanticism.

The corpus includes *Montgomery; or, the West Indian Adventure* (1812–13), *Hamel, the Obeah Man* (1827), *Marly; or, the Life of a Planter in Jamaica* (1828) and Michael Scott's *Tom Cringle's Log* (1833). Cyrus Perkins's "Busha's Mistress; or, Catherine the Fugitive" (written in 1855 but published in 1911) falls midway, chronologically and in other ways to be examined. Two later novels are Mayne Reid's *Maroon* and William G. Hamley's *Captain Clutterbuck's Champagne* (both 1862), which differ considerably from the earlier set. All exploit the "exotic" in landscape and folk, venture into the emotional intensity of individual passions, and engage the theme of freedom; all include in their action escape or release from confinement; all convey the perspectives of characters in some way separated from civilization. But in each the theme of the independent self is riddled with contradiction. It is a contradiction inherent to the cognitive environment that partly composes the context of each novel.

The physical and sociohistorical setting of Jamaica would seem naturally appealing to the romantic temper. Landscape might offer itself for emotive reference and for evocative description to reveal individual response and so to invoke selfhood. Physical surroundings used to create "exotic" atmosphere could combine with emotional symbolism and enable a novelist to exploit the gothic heritage. Here was a setting that offered opportunity to connect and to contrast outer and inner landscapes in the interest of undermining dogma, questioning the finality of reason, unsettling certitudes, and thus liberating the imagination. There is ample opportunity to loosen the cohesion of settled ideas, to cultivate incongruity, to achieve a new perspective, and so to introduce doubt. For many, these are defining features of romanticism (Stevens and Waterhouse 114).

However, distortions in literary representations of Jamaica at this time cannot be avoided. Crucial issues include problems of definition. What constitutes savagery, noble or ignoble, in the opinion of the writer who selects Jamaica as setting? Competent writers seek to satisfy conventions that generate meaning in their own systems. Most writers in the European literary tradition did not have the time, inclination, or social context to acquire some native Jamaican frame of thought or unlearn European values. Even direct experience of Jamaica was therefore drawn into a setting filtered by the cognitive environment of such an author.

Whatever native verse might imply, a European novelist of the period could hardly express Caribbean experience forged by dislocation, oppression, and confinement. Readers today might hope for fiction that questioned ideologically entrenched and institutionalized values of white creole society, distinguished creole values from those of Europe, or addressed moral issues surrounding the bartering of individuals. Such questions would destabilize fixed assumptions about civilization, and only in this way could such writers honestly explore, in a Jamaican setting, themes of selfhood and freedom. To expect such insight is to overestimate the mutual knowledge of nineteenth-century writers and twentieth-century postcolonial readers. Such deconstruction of societal values, which nineteenth-century novelists might indeed undertake using British settings, proves impossible in the Jamaican setting.

In any case, what is this Jamaican setting? Gerald Prince explains setting as "a set of propositions referring to the same (backgrounded) spatio-temporal complex" (*Narratology* 73). Propositions may rest on presuppositions or at least "nest" in other information. Eva Feder Kittay relates the "nestedness" of information, shell within shell, to linguistic truth and to the structure of metaphor. She points out that because all information is nested in other information, any particular signal is encoded by focusing on one piece of information and eclipsing another, and context "selects out" certain sets of meanings on the basis of pragmatic considerations such as differential or selective relevance (129, 167). British authors must have formed the set of propositions that composed Jamaican setting in their novels by a process of focusing and eclipsing information at their disposal. They could hardly eclipse the political relationship or the financial value of Jamaica to Britain.

Similarly, British authors could only rarely convey the creole perspective through its natural medium, Jamaican Creole, and they represented this code essentially to underline the strangeness of the Jamaican experience. Early and Eurocentric perspectives on alienation in Jamaica are necessarily framed by context to produce a vision of truth quite separate from anything twentieth-century readers might see from a different perspective or in the context of distinct information.

Visitors and Adventurers

The earliest of the novels merits attention as a romance authored "by a gentleman resident in the West Indies" and printed in Kingston. However, *Montgomery* is less anchored physically in Jamaica than are the rest of the group. Its action alternates across the Atlantic, beginning during the life of the hero's father, which occupies the first two hundred pages. The Jamaican setting is sporadic until early in the second volume.

Henry Montgomery arrives on the island midway in the evolution of his career from legal clerk to plantation bookkeeper and eventually to pastor. His adventure in Jamaica exposes him to deprivation, injustice, and corrupt influences in the lower ranks of white plantation society. In this social strata and burdened by false representations of his character, Montgomery sees his love for the daughter of a wealthy landowner as hopeless. However, Montgomery rises from this position of isolation and apparent lack of a future. His reputation cleared, he regains his rightful position in society, marries, and returns to Britain.

The spatial separation between the alternating loci of the action is crucial. Much of the action comprises the hero's repeated and extensive journeys. Moreover, spatial distance mirrors moral separation as the protagonist endeavors to maintain integrity and preserve an untainted mind in the midst of company hardened to a corrupt lifestyle (2:139). However, despite the moral issues debated between packed adventure and novel experience, Montgomery's character grows little. Although his career evolves, he begins and ends as nearly perfect, a formed character with settled ideas on controversial issues. Notably, these issues are never debated in the Creole. So Montgomery's confrontation with the Other is limited. His is an augustan rather than a romantic separation, an aloof reasoning rather than a solitary and brooding vision, a triumph of reason rather than of imagination. The physical journey perhaps mirrors an inner voyage of inquiry, but it does so without conveying psychological growth. Events merely prove him right. The narrative structure involves complications of action that raise doubts about him in the minds of other characters, and the narrative's resolution exonerates him.

Part of his characterization is his certainty of the slaves' humanity (2:121). The author is sensitive to the double standards of white society, which pays lip service to notions of equality while maintaining internal stratification by the rigid class boundaries that isolate the bookkeeper. However, the writer's own cognitive environment filters the admissible content. Glimpses of interaction between blacks and whites or among blacks are rare and limited almost entirely to the type of interaction imposed by slavery, such as brutal whippings.

Lacunae pocket the argument. The novel debates but never quite proposes freedom for Jamaican blacks. Indeed, it celebrates not freedom so much as the responsibility of those in power to act humanely toward those they control. Thus, the hero is socially and morally separated from other characters in the novel rather than from a belief system that ratifies the prevailing social structure of the author's time. His opposition to some aspects of the system is philanthropic instead of revolutionary.

In a sense, *Montgomery* displays a conflict between context and setting. The cognitive environment in which the text is composed presupposes a social order built on slavery, and nothing inside the text can resolve this issue, which, outside of the text in its cognitive context, is not an issue at all but hard set in presupposition. The text conforms to earlier eighteenth-century literary modes, in embedded arguments that search for intellectual solutions to moral issues, yet it selects the Jamaican setting to embrace romantic emotionalism about common humanity.

This confrontation of interests in the context constrains the outcome of the action, rendering it impossible for the hero to be absorbed by the Jamaican setting. He remains an observant outsider, and his return to England is a logical conclusion. Edward Kamau Brathwaite notes rightly that the author's imagination is "basically concerned not with the society but with 'the sylvan scene' " ("Creative Literature" 65). However, the novel reflects the romantic temper by accurately evoking setting through landscape, and occasionally the text yields glimpses of individuality among the slaves (such as one compassionate woman who, in her limited leisure time, mends the hero's mosquito net). So, tentatively, *Montgomery* reaches toward the Other, even as it cautiously circles the moral issues of Jamaican slavery. All in all, however, Montgomery's separation from others is that of the decent young man voluntarily and temporarily exiled from civilization and psychologically detached from local corrupt white society (2:153–58). Within this society, the vast majority of human beings in the setting command pity but are dimly perceived and rarely heard. The cognitive environment of the text excludes their perspective and preempts the issue of their resistance.

From the sprawling time frame of Montgomery, whose perspective changes temporally over generations and refocuses spatially through shifting geographical locations, the vision in *Marly: or, the Life of a Planter in Jamaica* narrows ostensibly to the consciousness of one hero, permanently located in Jamaica. *Marly* unfolds a thinner romantic plot—also one of lost property restored and an apparently inaccessible maiden won. The grandson of a Scots colonist, Marly arrives in Jamaica to make his fortune by reclaiming his grandfather's property, and Marly, like Montgomery, suffers social injustice before reinstatement and marriage. In focusing on its protagonist's perspective, the narrator admits a wide range of viewpoints through discussions that swiftly become extended monologues to which Marly is audience. The reader encounters Creole voices rarely and briefly. Nevertheless, the Jamaican setting is more strongly evoked than in *Montgomery*. The second chapter incorporates into the adventure events prior to the hero's arrival in chapter 1, including reference to preceding island history, such as the Maroon Wars. Thus, it frames the setting in a history of violent resistance.

Marly shows less complication than *Montgomery* and only loosely strings together embedded (often conflicting) arguments on issues associated with slavery. Within and between these embedded arguments are metanarrative comments, which confuse rather than clarify the narrative stance, leaving contradictions unresolved. The unfolding action is thin and relatively unrelated to the argument, leaving the protagonist's character undeveloped. Rather than synthesizing a coherent vision, the total structure is therefore fragmentary.

The discourse includes descriptions of plantation life and presents the realities of slavery, but it does not develop a logical connection between this vision of slavery and the conclusion of the narrative. After all Marly observes of the island's explosive social structure, he settles in the end for what is foreshadowed as a safe and moral life as a successful slave owner. Romantic questioning of entrenched values, curiosity about "primitive" consciousness, and engagement with issues of intellectual and personal freedom all motivate the structure of *Marly* and relate to its incidents and conversations. However, the action does not assimilate this polemic or logically link it to the resolution, and this gap in logical development frustrates the novel's motivating romanticism.

In addition to its narrative structure, the novel displays the structure of debate, which itself comprises other discourse types, including the speeches and monologues that sever the thread of action for extended portions of the novel. Because the debate and the narrative are not integrated, however, *Marly* is deficient in perlocutionary force. It cannot effect what a debate is intended to effect, which is a logical analysis and argument leading to a conclusion. Even as it recounts how Marly establishes his identity and achieves independence, the text denies the black community these qualities, which characters have debated throughout. The novel fails through nonrelationship between components of its discourse and does not in the end articulate a consistent point of view suggestive of its narrator's reliability.

Naturally, it also excludes any debate in the Creole that might permit an inadmissible perspective. Creole speech is local color, part of the setting, or a humorous touch to a description, or a negative feature of characterization.[2] It is never the medium of serious argument. Quite apart from this, in *Marly* (as in *Montgomery*), the issues debated within the text are often matters of social structure and worldview that are nonissues and matters of presupposition in that component of the novel's context that we have identified as the cognitive environment of the novel. In this sense, the novel's context precludes admission of Creole argument.

The novel does not achieve gripping characterization by portrayal of individual struggle for selfhood, as distinct from a struggle for purely physical and social success. Marly is a stranger, but his alienation is temporary, based on misunderstood identity. He conveys relatively little imagination and emotional sensitivity, and his reliance on logic is problematical, hinged as it is on the inconclusive debate of the entire novel. The text articulates his commitment to ameliorating the conditions of slavery and so establishes him as philanthropic, like Montgomery; yet persistent debate has exposed him to testimony against the humanity of slavery, and the reader's knowledge of the hero's knowledge marks this qualified philanthropy as wishy-washy.

The coda that concludes the discourse links the future of its characters to a gradual and "natural" drift toward emancipation. The narrator foresees that "slavery will . . . gradually cease—an increase in free laborers will be the consequence" (363). Meanwhile, the protagonist will settle (profitably) within the institution, beloved as a benevolent master. Marly neither returns home to Britain nor outwardly embraces and perpetuates the horrors of the system. A sort of comfortable blindness links the protagonist's character to the gap-ridden logical component of the larger debate.

Neither the coda nor any other metanarrative comments suggest authorial criticism of the protagonist. The reader can only infer that the vision is ultimately authorial, and the discourse confirms this supposition. For example, the writer of *Marly* does not appear to control the semantic drift discernible in terms for happiness, well-being, or contentment and in terms such as *civilization;* as a result, the discourse shows apparently unintentional irony: "As they proceeded toward the mountains, the country in the ascent from the seashore became more and more romantic; . . . it resounded with the sounds of civilization and subordination, in so far as the smacking of whips are a proof. In the prospect too, numerous gangs of negroes were to be seen, apparently gently enough wrought; and, if a judgement was to be inferred from their singing, they were quite happy"(17). Similarly, such presuppositions about the natural linkage of civilization with subordination expose the superficiality of explicit inferences regarding the happiness of slaves. Considering romantic concern for individual liberty, an ascent into a romantic landscape echoing with the whip is additionally contradictory. The problem arises because civilization in "imperial" discourse presupposes a dialectic of domination and subordination as a construct for order; in the Jamaican setting, this construct overrides the romantic revolution of contemporary British literature.

Because of this automatic override, various aspects of the novel as a literary discourse fail to elevate the value of the individual spirit above the interests of society (which are here clearly material), and the novel ultimately condones the bartering of humanity. Revolution, even spiritual revolution, remains unthinkable. In *Marly,* any potential for nobility in the "savage" is inconceivable except in terms of remodeling and even recoloring to suit society. Marly looks forward to a gradual dilution of the negro race by interbreeding to produce a higher (i.e., fairer) order of peasant class. Whatever a mere chronicle of his life events might lead the reader to expect, the protagonist never separates from the moral confusion of his creator's mind. A random assortment of personality features and perspectives remains uncoordinated, descriptions and events lack cohesion, and the self is unarticulated. The composite vision of *Marly* relays variant and conflicting views without arriving at synthesis or conclusion and without offering these views as alternatives that might imply plurality of meaning. Thus, the protagonist's assimilation in the Jamaican setting, as promised by the coda, is unconvincing.

This result is predictable, given the point of departure for the entire discourse. Eurocentricity frames the novel's dialectic of civilization and wilderness. The opening sentence of *Marly* defines Jamaica as "the grave of Europeans," and the introduction continues with a vision of the island as "a place to take one's chance," "a strange country," and a fit setting for the adventurers' hunt for gold. An elegant dinner is one "nearly in the same style as an English one" (11), and the narrator claims explicitly that Britain is referred to as home "by all inhabitants of the island, whether blacks, browns, or whites" (22). Similarly, the phrase "thinly inhabited" is used as exactly equivalent to "thinly white inhabited," which follows it in a few lines (14). Thus, even words that might seem unlikely to be loaded, such as *inhabited* (versus, say *elegant*), have semantic properties entailed by Eurocentrism.

The same point of departure that polarizes civilization and wilderness associates civilization with concepts of possession and belonging. The narrator ascribes to slaves as well as to proprietors the presupposition that structured existence involves possession of one group by another. The narrator elaborately explains a disclaimer by a slave who is caught stealing ("no tief from Massa . . . take from Massa" [41]). According to the narrator, "as she was his property, she formed part of himself, argal, what was his was hers." Yet this argument of "takee, no tievie," which recurs in other nineteenth-century Jamaican texts (Lalla and D'Costa 157), has a more credible explanation. It seems natural that slaves might deny guilt in living off land maintained by their forced and largely unrewarded labor. Direct speech in Creole is included to authorize the dominant perspective rather than to express the position of the dominated. The concept of civilization as involving domination and possession of one group by another constrains the narrator's interpretation of "takee no tievie."

Because the virtue of belonging to Britain is a crucial presupposition to this debate, the romantic tenet of individual liberty surfaces as self-contradiction. The narrative proposes that the slaves, if free to choose, would choose enslavement, as is conveyed by implication, for example where the birth of an heir to old Marly occasions "great joy to the parents, and the pleasure of their negroes, who rejoiced at whatever pleased their massa and missa" (21). The benefit to the black of remaining enslaved is also inferred by accumulating a proliferation of binary oppositions between, for example, barbarism and civilization, curse and blessing, cultivation and waste, para-

dise and wilderness, hut and palace, and preservation of the establishment
(as order) and revolution (92–93). Indeed, from the point of departure identified, freedom for the black is regressive for "in place of improving in the
arts of civilisation, they would retrograde from what they are at present, until
they became equally savage with their forefathers. . . . In all probability the
mountains would become receptacles for bands of banditti, and from our experience in the late maroon war, we were fatally taught the difficulty of con-
quering a handful of blacks when in possession of the ravines, or, as they are
called, the cockpits, in these forests" (247–48). From the perspectives presented in *Marly,* free blacks must be the ultimate outcasts. As far as freedom
is concerned, the narrator explicitly remarks that "few of the decent well-be-
haved negroes desire it" (91). In the universe of *Marly,* predicated on the de-
sirability of belonging to Britain, black freedom involves an ideological separation that is epistemically impermissible.

Tom Cringle's Log, by Michael Scott, achieves a partial view of independent selfhood, but it is a floating, offshore view. Like other novels of
its time, it envisions the protagonist as adventurer, but here it is as an un-
ashamedly swashbuckling adventurer, far less consciously righteous than
Montgomery. The perspective is that of a protagonist who is the speaker, directly recalling experience that lies largely outside of the plantation setting.

Cringle explores "exotic" lands from Jamaica to Panama and visits cities
that evoke danger and violence. However, the novel's unifying setting is Jamaica and its surrounding seas. Scott's account highlights emotions of humor and pathos in preference to wit and reason. The individualized perspective of the wanderer is blended at first with that of the child, fresh and testing
each experience from the beginning of the novel, when the narrator is thir-
teen, to his confirmation as captain and to his marriage. A refusal to accept
ready-made judgment, the autonomy of individual choice, and the absence
of explicit moral conclusions infuse the tale. At times, fast-paced action traps
the hero in moral dilemma and triggers confessional unburdening of the
soul. Portrayal of strangeness, of otherness, emerges through a fevered consciousness during an illness, through curiosity about the unfamiliar religious practices of slaves and through shipboard culture that blends the superstition and myth of varied peoples (2:35).

Scott skillfully exploits romantic interest in nonstandard speech and informal language through his accurate representation of linguistic variety
among the ship's crew and their contacts on land. Narrative language also
varies through brisk informality, exclamatory description, passionate reference to Cringle's beloved Mary, and fragmented impressions during illness.
Scott clearly contrasts the expression of a tortured mind, raving with yellow

fever (1:320–21), to the hearty familiarity of a narrator, who addresses the reader directly ("I say, messmate . . . " 1:328).

Yet despite many characteristics of romanticism, Scott conveys a confused or at least selective vision of liberty, of individual worth prioritized above social norms. The tale includes a description of an engagement with a slaver that is fired on and sunk "while five hundred human beings . . . split the heavens with their piercing death-yells" (2:165). Some slaves are rescued, but Cringle must assume the awful responsibility of firing on the rest to save his ship from overloading. He professes himself deeply affected by one of the rescued women, who jumps overboard to sink with her lover. Yet shortly after this harrowing description of what is recognized as human suffering, there follows a skit of obviously humorous intent. It ridicules the exclamatory style of an antislavery pamphlet that lambastes "those planters whose molasses is but another name for human blood" (2:183). This is greeted with "shouts of laughter" (2:185). Elsewhere, Scott describes black infants in the care of an old woman as "little, naked, glossy, black guinea pigs" and concludes his cozy picture of slaves dancing home happily from work, attractively dressed: " 'And these are slaves,' thought I, *'and this is West Indian bondage!* Oh that some of my well-meaning anti-slavery friends were here, to judge from the evidence of their own senses!' " (1:217). Scott's vision of Jamaica is accurate and sensitive in some places, such as his striking description of the island at daybreak, seen from the sea, framing the awakening activity of a people bursting with vitality, good humor, independence, and dignity. But these scenes are coordinated into an overall vision of a well-ordered slave society (1:179–82). Scott's approach does not synthesize its scattered sketches of black humanity to a universally applicable concern for independence and selfhood. Again, his protagonist is a curious and observant stranger, often distanced from civilization but not outcast.

Montgomery, Marly, and *Tom Cringle's Log* comprise a group unified not only by a physical setting exotic in contrast to British landscape but also by a social setting in which all members of the community are imports, either in their own generation or in earlier family history. In some novels, such as *Marly* and *Montgomery,* it is important that the social setting accords or withholds status according to the length of presence and degree of assimilation into the community and according to the presence or absence of ties with home. The expatriate protagonist is always isolated because he is unassimilated into the unfamiliar Jamaican community and separated from home. However, at no time does this alienation approach marronage. Each hero retains the option to return home, the ability to recover entry to civilization, and the claim to property that is rightfully his.

Fugitives and Romantic Warriors

Patterns of oppression, escape, and resistance spawn situations that produce solitary figures distinct from the adventurer-stranger type. One such familiar type in Caribbean postcolonial literature is that of the damaged woman, a victim both of male domination and of colonial exploitation. The first appearance of such a character in Jamaican fiction is in the earliest text believed to have been written by a local author.

This brief fiction, "Busha's Mistress," recalls a plantation setting in which the social system repels an attractive young visitor (Vernon) and introduces him to an overseer (Busha Jackson) and the overseer's mistress (Catherine). As Vernon observes the atrocities of the system, he comes to love a Creole, Celest, who turns out to be (imperceptibly) colored and to be his cousin. These love affairs are parallel, so that Vernon sees the rift that develops between Catherine and Jackson when she learns of his infidelity. Eventually both couples are united.

This is an unpublished and generally unknown tale. Its author, Cyrus Perkins, may have been the son of an army doctor in Jamaica, and "Busha's Mistress" is thus significant as fiction on Jamaica by a writer not only long resident in the island but perhaps native to it.[3] This warrants no assumption that the vision is creole. Both the language and outlook are those of educated literary Standard English. Cyrus Perkins appears to have been a minister or missionary on the island, and a brief preface to the work connects him with "planting" before he entered the local mission field. The same brief introduction claims that "Perkins did splendid work among the slaves, and cried out bitterly against the brutal traffic in human lives." Local or not, "Busha's Mistress" conveys an authorial perspective found in no other nineteenth-century novel of Jamaica.

The emotional significance of its physical setting becomes clear from the introduction, which points across a distance of time to the massive, moldering grandeur of a plantation great house and so recreates its past. The writer plays on contrasts between the dull monotony of toil and the bright lights and laughter in the stately sitting room, between the overseer's concern for his animals and his contempt for black servants (1). Elsewhere, the brilliant landscape throws into relief the darkness of the social system. Some ostensibly objective descriptions elicit reader response through lexical incongruity, as in a description of a whipping: "As one of these [women] was likely ere long to be a mother, she was considerately accommodated with a hole which was dug in the ground over which she was stretched" (1).

From this system various characters separate themselves. Vernon voluntarily distances himself from the values of the other planters. Catherine occupies a naturally isolated position from both whites and blacks as the brown mistress of the overseer (*busha*), then escapes the system altogether and returns only when it can no longer bind her. The overseer loses his position and, stripped of wealth and power, is reduced to vagrancy, to the scorned status of a "walking buckra." (*Buckra*, a polite variant of regular Creole *backra*, "white man," is originally from Ibo and Efik. See Cassidy and LePage, *Dictionary*.) As the *busha's* acceptability in his community declines, his alienation increases; conversely, his mistress's acceptability rises, and her isolation gives way to tightening bonds of friendship, family, and romance. Catherine's isolation from society in her original bond with Jackson is relieved by her rejection of him, and his resulting alienation not only from her but from his peers is relieved by reunion with her. Spatial separations between characters are thus crucial to both action and characterization. Lack of information about each other's whereabouts repeatedly intensifies the anxiety of various characters.

Temporal separation is also important. The reader experiences the distance of events through emphases on the time lapse that separates these events from the narrator's time. The resident narrator's view from within Jamaican society recalls a setting that is separate by time rather than space and also by moral depravity. However nostalgically he describes the flourishing greathouse, the writer also conveys the seeds of its destruction in the decadent revelry of the ruling class.

The physical island setting remains, even from a local perspective, exotic. It perpetuates some features of the stranger's vision, which earlier nineteenth-century novels conveyed. Among these persistent features are those that distance the Jamaican social setting from the reader by emphasis on geographical remoteness. Just as earlier novels introduce Jamaica by reference to journey and distinguish it by contrast to Britain, recognizing Britain as home, the resident writer presents Catherine's flight from her native Jamaica to Britain as a homeward passage. Arrival at this home frees, uplifts, and sanctifies her. Indeed, the escape to Britain is little less than a psychological pilgrimage.

The earlier novels could hardly have presented the flight of a slave in this light, and Perkins's fugitive is a distinct development because she escapes from a system both past and wicked. Nevertheless, the moral centricity of Britain underscores the virtuous characters' alienation from the Jamaican social setting, even where this setting is native to them. The writer also clings to British literary traditions. He does not describe the landscape in the fresh, immediate terms through which he relays the social setting. Where Perkins

sketches the physical setting, he tends to do so in ornate terms ("the feath-
ered tribe," "dulcet notes"), and the repetition of these exact phrases elsewhere in this short discourse marks them as stock phrases regurgitated for
the light romance.

Yet accuracy and precision are otherwise apparent. He vividly evokes the
social setting, drawing careful distinctions between the meanings of the
word *free* (free by law versus free by nature). Even his biased presentation of
a *myal* ceremony for shadow catching is evocative. He defines the *gumba* as
"a fantastic little drum," and the African origin of both the instrument and
the activities associated with it is immediate and offensive. Thus, the dance
consists of the "most ridiculous postures imaginable," of "subtle and fantastic movements" that are "wild," "tramping," and "sprawling." The songs or
outcries of the participants are "hoots" and "screams," and the associated
potion "bitter" and "nauseous" (18). However, although presented in loaded
terms, the social setting receives more attention than the landscape, and the
writer perceives and explores in his black characters dimensions of personality and areas of experience beyond those contingent on oppression or subservience.

Characterization is to some extent stylized; the brown housekeeper is
even identified as Miss Brown. Yet the visitor, Vernon, is individual, distinct from the majority of his peers, whose object is only to gain wealth: "Mr.
Vernon was not of this class" (2). Vernon's primary object in visiting Jamaica
is one of self-education and personal development. His objective observation
of slavery separates him emotionally from the planters. He concludes early
that "slavery has made the negro what he is; he is crushed beneath an over-
powering weight, and it is impossible to form any fair estimate of his moral
powers where there is no room for his development" (3). Perkins similarly
departs from stereotype by creating a feminine, local, and colored perspective on independence (4).

Such characters, highly individualized at crucial points in the narrative,
cooperate in assisting slaves who have been unfairly and brutally punished
to escape from the estate dungeon (7). The vision links confinement and corruption with mental decomposition. The motivating spirit behind the novel
is a need to free humanity from "this tomb of the living," to expose the "gan-
grene . . . in . . . the whole social system," to explore how "by association with
scenes of horror . . . the mind lapses into a state of indifference" (11). The
author unfolds a logical progression toward spiritual revolt. The death of the
old preacher, Williams, following brutal punishment "produced . . . sensation" (17). The slaves manifest their anger in insubordination, which the
novel presents as a logical development.

On the other hand, Catherine escapes the social, racial, and legal constraints of the island to develop her natural "nobility" in more conventional terms that reflect the language attitudes of the age (22). The narrative presents linguistic achievement and development in Standard English as a measure of success and excellence of character, and it identifies freedom with intellectual development and linguistic competence in the official code (33).

Jackson's character, like Catherine's, is crucially defined by the nature of his communicative skills. He is a speaker of British English, and features of Scottish dialect pronunciation separate him both from characters native to the island and from the more cultivated Vernon. Moreover, Jackson communicates by speech acts and gestures that distinguish him from those to whom he speaks. He summons, threatens, directs, and questions. Where Catherine is at first silent and breaks this silence only to whisper a warning to Vernon, Jackson whistles for both his slaves and his dogs and speaks through his whip (3). The narrator relates that after Catherine's departure, Jackson "grumbled, cursed or swore perpetually" (5). However, he is reduced eventually to pleading with her (6) before he is silenced. For Jackson, silence comes when he experiences total loss; his slave mistress departs for England, and he deteriorates until he is expelled from the estate to wander on foot. The turning point from his early volubility is Catherine's reaction to his promise to buy her. She dismisses this promise as "story talk," throwing off his oppression as she becomes more articulate.

The novel does not convey the perspective of the exploited woman directly but filters it through an observer. The period of observation is short, broken by her escape, and it is not until she becomes free and articulate in educated English rather than in Creole that the narrative properly shifts to Catherine's point of view. Until this time Vernon interprets and conveys her attitude, and for the earlier part of the novel Vernon's affairs receive a comparable degree of attention. When Catherine comes to speak and read educated English, the narrator enters her mind and eventually focuses on her search for Jackson after her return to Jamaica. Vernon reenters the narrative after Catherine and Jackson reunite, and Vernon's return and union with Celeste are viewed from Catherine's perspective.

Disturbingly, even as the tale concludes with satisfactory resolutions for the suffering of white and brown characters, the theme of black oppression and necessary liberation slips away. Central and approved characters, such as Catherine and Vernon, work toward liberation by peaceful and legitimate means, absolving Britain. Even in this local novel, central figures are white, near white, or brown—an important distinction from black in Jamaica— and by the conclusion of the tale all fall within the upper, educated social class.

Despite its explicit stand against oppression, "Busha's Mistress" offers no solution for black characters at the bottom of the social scale. Yet the authorial stand is clear, and reader response to the brutality of slavery is elicited forcefully, indeed almost in gothic tradition (17, 23).

At the end of this fiction compromise frustrates romanticism. The resolution happily unites Catherine with an overseer who has been little less dissolute or brutal than Fraser. We are assured that her Jackson has "been taught a lesson." But this purgatory of suffering and this "change of heart"—a sort of redemption by spiritual chastisement—produce no spinoff for the community. Once Jackson is freed of his own corruption, the subject of enslavement is dropped. The central figures thus gain freedom by coming to terms with a society earlier portrayed as corrupt and by finding a comfortable place in the system. The feminine victim estranges herself from an intolerable situation and becomes a fugitive, but only temporarily. Catherine undergoes rehabilitation to become a "proper" romantic heroine.

Curiously, the main narrative is broken midway by an account of a military response to a Maroon uprising. This portion of the text is fragmentary, but what survives clearly establishes the Maroons as a treacherous band, supposed to track runaway slaves but bonding with them in evading and resisting recapture and inseparable from them "as body and shadow" (20). This episode ends suddenly, shifting back to Catherine, an isolated fugitive contemplating the receding shoreline of Jamaica. The relevance of the foray against the Maroons is not clear, but it reinforces the Eurocentric orientation of the local narrative.

Although a flawed and relatively dull piece, "Busha's Mistress" marks an important stage in the literary history of Jamaica and of the Caribbean. A fusion of types, the exploited woman and the marooned consciousness, becomes increasingly familiar in later literature and offers crucial metaphorical expression to colonial schizophrenia. Catherine begins as a woman trapped in silence. She resists fraudulent discourse and becomes increasingly vocal in her struggle for freedom, which she ultimately achieves through compromise.

"Busha's Mistress" offers interesting contrasts to a later novel of the century. Mayne Reid's *The Maroon* (1862) is yet another tale of adventure in "exotic" surroundings among "savage" characters, but its governing temper is more characteristically Victorian than romantic in its metanarrative celebration of national decency. Comments on emancipation reflect this phenomenon (2–3) as well as general satisfaction with the progress of the empire. The tale was published well after emancipation although it is set immediately before it.

In *The Maroon*, a young Englishman (Herbert Vaughan) arrives in Jamaica to seek his only remaining family but finds his uncle (the custos) unwelcoming. Custos Vaughan looks forward to uniting his daughter (Kate) with a pretentious landowner, but a romantic bond develops at once between the young cousins, Kate and Herbert. In an effort to unite Herbert with his own daughter and so transfer Kate's inheritance to his own family, a neighboring Jew schemes with a vengeful obeahman (Chakra) and has the Custos murdered. Chakra abducts Kate and has the plantation torched. Meanwhile, Herbert has formed a friendship with a heroic Maroon leader (Cubina), the lover of Kate's maid (Yola, an African princess). Ultimately, both couples unite, the Jew and obeahman having been swept over a waterfall.

The novel is significant as the only extant nineteenth-century fiction in which a Maroon is a central character. The action also follows the revenge of an obeahman who has been brutally tortured, and it records the fury of his own unrequited love. Thus, the alienated black consciousness receives attention, though of the most negative kind, for in Chakra we see the black outcast as villain. Obsessed with a hatred that reinforces dehumanizing features, Chakra and his Jewish accomplice haunt the margins of the community both linguistically and morally.

The familiar plot of abduction and rescue goes beyond the shift in point of departure noted in "Busha's Mistress" in that *The Maroon* unites a heroic young Englishman with a colored wife—although the heroine is *mustee* and the "taint," as the book terms it, is invisible. "Busha's Mistress" stops short by revealing that both Vernon and his lover are the children of two sisters who are colored, and although the text also unites an ex-slave with an ex-overseer, Jackson can hardly be considered a romantic ideal. Reid's *Maroon* not only romanticizes intermarriage but suggests a relationship of equality between, on the one hand, the English and creole couple and, on the other, the Maroon and his African bride. So, melodramatic as the novel is, it reveals new possibilities for resolution, such as interracial marriage, liberation of blacks and their ownership of property, and outlandish poetic justice for the slave trader. (He is eaten at an African marriage feast!) Yet this qualified liberation not only comes later in the century than most romantic art, but it also demonstrates a self-satisfaction and concludes with a confidence in the perfection of civilization more characteristic of Victorianism.

Superior to *The Maroon* in both plot and execution, *Captain Clutterbuck's Champagne*, by William G. Hamley (1862), is tightly structured, realistically portrayed, and credibly expressed. Again, by this time, the narrator looks back on emancipation to view it as a triumph of civilization (218–19), and this novel is consciously lighter, articulated in a frank and humorous vein in contrast to the somewhat pretentious *Maroon*. Although it includes romantic jealousy, attempted abduction, and rescue like other nineteenth-century works, it does little to stir issues of individual liberation or selfhood. In fact, it rather takes these subjects for granted. Hamley presents Otherness as engaging instead of as terrifying or revolting. Incongruities amuse rather than alarm. Viewed in the Victorian tradition, *Captain Clutterbuck's Champagne* is orthodox in its worldview yet unburdened by heavy moral overtones, and it surprises in its sheer lightheartedness. Here, in contrast to *The Maroon*, there is relatively little distancing of characters to suggest marronage in theme or perspective.

The novels of Reid and Hamley are distinct from the five that appeared between 1812 and 1855, including *Hamel,* which is not yet examined. The authors of the earlier five conceive their narratives in the traditions of European romanticism, but confrontation of European values with Caribbean social realities constrains this romanticism. In an important respect, *The Maroon* differs substantially from the other novels examined. Montgomery, Marly, and Tom Cringle approach unfamiliar Jamaica with curiosity; home is available for recall. Despite their separation they have some support in the system itself. Herbert Vaughan has no such assurance, and the Maroon himself has no base outside of Jamaica. Even Catherine in "Busha's Mistress" is not irreversibly separated from her community. Her success rests on both physical and psychological escape, which are possible once she shares in that imperial discourse in which Britain is home.

The Maroon differs from the other novels so far examined in that it does not overtly locate home in Britain. At the same time, the discourse conveys a setting that is spatially, temporally, and ideologically remote. Its introductory pages sketch the mountains of Trelawny, "some blue peaks just visible in the distance" (1:4), and temporal references intensify this sense of separation by evoking "romantic interest equalling, if not surpassing, that which attaches to the vanished halls of the Moctezumas [*sic*], or the ruined palaces of the Peruvian Incas" (1:4). References to unfamiliar objects by terms foreign to English (*goombay,* 1:6) reinforce this sense of strangeness. In addition, the narrator claims an ideological stance that ranges him with the inhabitants of this remote world and against established interests and sympathies, as he implies this in his "enthusiastic admiration for those brave black men, who, for two hundred years, maintained their independence against the whole white population of the island" (1:5).

The narrator remains independent of the action, claiming to convey a tale related by an ancient Maroon warrior, Quaco, about "affairs of the olden time" (1:8). However, Quaco himself is not only peripheral to central events but also absent from most of them, and none of the events are filtered through his consciousness. Even Cubina, the Maroon himself, appears only briefly in the first volume, glimpsed through the consciousness of the young Englishman, Herbert Vaughan.

Virtuous characters conform to European values in various ways and speak the official language for the most part. The greatest distortion measured against these traditional norms is the character of Chakra, the obeahman. Reid draws this character through repeated references to bestiality and ugliness, which relate closely to his African culture and physiognomy as well as to a physical deformity that the text renders indistinct from racial features. He gradually becomes more monstrous, until he eventually constitutes a nightmare that the Custos encounters on the verge of death. On the other hand, the writer takes pains to emphasize that Yola and her brother lack the physical features commonly associated with Africans but instead possess "arabic" facial features and hair (1:31–32). Kate, although self-disparagingly styled "only a mustee" (3:312), is indistinguishable from white residents both physically and behaviorally despite Reid's apologetic references to "the taint" (1:29 and throughout). The Maroon himself, half brother to the beautiful Kate and resembling her, is the son of a quadroon. Curiously, his language is devoid of Creole.

The Maroon is not the central character of the tale. Early reference to Maroon aspirations for liberty and to the breaking of bonds provides background for the plot. This struggle forms no part of the action, which is set later, when the Maroons are bound by treaty to retrieve and return runaway slaves. Congruent to the "queer encounter" that the narrator describes as throwing him into conversation with Quaco and informing him of the circumstances he narrates is the chance meeting between Herbert Vaughan and Cubina, the Maroon. Herbert, the young Englishman, is central to the action. Isolated by the death of his father and by his uncle's rejection, alone on a strange island, lost in the forest, he is vulnerable to exploitation by the Jew, susceptible to compassionate maidens, and open to friendship with inhabitants of the wilderness.

Apart from Chakra, the blacks are warriors or slaves. The latter evoke sympathy rather than respect, "dark-skinned victims of human cupidity brought from below, and submitted to . . . demoniac anointment—to which one and all yielded with an appearance of patient resignation, like sheep under the hands of the shearer" (1:50–51). Grammatically, lexically, and metaphorically, the writer conveys their passivity. In the end, even Cubina and Yola will enter Jamaican society through the action of Herbert and Kate, who will not only accept them socially but also give them a portion of land.

Cubina's character does not break with stereotype. Reid merely selects the stereotype of the black warrior and romanticizes it. The narrator recalls the Jamaican Maroons as an essentially peaceful group in exotic surroundings where "when war was forced upon them, lay the scene of their valorous achievements" (1:6). Cubina, as leader of these inhabitants of the greenwood, fights injustice and entertains wanderers and refugees; he is a brown Robin Hood rather than a Jamaican Maroon, and the narrator explicitly makes this comparison (1:261).

Although *The Maroon* does not explicitly locate Britain as home, the island setting is conveyed as spatially remote, its wilderness as exotic, and its dwellings as civilized insofar as they accommodate European tastes. Characters are virtuous or evil as they conform to or depart from British values, and they are fortunate or pitiable as they achieve or are deprived of colonial possessions. The central consciousness turns out to be that of an English adventurer, whereas the Jamaican Maroon is supportive and is envisaged in terms of a traditional British hero. He is distinct from his own band—more European in dress, in features, and in speech. Reid verbally marks his otherness only by scattered exclamations (*Crambo!*) to recall historical association between the Maroons and the Spanish. Cubina's participation in the action, his character, and his language link rather than distance him from civilization. The Maroon conveys no sense of marronage.

The Rebel in Search of a Voice: *Hamel, the Obeah Man*

The writer who selects a Jamaican setting confronts decisions about alternative language codes that may relate to each other as discourse and counterdiscourse. The writer may adopt official or marginal codes to convey perspectives that are central or peripheral.

By selecting a code for direct speech by a character, nineteenth-century writers indicate how and to what extent that character fits into the social setting of the novel. Moreover, as language attitudes are crucial elements of the cognitive environment that forms part of the novel's context, the choice of code for a character reveals other pertinent features of personality. In *Montgomery, Marly,* and to a lesser extent *Tom Cringle's Log,* the Standard English–speaker encounters Jamaican Creole as one component of the adventure in an exotic land, as an aspect of the unfamiliar or the bizarre that challenges the protagonist. "Busha's Mistress" exhibits the most varied use of the Creole but marks the assimilation of the heroine into civilization by acquisition of the official code.

The writer of another nineteenth-century novel, *Hamel, the Obeah Man,* does not attempt to render the Creole but makes clear that it is one feature of its hero's Otherness. Hamel provides a perspective that is off center, non-civilized. He is an incomplete and inconsistent character, more than a Caribbean Caliban or a voiceless savage yet less than an embodiment of black self-hood. His marronage most volubly expresses itself in his voicelessness. The most nearly conceived black consciousness in the nineteenth-century texts is not reported by reference to his own language.[4]

The voicelessness of black Jamaica is nowhere more apparent in the nineteenth century than in *Hamel, the Obeah Man*, yet *Hamel* is a landmark in the development of characterization in the Jamaican setting. The text is overtly a romance, and its Eurocentric values reach deep into its underlying purpose, which is antimissionary. Yet this text is disrupted by a subtext that focuses on a black protagonist.

A white missionary (Roland) incites the slaves of a plantation to plan rebellion and to establish a black king (Combah), but Roland creates the plot for his own selfish, sensual ends rather than out of concern for their humanity. An aging obeahman (Hamel) directs the plan but later averts it in the interest of a young adventurer (Fairfax) who is in love with the young woman whom Roland seeks to abduct, the daughter of the plantation owner on the threatened property. Fairfax disguises himself as a Maroon in an attempt to rescue her, but the obeahman actually restores order.

The gap between imperial values and Other is more profound and explicit in *Hamel* than in any of the other texts discussed. In *Hamel* the center of focus shifts to highlight different dimensions of otherness. Although Roland proclaims equality and encourages the slaves to rebel under the leadership of a black king (Combah), his concept of liberation is deformed. He intends to control the entire community through Combah and to gain power over a young white creole woman. Roland's mental distortion approaches lunacy, while Hamel emerges as the thinker who has masterminded preparations for the rebellion but who ultimately averts it (2:196).

In its recognition of black consciousness, the novel demonstrates romantic interest in the foreign, the "savage," the poor, and the unlettered. The obeahman is an enigmatic figure who inhabits a remote cave above a gorge in wild landscape rent by violent storms and floods. This enigma in characterization at least partly results from a fractured narrative vision of freedom. Alternately threatening and reassuring, Hamel wields enormous psychological power over the slaves, on whose obedience hangs the security and sanity of the ruling community. By the conclusion Hamel has achieved heroic proportions, but for much of the tale he is ambiguous and obscurely threatening. Throughout he is presented as isolated, brooding—an individualized and uncontrollable assessor of social norms. The novel closes with him rowing out alone "to the land of [his] birth" (2:326). He turns eastward on a vast ocean whose far shore is so distant as to have passed into myth.

Interestingly, the narrative reverses the reader's initial expectations and responses to hero and villain. Roland appears at first to be the central consciousness, possibly a hero of recognizable type—the daring adventurer. The novel opens with him engaging in monumental struggle with the storm that drives him through wilderness and flood into the habitation of the obeahman (1:17). Early on, he finds himself longing for emancipation from the obeahman's abode and power. Actually, Roland turns out to be a villain of gothic dimensions, loading the novel with that danger and sexually tinged larger-than-life evil familiar in romantic fiction (1:23).

The causal relationship between Roland's actions and those of others implies power on his part and weakness or malleability on theirs. Threatening black characters are no match for him; their crimes are confused reactions to his misinformation and bad influence. Within the belief system that underlies the novel, Roland, the preacher, is a corrupting force who misleads slaves into a sense of equality. His religion is presented as deviant, raving, supportive of murder and anarchy.

In describing *Hamel* as an antimissionary tract, Edward Kamau Brathwaite ("Creative Literature" 67) recognizes a crucial link between social context and a genre of discourse. The antimissionary tract is a form of discourse that highlights and seeks to perpetuate separation between social groups. Distancing techniques associated with the genre include a lexis that is emotionally loaded. The novel denounces clergy outside of the established church as white obeahmen who for their own aggrandizement seek to overthrow divinely ordained social order by inciting blacks to freedom. Such lexical choice is all the more potent for being placed on black lips, especially on those of an obeahman. From the point of departure where black strength is threatening or African belief is revolting, the writer not only sets up an equivalence between offending white clergy and black "power" but places this denunciation in the mouth of the book's most noble and intelligent black. In fact, Roland turns out to be a twisted version of Hamel.

Combah's group is potentially a Maroon society. The planned uprising is a bid for independence that will place its participants outside of imperially defined civilization. The rebels perceive, beyond violent resistance, a structured society of their own, and they reject the model of European domination. Hamel is divided between this commitment and a sense of obligation to one member of the dominant group. The obeahman stands poised on the edge of action that could constitute an intervention in imperial history.

However, the group that Roland seeks to stir up to rebellion does not in fact comprise men of Maroon caliber. Indeed, when the missionary displeases them, Fairfax is able to save him by terrorizing them by shouting that the Maroons are upon them (1:169–70). Maroons participate in the action, but they do so on behalf of the planters, tracking and retrieving runaways as agreed by treaty. The narrative establishes their motivation as monetary gain rather than heroism (2:213). Hamel demonstrates absolute withdrawal, and he plans and is capable of implacable resistance to the established order. The first setting in which we encounter the obeahman locates him outside of civilization and suggests his desperation.

Within Combah's group there is argument and discussion regarding their relationship with the Maroons, whose skill and aggression they fear. Combah encourages collaboration and proposes joining the Maroons with his followers. Unlike these rebels, however, the Maroons are presented in an honorable light as a group committed to abiding by a treaty with the whites. Yet this too turns out not to be a picture of honor among blacks; the "Maroon" leader is no other than Fairfax in disguise (2:259).

Hamel is a tale of intrigue within intrigue. Hamel himself lacks background, and references to his future are cryptic. Hints that the obeahman has his own obscure agenda are never explicated. Instead, the writer takes us into the mind of the preacher, who plots abduction and rape with the assistance of the confused Combah. Similarly, we know that Combah, like Roland, plans to keep the victim for himself. However, Hamel is isolated by gaps in our information about him, by perspectival choices that exclude the reader from his mind.

Within the setting of the novel, Hamel is isolated by the bipolar racial differences between himself and the white characters, but the features that isolate him relate to the power structure among the characters. The writer conceives these characters within a context of certain social expectations, but Hamel departs from stereotype when he disturbs shared expectations of black powerlessness. His potential for disrupting the status quo, for contriving an alternative history, undermines the novel's Eurocentrism.

The weak black characters are devoid of enigma, and the most vulnerable of the "ruling" characters is also entirely comprehensible—the woman as victim. The predictable essentials of her character are innocence, virtue, beauty, and above all a racial purity equated with moral spotlessness. Combah, the black stereotype, is all the more stupidly presumptuous for aspiring to possess her; Roland is all the more evil for offering to betray her to primitive lust. Roland threatens betrayal of the divinely ordered white power structure from within. Hamel occupies a position outside of this structure that is undefined by any visible power base of his own yet quite distinct from all the other black characters, who fall obediently into stereotype.

Inner conflict strengthens the character of Hamel where it undermines that of the dissatisfied slaves. Within the later discourse, contradictions in the presentation of the rebels are all ascribed to the warped consciousness of Roland. He describes the very slaves whom he credits with souls as "brute beasts—guided only by their passions" (2:79). Obligation to their masters binds the blacks securely, constraining even Hamel to the decision that Fairfax is his friend and that "there will be no rebellion" (2:80). His declaration of this decision is a speech act that conveys its speaker's power. It parallels other actions, like that of turning over his cache of weapons to Fairfax (2:323), that indicate volition in his abnegation of power. Beneath Hamel's loyalty churns recognition that "there is justice upon the earth, though it seems to sleep; and the black men shall, first or last, shed your blood, and toss your bodies into the sea" (2:197). This explosion of emotion, credible in a Jamaican setting that is socially as well as physically realistic, cuts through the more contrived discourse that relays doctrine.

Indeed, Hamel's character gathers force to such intensity in places as to take over, conflicting with the polemic. Speech acts of warning and threat, as well as command and explanation, separate Hamel from other black characters, even as ethnic differences isolate him from the ruling class. *Hamel* remains Eurocentric narrative, haunted by recent horror of the Haitian revolution. Nevertheless, this novel marks a major development in the foundation of a Caribbean perspective in that its ultimate protagonist is black. Although Hamel functions in the action to preserve white supremacy, his independence constitutes a conflicting subtext to the doctrine of black subservience. Selfhood in the personality of Hamel struggles with authorial ideology.

Conversely, intrinsic inferiority fetters Combah. As the black figurehead for the rebellion, he seems built to self-destruct. In the presence of the young woman whom he has attempted to abduct, "a beautiful and elegant white maiden, an accomplished European and Christian . . . he sank even in his own estimation into nothing" (2:218–19). Similarly, racial difference blocks Michal, the fascinating quadroon girl, from lovers too dark or too white for her, and she accepts the loss of the (white) man she loves, satisfied to "see him happy, contented, with his white and beautiful wife" (2:319). She too is isolated by castelike racial distinctions that the novel supports; but here too, portrayal of her earlier pain and sensitivity argues an equal humanity within the very discourse structure designed to perpetuate inequality by denouncing resistance.

The psychological alienation of the preacher is central to this design yet begs comparison and contrast with the remote yet controlled and stable stance of the obeahman. Roland's psychological marronage unstructures his mind, while Hamel's physical, emotional, and psychological distance increases his control over events. Roland's fevered mind twists increasingly toward violence as the tale progresses. His imprisonment finds him on the verge of absolute breakdown; the prison scene is one of nightmare desperation. He escapes by stabbing his guard with a poisoned blade, establishing at the physical level of the action the poisonous influence stemming from his moral and psychological corruption.

From his remote contemplation of this destructive passion, Hamel rebukes white society for tolerating "the cunning, sneaking, fawning, fanatical, murderous villain, who tampered with the passions of their slaves" (2:316–17). The obeahman's address to this gathering is both outspoken and contemptuous. In context, this register is appropriate for denouncing the reversal of white values, which Hamel's character has been invented to attack. However, in an important sense, this register is inappropriate in its context, which includes the mutual knowledge of white nineteenth-century writers and readers that a black man is addressing "civilized" white society. Hamel's register at the end of the novel confirms the modern reader's inescapable conclusion about who is in charge.

Romantic heightening of feeling emerges in *Hamel* in the passion of the adventurer Fairfax, in the black characters' tentative but doomed search for freedom or love, and in Roland's twisted yearnings (political, religious, and sexual). Strangely apart from these feelings stands the obeahman, self-possessed, controlling the action, acclaimed eventually as hero for preventing catastrophic interference with the existing power structure. Yet the logical thread of the discourse knots in places, severs in others, always through the intervention of this illogically empowered black. Hamel orchestrates the original gathering of dissatisfied slaves to plot violence and to take a bloody oath of rebellion. In the end, Hamel not only renounces but denounces both abolitionist preachers and their cause of revolutionary freedom. Inevitably, he turns away from the entire community, which cannot, in literary discourse within this genre, accommodate a character that is both black and powerful. His ultimate act of independence and quest is the solitary journey onto that sea that separates the black from his past and across which he normally returns home only through death. Guinea, the far shore, is apotheosized in early Jamaican worldview.

In one sense, the dialectic between black and white values produces structural incoherence, contradictory points of view, and confusion in meaning that inhibit full development of a romantic worldview in this novel. At the same time, heightened feeling, unfettered imagination, and fascination with landscape lead the writer first to a Jamaican setting and later to themes of awakening black consciousness and uneasy bids for independence. In truth, social norms retain primacy over individual needs, and the self is not fully privileged. Yet the character of the obeahman, riven by conflicting loyalties, is memorable. Hamel is a character of strength, dignity, and self-possession, glimpsed through the distorted vision of a narrator who cannot enter the black mind. Herein lies the otherness that preoccupies the romantic. "What a strange fellow," mutter the whites as Hamel recedes from vision at the end (2:326).

Although Hamel, like the expatriate heroes of *Montgomery, Marly,* and *Tom Cringle's Log,* is isolated, is a stranger, and is far from home, Hamel is additionally isolated by the inaccessibility of his mind. He is remote not only physically but also psychologically. His own references to home are cryptic, devoid of that wealth of associations that accompany such references by protagonists in other texts. Moreover, in this novel no one else remotely resembles the hero. He not only encounters the unfamiliar, he is the unfamiliar. Finally, he is more frequently alone physically than any of the others. The stranger/visitor type is separate from civilized community by virtue of unfamiliarity and impermanence. But a greater number of the definitive components of civilization, as used in imperial discourse, are absent from the representation of Hamel than from that of European strangers such as Cringle, Marly, or Montgomery. What defines his separation as more extreme is the absence of such crucial components as location in community, history, codified language, and status appropriate to race.

In Hamel we meet the genuine recluse, distinct from all others in the community and unapproachable except on his own terms. This is the only major character in the nineteenth-century novels whose existence outside of his community must be permanent because he threatens by his very nature all that holds this community together. When the community recognizes him as a hero, he becomes even more impossible to assimilate. The inchoate black protagonist has spiraled beyond control even of his author. Thus, he remains an elusive character, barely definable as "a strange fellow," receding toward the unknown from which he came.

Hamel's perspective remains at least partially hidden, yet it is clear that he retains a clear concept of home. In this he contrasts with the ineffectual rebels. Simon Gikandi points out that what needs to be "foregrounded in Patterson's theory of slavery as social death, and indeed in Caribbean culture as a whole, is the extent to which slaves were denied a consciousness of their historicity" (6). Hamel is the most self-aware black character of the time, partly because he retains a sense of his own background. The strength of this retention intensifies his own marronage because he does not claim Jamaica as home. His ultimate direction is also uncertain. In a view of the distant sea, he points to the subjects of King Combah "going back to the land of freedom—Haiti—with some of the wretches whom it vomited forth for your destruction, at the recommendations of the Obeah Christians in England" (2:323). One member of the planter class in the novel believes that Hamel too will go to Haiti "to deliver himself up to the rebels whose triumph he has spoiled," and Fairfax appears to share this view (2:326–27). Yet Hamel announces his destination as his mother's country, the land of his birth, and it is not certain that this is Haiti, considering that his Creole is intelligible to characters native to the Jamaican setting. The author renders the protagonist more mysterious by highlighting gaps in content—unknown background, denied history, and ultimate fate.

Hamel is also elusive because he speaks a language that is never heard. The text accompanies Standard English dialogue with occasional narrative reminders that the actual usage is Creole. Perhaps even the author who selects a black protagonist in the period of slavery finds it impossible to achieve serious characterization using a medium traditionally linked with comic intent. Or perhaps the author simply lacks linguistic competence in Creole. At any rate, the writer who identifies the obeahman as Other repeatedly underscores this Otherness by reference to the character's speech in a marginal linguistic code. The narrator assures us that "Mr. Hamel used the dialect of his country, the creole tongue; sufficiently understood by all the assembled party . . . to make a considerable impression" (2:317).

In Hamel the persona of protagonist and outsider come most closely together, however inconsistently. No other hero is as alienated, and no other character, however distanced from civilization (as the obeahman must always be) achieves Hamel's stature. As powerful outsider, Hamel weaves schemes barely discernible to other characters. His planning is effective, and nothing forestalls his intentions unless he redesigns his scheme. He outlines strategies for others and intervenes in other characters' courses of action, recharting their futures. He advises on procedures for maintaining a hated system for the time being but foresees the destruction of this system whose preservation or overthrow lies in his hands. In a context where physical constraints on blacks are taken for granted, Hamel comes and goes at will and at last rows coolly out of sight.

Although Hamel's code must be the marginal language of the blacks for his character to be convincing, his words must be rendered in the language of serious affairs. Otherwise, the requirements of the overriding discourse type (the antimissionary tract) cannot be satisfied. Even for the purposes of characterization neither his pent power nor the cogency of his arguments would in the context of literary tradition at that time be renderable in Creole. Inconceivable as this constraint may be to twentieth-century readers, the nineteenth-century readers who shared the cognitive environment of the novelist could understand that Hamel speaks Creole without the actual Creole intervening in their comprehension of the obeahman's power. The obeahman must gain strength not through what readers would perceive as bogus African trappings but through some indefinable trait, some mysterious property of his Otherness. He is distanced by our inability to hear him directly, as the narrator articulates his character's message in a universal rather than an obscure tongue. He is distanced, conversely, by the reader's knowledge that this tongue is obscure.

Thus, Hamel retains the voicelessness expected of the savage. He supplies the imperial need for a Caliban in the wilderness. As Michel de Certeau points out, in such imperial discourse the New World is "a blank, 'savage' page on which Western desire will be written" (219). At the same time, Hamel's dignity and influence demand that when he does speak he must use the master code of the time, especially if he is to deliver the antimissionary message that is the imperial purpose of the text. This message from this powerful personality must be rearticulated in language dignified by social acceptance and learned usage.

The works considered here provide a more authentic setting than do novels such as *The Koromantyn Slave*, whose author lacks firsthand knowledge and depends on other writers' descriptions of residents or visitors. At the same time, the limited understanding of those authors considered (regarding the condition of the masses) subscribes imagination. This constraint limits access to types of individual experience that lie at the heart of a Jamaican setting that is internally experienced rather than externally recorded. Certainly, no author of the time enters the native consciousness in the way Michael Scott enters that of the adventurer.

Fictional writing on Jamaica shows limited development in the theme of selfhood that is central to European romanticism. Jamaican songs treat selfhood more successfully, but the theme as voiced by native Jamaicans has implications that run counter to European interest. Self in the nineteenth-century Jamaican setting is quite distinct from self to the English romantics. The heroic ideal in European romanticism defines quest as a search for something beyond one's self. Self-absorption is only a middle point toward a larger passage—a cosmic consciousness that brings true union with humanity, and in this context Wilson James explores what he identifies as an aesthetic quest for self-annihilation. Development of self and development of community may thus fuse in European romantic vision. However, fiction set in Jamaica but Eurocentric in perspective preserves entrenched social barriers as paramount to survival of the writer's social group, and ambiguity inevitably riddles the treatment of selfhood and its relationship to community. Not that ambiguity or conflict is foreign to romanticism—quite the reverse. The movement through romanticism to Victorianism culminates in explorations such as Tennyson's extensive charting of inner landscape to highlight doubt. However, successful romanticism directs ambiguity so as to result in conscious irony, as Lillian Furst demonstrates (28). In British novels of Jamaican setting, semantic anomalies betray apparently unconscious irony.

It is unsurprising that fiction of this time should contrast sharply with Jamaican verse. This verse takes two forms. One is folk song, expressing the longing of the individual, native self. This is the peasant, oral, Creole voice. The other survives in rare literary verse. In the latter case, the native black and native white poets are grounded in European tradition yet steeped in the Jamaican experience. Pamela O'Gorman's reproduction of Samuel Felsted's *Jonah* preserves a cry for freedom that spans oceans, races and cultures:

> Billows foam around my head
> I am counted with the dead
> Save me, Lord, revoke my doom
> Nor leave me longer in my tomb. (17)

However, the romantic fiction shares little with local oral tradition and differs substantially in its perspective from educated verse of the time. The fiction reflects the spirit of the age in the desperate search of its heroes for meaningful love relationships, in the fascination with far-flung lands, and in curiosity about mental processes of the aged, the feminine, the poor, the troubled—the inquisitive pursuit of otherness. But this fiction does not and cannot blaze with revolutionary fire and unambiguously uphold the supremacy of selfhood for the re-creation of society.

Hamel most closely approaches true revolutionary romanticism in the character of its black protagonist because of inherent conflicts in presentation between power and independence of the spirit in the hero's character on the one hand and suppression of the black in the ideological context that the character has been invented to support. Thus, even in *Hamel*, worldview is fractured through narrative inability or unwillingness to convey black selfhood in its own terms, a rift in observation between outer and inner landscapes. Hamel's separation from civilization and his own ultimate inaccessibility lie partly in the reader's inability to hear the character's own voice, to enter his consciousness through his own code. His thoughts are filtered by a Standard English rendition, which contributes to the strange riven character of the earliest black protagonist in an authentic Jamaican setting, although some of the contradiction lies in sheer incompatibility of content.

As an imperial text, *Hamel, the Obeah Man* displays what Gikandi itemizes as the central paradigms of colonial historicity: systematization, chronology, and closure (8). Beneath this imperial text, however, *Hamel* is Jamaican in the protagonist's resistance, in his lack of historicity, and in the open-endedness of his departure.

The nineteenth-century writers who selected Jamaica as a setting conveyed a sense of distance between this locale and that of Britain, to which Jamaica is at least implicitly compared. Thus, the writer conveyed the ensuing isolation of the protagonist, often a stranger or visitor, usually representing civilization in an encounter with otherness. The writer may overtly highlight otherness in the Jamaican setting by indicating savage or bestial features (which may include what the writer conceives as distortions of language), as in Reid's presentation of the obeahman. Or the writer may covertly highlight otherness by imbuing the character with mystery, by imposing silences or lack of articulation.

The separation conveyed may be temporal distance (from an idyllic past, as in Montgomery's recollection of childhood), or the separation may be spatial distance from civilization, which the writer may achieve by defining the boundaries and limitations of the island community. Black characters are normally removed from the center of the narrative and presented as deviant. Eurocentricity inscribes ex-centricity on non-European characters but conceives them in terms of recognizable types—the scheming villain, such as Reid's Jew, or the outsider who revels in his withdrawal to the greenwood, such as Reid's Maroon. Only one text appears to subvert this ideological perspective by convincingly representing an anti-imperialist perspective. At the same time, this text conveys the divided mind of the colonized black consciousness. In *Hamel*, the obeahman's rebuke of white creole civilization constitutes the beginnings of a subtext to the imperialist tract.

On the whole, in the traditional British discourse, the romantic movement embraces the Jamaican setting but is frustrated—at least in part by suppression or contextual restriction of the Creole voice. Narrative expressions of cosmic awareness are muted; implied or stated attitudes to liberation are contradictory, not necessarily by authorial design but by divided point of view; and irony and conflict surface as prominent but often unintentional. The maroon as a fictional type (not necessarily tied to the Maroon as a sociohistorical entity) begins to take form, growing in independence, a speaker awaiting a discourse. However, in the fiction of this period, the unshackling of imagination remains partial, commitment to selfhood continues inevitably color coded, and the articulation of freedom is constrained in the twilight recesses of narrative consciousness.

3

The Jamaican Outsider
in the Caribbean Canon

But we were not in their ranks.

—Jean Rhys, *Wide Sargasso Sea*

JUST AS JAMAICA's remoteness and exoticism presented nineteenth-century British writers with a setting for adventure on the far side, Jamaica also offered the nineteenth-century literary temperament a source for characters who might exhibit pathologically extreme alienation in British settings. The Jamaican protagonist as misfit is foreshadowed but not fully realized in some characterizations of the stranger, such as Marly and Montgomery. Besides, both these protagonists encounter local whites of strange temperament, distorted by separation from civilized influences. The most deluded and dangerous of such characters in the nineteenth-century corpus is Roland, the missionary in *Hamel*.

Characters who are Jamaican by birth and displaced to a British setting introduce a new dimension of alienation. Charlotte Brontë's shadowy creation of Rochester's mad wife implies again, quite naturally, a Eurocentric view in which the Caribbean is Other. Bertha is Rochester's dark secret, an obstacle to the heroine, Jane, the logical explanation for strange events at Thornfield Hall. In the nineteenth-century British canon, the Jamaican's shattered reason requires no explanation. It is a Caribbean author, Jean Rhys, who explores the fragmented self of the dislocated Jamaican in *Wide Sargasso Sea*.

Wide Sargasso Sea has enjoyed a widespread critical acclaim that establishes it in the canon of English literature even as the novel itself deconstructs values entrenched in the British classic by Brontë. International readers unfamiliar with Caribbean literature categorize *Wide Sargasso Sea* as a modern British classic. However, the position that there is now an established and growing Caribbean canon, defined on the basis of an established body of authors in all genres, is crucial to this book. The work of this growing number of successful and professional authors has both international currency and acclaim, as evidenced in nominations and awards of prestigious international literary prizes. Caribbean literature now claims a place among areal subdivisions of the discipline even in conservative university programs. Caribbean criticism owes much to black studies and postcolonial criticism but flourishes independent of such approaches and significantly contributes to them. More and more, educational systems entrench Caribbean texts by inclusion on syllabi for regional and international examinations.

The growth of a canon gives rise to the emergence of patterns, norms, and expectations regarding themes, characterizations, settings, and even narrative structures. Before attempting to trace national as distinct from regional patterns, this chapter will consider how a novel that has contributed to the formation of a Caribbean canon rewrites the character of an alienated Jamaican woman, initially conceived as a creole lunatic in traditional literature of the British canon.

Motherland and Dislocation

Neither Brontë nor Rhys had ever lived in Jamaica. For nineteenth-century creators of characters who were Other, it was simply enough to cite Jamaica as a source for alien and incalculable behavior. Rhys, on taking up Brontë's Bertha, involuntarily took up Bertha's birthplace. But Jamaica is more than an involuntarily acquired setting for *Wide Sargasso Sea:* it convincingly represents the wider Caribbean. Its association with refugees from revolution in the French Caribbean makes it a reasonable location for characters of French as well as British Caribbean extract. Considerable movement between the islands takes place in *Wide Sargasso Sea,* as it does in other novels of the period in which *Wide Sargasso Sea* is set. The offshore perspective of Tom Cringle reveals non-Jamaican residents in Jamaica from a variety of origins. In Cuba, Cringle also meets a Jamaican who has made himself at home. Antoinette's movement between the islands is not unusual for the period and renders her thoroughly Caribbean as well as thoroughly Jamaican.

The preceding chapter examined texts whose authors had direct experience of Jamaica—as far as could be determined, considering the anonymity of some novels. This chapter relaxes this requirement to consider the re-creation of Jamaican setting and character by writers of Caribbean worldview and regional rather than national focus. Rhys's own unfamiliarity with Jamaica did not prevent her from evoking it as a physical and social setting similar in many ways to her own island. In any case, *Wide Sargasso Sea* conveys a perspective on Jamaica that is not the vision of the direct and dispassionate observer. In this novel, the Jamaican past is recollected through flame by a shattered psyche.

The discourse recalls through the symbol of Jamaica the Caribbean setting of Rhys's own early experience. It explores the mind of a Caribbean woman adrift in murky passage between her Jamaican beginnings and an attic in Britain. The narrator, dislocated in space, produces an account that is superficially sequential but embedded in a frame that is dechronologized. In setting out to supply the Caribbean background of a well-known character of British literary tradition, Rochester's mad wife in *Jane Eyre*, Rhys seizes on those physical, sociohistorical, and sociolinguistic characteristics of Jamaica that are familiar elsewhere in the Caribbean.

Topological extremes, such as high mountains, concretize the social barriers. The exotic green vegetation (with vast ferns and massive bell-shaped flowers) clusters, blooms, towers, runs wild, writhes, and decays, and with it falls apart the plantation system in all its crumbling wealth and decadent lifestyle. The confines of the island hold mounting resentment, gathering black threat, and spiraling white fear and suspicion. From beyond trickles a continuous inflow of outsiders from home, legendary Britain, to whom this island is a wilderness. Thus, the setting induces conflicting values and perceptions forced into confrontation in a cramped space with pressure building to uncontrollable eruption. The compressed violence explodes in the burning of Coulibri estate, which consumes the whole world of Antoinette's childhood. The backward glance branded on her mind is "the house . . . burning and the yellow-red sky . . . like sunset" (37)—a vision that flares up again as she breaks from her confinement in the attic: "Then I turned around and saw the sky. It was red and all my life was in it . . . and the tree of life in flames" (155).

The nineteenth-century parallel to this painful recollection is an inside view of hell, for thus Brontë's Rochester perceives his Jamaican marriage according to the account he gives to Jane of "a fiery West Indian night. . . . The air was like sulphur-streams. . . . The sea . . . rumbled dull like an earthquake—black clouds were casting up over it; the moon was setting in the waves broad and red, like a hot cannon-ball—she threw her last bloody glance over a world quivering with the ferment of tempest. . . . My ears were filled with the curses the maniac still shrieked out: wherein she momentarily mingled my name with such a tone of demon-hate, with such language!" (335).

So Rochester escapes the infernal wilderness, turning home with "the sweet wind from Europe . . . still whispering in the refreshed leaves, and the Atlantic . . . thundering in glorious liberty. . . . 'Go,' said Hope, 'and live again in Europe' " (335–36). But he carries with him this Creole hell, which is the secret underlying the angst of the dominant but tortured lover whom Jane persists to the end in addressing as "master." Critics have recognized the parallels between Jane and Antoinette as feminine outsiders struggling with masterful men (Thorpe 104), but Brontë's Rochester sees only the opposition between Jane and Bertha, which he expresses in terms that delineate spatial direction and distance. He describes the woman who suits him as "the antipodes of the Creole" (338).

The Caribbean view of the disturbed creole is more than Rhys's chronological account of Bertha's past. In *Wide Sargasso Sea*, sequentiality is apparent rather than real. The action consists of remembered losses in series. First comes a neighbor's suicide, identifying a way out by sea as a way out through death. Antoinette loses, in turn, her mother, her social circle, the friendship of her peers, her home (and incidentally her brother). All had seemed protected from strangers by the barrier of the sea when she lay womb-safe in Coulibri after her mother had covered her up in bed (23). Antoinette also loses the shelter of the convent and its religious support, her sympathetic aunt and mildly supportive stepfather, her inheritance and the limited love/lust of her husband. Her passage to England finally deprives her of her homeland, her region, her identity as Antoinette (for her husband insists on renaming her Bertha), and even the certainty of her own sanity. Through the flames of displacement and exile Rhys rewrites irrationality as dislocation and psychological marronage.

Various circumstances turn Antoinette physically, mentally, and emotionally adrift. This effect of a floating consciousness is achieved by suspension in time, by dislocation in space, and by the cutting of communication (Lalla "Sociolinguistic Approach" 10). Events of the novel, built into its social setting, disconnect the speaker from context after context, leaving her ultimately in a void. In Brontë's novel, Jamaica truly represents a setting in the void, for in Brontë's context Jamaica is the largest and best-known British holding in the distant Caribbean and an island geographically isolated from the other British islands. For the Caribbean author, the void lies beyond the island home, in an illusory England.

Yet Antoinette's condition of "unbelonging" begins in Jamaica. Antoinette recalls not only a past denied but a past in which she never fully belonged and outside of which she has no reality. Dispossession of setting is crucial to the fragmentation of self that transforms Antoinette into Bertha. Because of the special circumstances of the creole woman who is the central character, however, *Wide Sargasso Sea* displaces the *origo* or zero point that specifies I, here, and now in raising questions of who, where, and when. Not only does setting provide the margins by which to define the protagonist's alienation, but the shifting setting from Jamaica to elsewhere in the Caribbean and then to Britain contributes to the multidimensionality of the boundaries that exclude this outcast. The Jamaican setting also makes possible the experience of an island under British rule and sensitive to the nearby French experience of revolution. Insecurity within Jamaica is the beginning of Antoinette's tragedy.

Rhys sharply defines physical settings in *Wide Sargasso Sea.* Coulibri, the estate of Antoinette's earliest memories, takes form through the voice of a hurt child; every discomfort of the garden is "better than people" (24), who belong to groups from which Antoinette is excluded. The narrative encodes this exclusion in terms of negation ("we were not in their ranks," 15). The liturgical phrasing of a growing girl's Catholic instruction frames the description of Mount Calvary Convent and interlaces the episodes of her life, "now and at the hour of our death" (47). The scene shifts from Jamaica to the French island with a change of narrator. Beyond Massacre, along a road climbing upward to Granbois, is a scenery "wild and menacing" to the English stranger who has married Antoinette, and its brilliant "too much" reflects Antoinette's passion and threatening otherness (59). The final parting is with Sandi, the love that might have been, for the transoceanic voyage that completes Antoinette's alienation (152). The narrative tears away each remembered setting to reveal one of greater confinement and isolation. Grace Poole's reflections reinforce our sense of Antoinette's separation by "thick walls. . . . Past the lodge gate a long avenue of trees and inside the house . . . the thick walls, keeping away all the things that you have fought till you can fight no more" (146). Each setting is insular, reflecting the alienated world of the creole self that is, after all, the ultimate setting of the entire discourse, for the speech act is internal. The original island setting naturally implies the sea, which both confines and sunders, and here as elsewhere this island setting contributes significantly in defining the outcast or exile as a familiar persona in Caribbean literature.

Apart from its title, the novel makes limited overt reference to the sea. Yet the presence of the sea is implied in the central themes of journey, exile, and marronage and is essential to the tale of Antoinette's dispossession, which involves her actual transshipment to England. The casting of her husband as conqueror/colonizer also implies his own voyage of adventure. Metaphorically too, the confining sea is implicit in all suggestions of insularity that support the theme of Antoinette's increasing isolation and eventual imprisonment. The Jamaican society of her childhood is insular, waterlocked.

The sea divides, it defines borders of existence, and to the Caribbean mind it represents the original paths to exile in the Caribbean itself.

Although Helen Nebecker examines development as journey, she does not pursue a link between transshipment and abortive birth. Antoinette epitomizes the unrealized self, becalmed on the Sargasso. Her physical voyage completes her psychological passage of dispossession and finalizes her deprivation of mother, of motherland, and of mother tongue. Separate from society and indeed never fully part of any civilization, Antoinette quests for existence and identity. The actual account of her physical passage across the Atlantic occupies less than a paragraph, but her psychological journey composes the entire novel, a study of emotional darkness, isolation, and confinement in which she battles for existence.

Elsewhere in Caribbean literature the Middle Passage has figuratively associated the sea with childbirth. In comparing the trauma of transshipment to that of birth, the narrative may focus on the tortured consciousness of either mother or child. The link between passage in the great triangular route of the slave trade and passage in the birth canal recurs, as in John Hearne's *Sure Salvation*, where the frustrated womb of Eliza Hogarth reflects the becalmed slave ship. The passage of Eliza's nightmare labor bears death and madness. After the stillbirth she is at sea in many senses, self-condemned to isolation in her sterile cabin. Close at hand the hold confines a cargo of slaves until the whole shameful enterprise is violently aborted. Similarly, Jennifer Rahim's "Still Birth" explicitly links the birth struggle and sea passage in ways that recall the movement down the dark passage at the end of *Wide Sargasso Sea* to a point that, in Rahim's words, "will end one journey and begin another" (Watts 65).

En route from her motherland, Antoinette tries to smash the portholes of the confining cabin, but her captors drug her into deep sleep: "It was that night, I think, that we changed course and lost our way to England. This cardboard house where I walk at night is not England" (148). Torn from her motherland, Antoinette never arrives at the civilization she has imagined.

The link between transshipment and unsuccessful parturition is far reaching. The stranger/husband's preconceived vision of Antoinette stunts her development as a separate identity from her mother and aborts her independent existence. Rhys approaches the passage as a psychological voyage of the "white nigger"/bartered woman in a study of identity crisis through transportation from the Caribbean to England. It is unnatural separation, abortive rather than maturing to independent identity; her passage is miscarriage. In addition, Rhys has set out to fill a gap, to supply the Caribbean background to Brontë's Bertha. *Wide Sargasso Sea* is thus a psychological journey through recollection by the "madwoman" in the attic, a woman in whose development separate identity from her mother has been stunted. Psychologically, Antoinette tangles in her mother's cord, just as she psychologically tangles in the Sargasso on being torn from Jamaica. Deborah Kelly Kloepfer analyzes the mother-daughter relationship in detail but does not explore the methods by which Rhys fragments time, setting, and point of view to support the controlling theme of this tortured and disoriented psyche, stripped of its every support and suspended in a timeless void.

Here the narrator retrieves all the remembered settings into a discourse whose eventual setting is the British attic, dark and cold until she rekindles Coulibri's last sunset. Conflicts between the perceptions of Caribbean settings (by Antoinette as narrator and by her husband as narrator) are related to oppositions underlying the semantic structure of the entire discourse. Her husband's Eurocentric vision of civilization redefines all that Antoinette would consider civilized as savage.

Antoinette's alienation is multidimensional, partly because her vision of civilization contrasts with that of her husband and also because her vision of wilderness is not necessarily a simple negation of civilization. The wildness of setting for the honeymoon cottage is positive in her view, and she resents her husband for negating it (121). Kristien Hemmerechts's structural analysis of *Wide Sargasso Sea* refers to the presence of complex and neutral terms that allow each semiotic square to be extended to six terms. The sememic oppositions of wilderness and civilization involve association of wilderness with noncivilization and of civilization with nonwilderness, but Hemmerechts points out that the space of the attic to which Antoinette's husband relegates her is a place that is noncivilization and nonwilderness (358).

This is another entrapping void reinforcing the metaphor of the Sargasso. Mad Bertha is a male invention by which Antoinette's husband transforms her to a figment of his imagination. We may take Antoinette as the classic Caribbean type of the exploited woman because she not only undergoes social and racial marronage but also experiences multiple colonization in the Caribbean by incomprehensible male and British culture, only to experience marronage again in exile to a space beyond all definition of civilization or of wilderness.

Although the intricacies of mother-daughter alignment and estrangement are a background to Antoinette's sexual confrontation with a stranger/ husband, this mother-daughter alignment is significant because it underscores the fact that Antoinette's dispossession precedes her abuse by the world of men. The text foreshadows this in the fate of her mother, early established (16).

Not only gender but class, ethnicity, and even language isolate the white creole woman in her Jamaican setting. Antoinette's separation from her French Creole mother exacerbates this loneliness: "She pushed me away, not roughly but calmly, coldly, without a word, as if she had decided once and for all that I was useless to her" (17). Yet the same isolation also identifies her irretrievably with her mother. The daughter begins to mirror the mother's expressions and gestures.

Antoinette's alienation increases as society begins to impose on her the expectation of madness. Much of her vulnerability lies in her typically Caribbean fatherlessness, and domestic and social circumstances that at once sever her from her mother and doom her to "become" her mother ensure her eventual tragedy. Society's and her husband's preconceptions tie her fate to Annette's by locking their identities together. They are never allowed to separate effectively. Yet the mother's rejection drives the daughter repeatedly to mother substitutes such as Aunt Cora and Christophine and traps her in the endless trauma of successive separations. The loss of her real mother entangles her in memories of repeated yearning and rejection: " 'I am here,' I said, and she said, 'No.' . . . and flung me from her" (40).

In rewriting *Jane Eyre*, *Wide Sargasso Sea* draws on archetypes of dream/vision/hallucination and of exile and voyage and explores consequences of male domination. But this novel also conveys and implicitly compares identity crises associated with colonialism through images of prenatal development, birth trauma, and mother-daughter relationship and separation. In addition, it compares the experiences of transshipment and bondage with those of feminine travail. The elements that convey spatial orientation in the narrative (encoding distance and separation) also present ideological and psychological perspective.

Aborting the quest for selfhood in *Wide Sargasso Sea*, the colonizer/husband becomes the first-person referent rather than the third and so presents an intervening perspective on Antoinette's consciousness. Isolation from her own social set, separation from her mother and mother-substitutes without independent maturation, and confinement to silence all lock Antoinette into the role of an unreliable persona. For Antoinette, there is no return from exile. The Caribbean that the British stranger sees as wilderness is the only home that the white creole knows, but it has never been wholly hers. The fact that (by virtue of ethnicity and gender) she has never fitted completely into any of the settings she recalls intensifies her dislocation.

Various strategies displace Antoinette even as speaker from the center of her own discourse. The most obvious is the interruption by her husband to reinterpret her from a "sane" point of view, but the unfamiliar Caribbean disturbs him to the edge of neurosis, just as loss after loss of every support in the Caribbean traumatizes Antoinette. This undermining of the speaker's integrity destabilizes the discourse and spawns question after question: "What am I doing in this place and who am I?" (147); "We lost our way to England. When? Where?" (148). As the text conveys increasing dislocation of the speaker from normal orientation at the center of her own narrative, at the center of her own account of life experience, the feminine narrator becomes a disembodied voice. Unable to recognize herself ("It was then that I saw her—the ghost," 154) she refers to herself in the third person. She also refers to herself as indefinite when she recalls, "Someone screamed and I thought, *Why did I scream?*" (155).

Interestingly, Hemmerechts sketches sememic oppositions of life and death to parallel those of civilization and wilderness (359). For Hemmerechts, the semantic universe of *Wide Sargasso Sea* "is encompassed by the tension between wilderness and civilization on the one hand and life and death on the other hand. These two sets of binary opposed sememes coordinate the semantic space of the text" (359). Thus, in the attic Antoinette is relegated to a place that is noncivilization and nonwilderness and a state that is nondeath and nonlife. Repeated references to ghosts and zombies underscore this situation, accumulating in the global semantics of the text to a theme of alienation from life itself.

Hemmerechts's scheme of sememic relationships illuminates Antoinette's multiple colonization and resulting marronage. Politically as well as physically and psychologically, she remains adrift in the void between nonwilderness and noncivilization, between nonlife and nondeath, and her ultimate locus remains unknown. As a Caribbean creole white she has always been and can never be other than peripheral to every sphere of existence she has known. Ultimately, she exists in a nowhere, miscarried ("We lost our way to England," 148). She recalls the physical voyage as she walks the cardboard passages of the mansion in which her husband has entombed her (148). Indeed, *Wide Sargasso Sea* presents a matrix of relationships between the civilization/wilderness dialectic earlier described and the life/death dialectic. Antoinette's shadowy existence in the attic is broken by her occasional manifestation in her husband's mansion as "the ghost" (149).

The narrator not only is dislocated in space but also produces an account that is only superficially sequential and organized in a time frame that is dechronologized. By suppressing tense in favor of exploiting aspect, *Wide Sar-*

gasso Sea delivers tightly organized packages of recollection, curiously unified by its fragmentation of time, which supports the controlling theme of a tortured and disoriented psyche. Although the narrative begins with Antoinette's childhood and seems to move chronologically, it is fed retrospectively by memory. Each setting moves the novel prospectively toward the "dark passage" out of Antoinette's confinement. Each episode is part of the feverish dream vision with which the novel ends. The beginning and end blend in a fiery haze. The narrative structure and the setting of *Wide Sargasso Sea* depend on disconnection within the time frame as well as dislocation in the spatial organization of the speaker.

Rhys suppresses temporal reference points in her linear time frame in a variety of ways. First, the denial of time is a matter of explicit statement. As Antoinette says, "Some things happen and are there for always even though you forget why or when." Grace Poole says to her in the attic, "I don't believe you know how long you have been here, you poor creature," but Antoinette responds, "On the contrary . . . only I know how long I've been here. Nights and days and days and nights, hundreds of them slipping through my fingers. But that does not matter. Time has no meaning" (151).

In addition to such explicit statements, the text draws time into question by implicature. In the temporal structure of the whole narrative, past and present are entangled. It is true that recollection implies past and that the discourse content is ordered so that it opens with Antoinette's childhood and leads through her tragic marriage to the attic where she dreams of burning the house. However, it is not a smooth sequence of events but a series of losses and deprivations. Constituents of the narrative are conjoined settings. Antoinette's dislocation from each disembodies her until she becomes a living ghost, dreaming her own existence and hallucinating her escape from the room/womb/tomb of the attic. What passes at first glance as conjoining of episodes into chronological order is in fact conjoining of settings chronologically parallel in memory, thereby involving complex manipulations of time.

First, references to the end (indeed to the very existence) of the well-established text, *Jane Eyre,* seem to lock us on a preordained path. The reader expects and at first glance appears to be offered chronological progress from fire-struck childhood to consuming lunacy. However, the foregrounding of images of fire and blindness in the earlier part of the work trap readers in backward/forward movement between the now of the speaker in the attic and the now of remembered events as they are relived. Similarly, analepses in part 1 fill gaps in information (such as Pierre's death) while downplaying the status of that information by the shift from chronological order. Analepses in part 2 are interspersed with prolepses such as Antoinette's prophetic dreams (see Hemmerechts 403–4). The prolepses increase in her husband's consciousness as he plans Antoinette's future while the analepses increase in the glimpses of Antoinette's consciousness that intersect his view.[1]

Rhys also achieves timelessness by recalling through her intersecting narrators not only parallel strands of events but also parallel situations and experiences that may be chronologically distinct. For example, Antoinette's relationship with her mother and mother substitutes parallels her husband's relationship with his father and Antoinette's relationship with her husband. Just as Antoinette undergoes the name shifting that undermines her identity, her husband remains nameless throughout the novel. Only readers of *Jane Eyre*, transferring their knowledge of Bertha's husband to the stranger/husband of *Wide Sargasso Sea*, identify Antoinette's husband as Rochester.

Some elements that are parallel in time contrast in action. Chronologically, the husband's visit to Cosway parallels Antoinette's to Christophine, but in effect these visits contrast, for Cosway willfully distances Antoinette from her husband and Christophine unwillingly supports Antoinette's efforts to bridge this growing gap.

In addition to such parallelism in textual structure, frozen events and iterative events deflect attention from an "outer" time sequence that might link complete events. Instead, these discourse strategies focus attention on the internal structure of each event. The text repeatedly indicates interruptions in the normal passage of time. Antoinette describes leaving Christophine in terms that interrupt the normal chronological time frame, suspending her temporally: "I can remember every second of that morning. . . . But now I see everything still, fixed for ever" (98). In effect, the time of the event is continuously transposed to speaker time, which is achronal. Another traumatic recollection is of her mother locked in the embrace of her keeper, and this is iterative, returning to haunt her. It is a scene Antoinette later recalls herself reenacting on the voyage during which she "lost her way to England" (148).

The discourse is thus not temporally linear in its sequence of events. In the overall structure of the narrative, what is more frequently specified is the dispersion of events at a particular time—their duration, continuity, or completeness.

Aspect, nondeictic and nonrelational, does not locate the speaker in time from an external standpoint. Exploitation of aspect rather than tense facilitates the description of gaps in time and enables the viewing of action analytically from the inside, disregarding its endpoints ("She still rode about every morning" 16). At times the speaker so locates herself within event time that she switches to narrative present, which marks aspect as imperfective, as it dispenses with past tense ("Now Sister Marie Augustine is leading me out" 50; "But I lie watching the fire die out" 147; "There is still the sound of whispering" 148).

In addition, Antoinette's recollections are threaded with snatches of Creole in which tense is unmarked and where occasional phrases may be read either as Standard English fragments of disturbed recollection or as Creole sentences. Such ambiguity of code is appropriate for conveying glimpses of Annette, "fixed forever" in Antoinette's mind ("a white woman sitting," 40). The unmarked tense is often exploited to merge past and present, for example in identifying the fate of the mother with that of the daughter. "They tell her she is mad," Christophine reflects (129), and both the ambiguous pronoun reference and the unmarked tense of *tell* confuse mother and daughter. As their chronologically separate situations link paradigmatically through parallels between events and circumstances in which they find themselves entangled, their experiences also entangle in sentence structure.

Another strategy for muting temporal progression is that of contrasting interpretations of the same event—contrasting, for example, what is said to what is meant:

I was prepared to pay very liberally
—so long as   they keep their mouths shut,   I thought
—provided that   they are discreet,   I wrote
(134).

Here, parallelism also separates expression from thought, marking the husband's linguistic subtlety and moral duplicity.

In addition to the effects of parallelism in suppressing temporal progression between events, the chronological dimension is muted by all that is left unsaid. There is nothing particularly unusual about the fact that the text dates few events or even about the fact that it does not measure explicitly the time between events. However, the text is unusual in the extent to which it embeds the past in the nonpast and specifically in a nonpast that appears to extend beyond the expected lifespan of the speaker. Past events are relived as now even while the reader filters the message through terminal events presupposed on the basis of a different text. Transitional devices suggestive of time, such as *then*, occur within episodes to sew them tightly together internally but are less frequent between episodes, so that the time lapse between one episode and the next often remains indistinct. Infrequency of obvious connecting words, spliced and run-on sentences (16), and disconnected phrases or words (11) contribute to the sense of disconnection and dislocation of the troubled narrator.

Tense-switching assists in destabilizing the narrative and in suggesting oral presentation (cf. Fleischman 9, 10); it supports the impression of the madwoman talking to herself. At the same time, rather than tracking complete events and overriding inherent duration (cf. Fleischman 37) the text replays action mainly through the imperfective. The imperfective conveys distance in ignoring boundaries of events and links with other events and in backgrounding events. Commonly, too, it is used for states removed from reality (cf. Fleischman's vertical matrix of semantic implications, 60). Through this matrix of features associated with the imperfective, Rhys achieves the narrative perspective of an isolated consciousness fed almost exclusively by deep memory.

The imperfective in *Wide Sargasso Sea* is not only lexically marked by auxiliaries but frequently implied through context for verbs that appear in the simple past. Antoinette retraces the pathless past of her loneliness at Coulibri in verbs marked as for the simple past (italicized below), but it is a past whose crucial feature is not its boundedness or completion but its ongoing and recurrent pain: "I *took* another road, past the old sugar works and the water wheel that had not turned for years. I *went* to parts of Coulibri that I had not seen, where there *was* no road, no path, no track. And if the razor grass *cut* my legs and arms I would think 'It's better than people' " (24). One verb phrase, *would think,* lexically marks the habitual, but numerous occurrences marked only for the simple past imply the habitual just as surely. In other places, actual tense shifts fuse speaker time with event time as the speaker passes from retelling to reliving the past: "Now it had started up again and worse than before, my mother knows but she can't make him believe it. I wish I could tell him that out there is not at all like English people think it is" (29). The emotions expressed not only pertain to the relationship between Annette and Mason but also are relevant to that between Antoinette and her husband. The second sentence is not only a reliving of past misunderstanding but an ongoing and endless yearning to communicate.

This Caribbean novel, whose central consciousness is an alienated woman, thus takes on a narrative structure that is not at base chronological. The relationship between aspect/tense functions in Creole syntax and Caribbean conceptual patterns broadly referred to as worldview has not been articulated and may well defy objective description. *Wide Sargasso Sea* raises the question of correlation. Rhys does not pattern the narrative so much on the passage of linear time (projected grammatically through contrasts of tense as crucial to the ordering of events), so much as on a set of relivings, of durations, of movements from one now to the next. Her protagonist recaptures from deep memory and relives experience in setting after setting, portrayed in the imperfective. These locales are contexts for each constituent of the discourse, and their loss deprives the speaker of context after context. Sentence elements that normally supply spatiotemporal anchors for the discourse are manipulated to produce discontinuity and to reinforce the sense of Antoinette's dispossession and her status as outcast in and beyond Jamaica.

Mother Tongue, Communication Gap, and Intertextuality

Rhys handles meaning in *Wide Sargasso Sea* in ways that accumulate to preclude closure at the conclusion of the novel. This is not a Caribbean innovation. However, Rhys achieves this effect by manipulating possibilities offered by the linguistic complexity of the Caribbean. Because meaning is not only confined to linguistic components of speech and writing but also implied by usage, a character's use of a particular linguistic code in a multilingual setting implicates meaning. Language attitudes displayed by characters in the novel also contribute meaning, defining their evaluations of each other, indicating distances as well as vertical and horizontal relationships between the characters. A disruption of communication links substantially contributes to Antoinette's alienation, and one crucial dimension of this is a denial of her mother tongue.

The Jamaican setting is not only physical but also sociohistorical and psychological. The social hierarchy of nineteenth-century Jamaica is reflected in the language of Rhys's characters, and language variation is thus crucial to setting. At the same time, Antoinette's monologue springs from her deprivation of her native setting and from confinement to the attic. The language variation that is crucial to characterization is a variation not only between linguistic codes but also between types of discourse within these codes.

The novel continuously reminds readers that the characters speak French, English, French patois, and Jamaican Creole as well as varieties in between the creoles and their standard languages. Rhys achieves this linguistic aspect of the Caribbean setting without loss of intelligibility by supporting narrative comment with careful installation of the text's few non-English expressions so that they remain comprehensible in their context. (Ludger Hoffman discusses such installation in his examination of intercultural writing, 183.) Most obviously, the ex-slaves are distinguished from the white creoles linguistically, but this binary distinction is broken down further in crucial though more subtle distinctions, particularly in the case of the central character, who is the victim of disintegration in intercultural communication.

What is Antoinette's mother tongue? Not only is Antoinette's mother French Creole, but her nurse, Christophine, is identified as a woman from Martinique. These facts do not categorically define Antoinette's mother tongue. First, Annette cannot be associated exclusively with French any more than Christophine can be connected exclusively with French Creole. Moreover, the novel emphasizes the distinction between Creole (of whatever base) and Standard, rather than between French and English or between French Creole and Jamaican Creole. The most vocal of Antoinette's "mothers" is Christophine, who speaks the English-based Jamaican Creole as well as her native French Creole and who is normally presented as a Creole speaker. But it is explicitly stated that she is also competent in Standard English and French. What she speaks is to some extent a matter of performance rather than competence. Unlike most blacks in her station, she selects her code as a feature of register according to situation (18). Her command of linguistic codes of different social levels and her use or disuse of the language of her masters by choice indicates her power. One of Christophine's roles is, in fact, to define choice. She advises, "A man don't treat you good, pick up your skirt and walk out. Do it and he come after you" (91), and her language itself demonstrates fewer competence constraints than performance constraints of a social nature (cf. Rickford 74). Her use of patois is consistent with what Robert Le Page and Andrée Tabouret-Keller might term an act of identity, as is her occasional use of the standard language in which she is competent though constrained by conscious response to expectations associated with her social standing.

The multilingualism of the central character operates quite differently. Antoinette's multilingualism has two major effects on characterization. First, it relays credibly the distinguishing and shifting codes of other characters as she perceives them. Second, it reflects her own lack of definition as a "white nigger." Although she speaks Creole to Creole speakers and addresses Mason in his own tongue, even mockingly as "white pappy," she repeatedly reminds us that different worlds are confronting each other without understanding and that she can never fully be a part of any of them. "You don't understand at all," she explains quite patiently as she tries to describe to her husband how Christophine thinks. He confirms that he does not "always understand what they say or sing" (85). Antoinette relays the terms in which she is rejected by black and white (*white cockroach, white nigger*) and stripped of definition; "So between you I often wonder who I am and where is my country and where do I belong and why was I ever born at all" (85). Her multilingualism does not fully admit her to any world; indeed, her communication with each world prejudices her acceptance in others.

Antoinette is both colonized and excluded by language. Unlike the Caliban described by Simon Gikandi, she does not demonstrate through her discourse "the freedom to transcend the Manichaean spaces that previously defined the relationship between the colonizer and the colonized" (41). On the contrary, these spaces entrap her and distance her from every community.

The problem of intercultural communication in *Wide Sargasso Sea* has dimensions even within conversations in Standard English. Antoinette's competence in Standard English is localized, informal Caribbean; it does not extend beneath the surface of her husband's expression to a grasp of that part of his content ordered by an alien culture. He is even more inept at interpreting her; the creole mind, white or black, is an illegible text. Apparently this unintelligibility exists at the level of nonverbal as well as verbal communication. Various gestures of the creoles irritate or bewilder him, and facial expressions are unreadable. Colored Amelie is attractive but unintelligible when he looks "into her lovely meaningless face" (115). Similarly, Antoinette's language and that of her husband remain on some levels mutually unintelligible, her face a blank that convinces him of her madness. In the arrogant logic of the conqueror/colonizer, he cannot read her; therefore, she is mad. Unless he defines her, she is meaningless to him (111). When he renames Antoinette, denies her reason, transmutes her existence, he catapults her into the chasm between gender-defined approaches to language, and our understanding of this opens a new dimension on the definition of *mother tongue* in the Caribbean.

For the husband, the woman he does not understand can only chatter nonsense—lies, foolishness, meaningless sounds. She is a doll to him; he calls her Marionette. In denying her meaning he proves her to be an object. To the extent that language controls perceptions of reality by defining thought, his patriarchal language redefines Antoinette according to both a male and a Eurocentric value system. From his point of departure, the masculine is not only unmarked and generic but rational, whereas the feminine language of Antoinette is expected to be nonrational, instinctive, or hysterical. His perception (presented as classically patriarchal) distinguishes even amount of discourse as gender associated, absence or excess of discourse being perceived as feminine. His approach to language presupposes feminine silence or cacophony.

Antoinette's mother tongue is presumably composite. She has grown up understanding the language of Annette, Christophine, and Tia but also that of her father, whose people, according to Daniel Cosway, have been "slave-owners for generations . . . in Jamaica" (80). She talks to Aunt Cora, under-stands the Jamaican servants, and picks up gossip among black and white creoles alike. Later, but still in her early childhood, she encounters her English stepfather, Mason. Then follow years of instruction in the convent school in Spanish Town. Antoinette's history suggests equal facility in French, English, and their Creoles. Her idiolect is presumably a range of speech containing various lects, each with its discrete grammar. This competence in more than one lect renders her performance variable, as demon-strated by her ability to communicate competently with speakers of quite distinct languages. Even her husband, who notices everything alien about his new wife, mentions nothing foreign about her speech to him. It is the inti-macy of shared knowledge of Creole that aligns her with all that is alien to him. This facility in Creole among local whites, and particularly local white women, is well documented in early Caribbean records, as is the contempt of observant visitors (Nugent 98: Moreton 116–17; *Marly* 210–12, 318; *Short Journey* 36). The husband's anxiety to redefine his wife is unsurprising.

Of course, Antoinette lets him redefine her. She does not "pick up her skirt and walk out." She authorizes her husband to rearticulate her existence, her transformation from subject to object of the narrative action. In Hem-merechts's model (387), through her own death wish she orients herself to-ward nonlife on the semiotic square. When they make love, she says, "Say die and I will die" (77), so it is easy for him to inscribe madness on her: "She's mad but *mine, mine.* . . . My lunatic. My mad girl" (136).

The "I" that is the husband confronts the "I" that is Antoinette (together with her motherland, her mother tongue, and all references to her mother and mother substitutes) with all the contemptuous incomprehension of con-queror/colonizer. His adjectives are judgmental: Amelie is "sly"; the sea, "stealthy"; the patois, "debased"; Antoinette, "alien"; and her mother, "infa-mous." The points of departure in his discourse place others in the wrong; if Antoinette cannot hear him it is because "she [is] too far ahead" (59). In-deed, he asserts, "If these mountains challenge me, or Baptiste's face, or Antoinette's eyes, they are mistaken, melodramatic, unreal" (85). The hus-band's character and his effect on Antoinette are best understood in the con-text of language as a reality-creating social practice. In this context, language variety is vertically stratified because it changes according to circumstances that confer power and opportunity differentially. Language thus becomes an instrument for maintaining a power differential between groups, "the authority of the one and the powerlessness of the other" (see Fowler, "Power"

62, 67). By reflecting and manipulating language attitudes, Rhys thus conveys ideological perspective in the novel.

For the white creole woman of the nineteenth-century Caribbean, the composite mother tongue of the Jamaican "white nigger" is not the language of power. The English husband controls the defining language. Antoinette's mother tongue is the vernacular, a composite that includes the Creole. International English is the father tongue, the language in which the English husbands in the novel direct the lives of wives and servants and transact marriage agreements and proposals on behalf of their children. This is the language in which the law seals Antoinette's dependence, in which her husband writes his father about the business transaction (arranged by men) that has sold Antoinette to him body and soul, in which he writes for information with which to legally control Christophine, in which he inscribes madness on Antoinette, in which he writes directions for her confinement in the attic. Antoinette's composite mother tongue is not a multilingualism that enables her to switch codes completely enough to control the full span of social variation in the standard code.

Her British husband speaks an English that is a more elaborated code than hers. His lexicon includes words that are probably meaningless to her or at least not part of her normal usage: " 'Why do you hate me?' she said. 'I do not hate you, I am most distressed about you, I am distraught,' I said" (104). The husband's English is the textualized language in which truth and meaning are confirmed by documentation and by the support of other texts, in which the text is arbiter and the written word established truth. Antoinette is trapped in a world of cultural diglossia and cleavage between worldviews, one of which is defined by texts (the literate world of English) and one by orality, Creole tales, songs, and folk wisdom. Antoinette communicates with speakers who are practically confined to their own worlds. Even Christophine asks how Antoinette knows there is any such place as England, and her husband confirms that he understands nothing the Creoles say. Antoinette recognizes herself as excluded from both worlds: "We were not in their ranks" (15). The struggle to bridge the communication gap is not assisted by her husband's elaborated code, which presents her with a web of deception: " 'Justice,' she said. 'I've heard that word. It's a cold word. I tried it out. . . . I wrote it down. I wrote it down several times and always it looked like a damn cold lie to me. There is no justice.' " (121).

Antoinette's evaluation of the term reveals that it is part of her own lexis. But her husband's elaborated code is distinguished not only by the inclusion of words not in Antoinette's vocabulary but also by the added specialization of terms that in her speech may have only generalized usage. Law and justice constitute a domain that is crucial to the semantic organization of the book and whose speakers utilize associated terms with very different degrees of specialization. The legality of male/imperial control locks Antoinette away.

In view of Rhys's concern with polarization between the sexes, it is unsurprising that feminist linguistics assists us in tracking the perceptual and conceptual orientation of the center of consciousness to events, situations, or other characters in the discourse. The importance of presupposition in patriarchal approaches to language reinforces its significance in language attitudes that characterize Creole/Standard contact situations. Once Antoinette is automatically excluded (in her husband's thinking) from the possibility of rational discourse, every speech places her further beyond his definition of sanity. At the same time, each silence confirms his preconceptions. Deborah Cameron records an interview with Luce Irigaray on the importance of silence as an aspect of the language of madness in women as distinct from men (94), and Antoinette's husband certainly interprets her silence as madness: "I looked at her. She was staring out at the distant sea. She was silence itself. . . . She lifted her eyes. Blank lovely eyes. Mad eyes. A mad girl" (138–40).

The redefinition of Antoinette blurs her to the status of rumor: "I too can wait for the day when she is only a memory to be avoided, locked away, and like all memories a legend. Or a lie" (142). Her own silence combines with conflicting gossip about the family and with the interpretation by her husband, who should be a reliable speaker. How has Antoinette arrived at silence? At first it is a refuge, tentative and conditional ("I thought if I told no one it might not be true," 16), but eventually she simply becomes realistic about communication with her husband: "I have said all I want to say. . . . I will tell you anything you wish to know, but in a few words because words are no use, I know that now" (111). The Creole woman's quest for selfhood brings her into continuous confrontation with the language of power: "Bertha is not my name. You are trying to make me into someone else, calling me by another name. I know, that's obeah too" (121).

Redefining Antoinette's Jamaican identity involves repudiating her mother tongue and denying her reason. It means challenging her reliability as speaker with the reliability of other discourse within the novel. Some of this discourse is of a particular type that is normally quite unreliable—discourse of the rumor and hearsay type. Ultimately, the full discourse of the novel discloses a linguistic crisis that is a confrontation of versions, Antoinette's perspective versus the accumulated views of the stranger's first impressions, the poison-pen letter, and fragmented rumor.

Rather than a single narrative composed of conjoined episodes in chronological order, the text presents a major discourse in which are embedded minor discourses, such as the gossip at Annette's wedding and the chips of rumor flying in the social upheaval after emancipation, each with the characteristic structure of hearsay (described by Fine 229ff). As the rumor of madness in the Cosway family grows to take control of actions and personalities, we define classic phases in the process of rumor distortion: leveling (the forgetting of details), sharpening (highlighting of specific details), assimilation, social constructiveness, information management (the individual's reconstruction), and network diffusion. The husband reconstructs information along lines of importance to the group of which he is a part. Antoinette relates denial and destruction of the past in her claim that "no one speaks of those days now. They are forgotten, except the lies. Lies are never forgotten, they go on and they grow" (108). Indeed, the book opens with hearsay, with a tone of popular chatter about the same social constraints that define speech groups and intensify solidarity and exclusiveness. The opening phrase ("They say . . . ") is a traditional frame for the type of discourse termed hearsay, and it merges into another type, the proverbial: "They say, when trouble comes close ranks, and so the white people did. But we were not in their ranks" (15).

The overall narrative structure thus accommodates embedded texts that are the many stories, rumors, or lies in circulation constructing the reader's many-faceted view of madness in the central character (see also Hemmerechts 430). Indeed, the central question of speaker reliability is raised through these conflicting embeddings.

Most of all, the shift in reference to the first-person narrator (from Antoinette to the husband and back to Antoinette) offers a contrast between early and late Antoinette, highlighted by her husband's intervening voice only to be undercut by intrusions of Antoinette's pervading voice. At times names are withheld so that the traumas of central characters intersect: "Now every word she said was echoed, echoed loudly in my head" (126); " 'You bring that worthless girl to play with next door and you talk and laugh and love so that she hear everything. You meant her to hear.' 'Yes that didn't just happen. I meant it.' (*I lay awake all night long after they were asleep*)" (127).

Close attention to the status of different linguistic codes in the text sensitizes the reader not only to the trauma of the victim but also to the tragedy of the conqueror. On the verge of betraying his wife, the husband is haunted by his own textualized linguistic code: "Words rush through my head. Pity is one of them. It gives me no rest. Pity like a naked new born babe striding the blast" (135). His self-revelations alter readers' presuppositions that he is reliable and also create an understanding of his own isolation and inner shipwreck. His status as speaker also genuinely shifts our perception of Antoinette, opening her vision to question however much he undercuts his own. The reader is repeatedly diverted from one point of reference to another. The husband's intervention in Antoinette's monologue separates its major constituents of Jamaican and British settings by his vision of the Caribbean wilderness and its savage inhabitants.

The text thus intimately involves readers in redefining Antoinette as mad through confrontation with patriarchal and prestige/standard language in the Caribbean diglossia. The mother tongue is "degraded," the mother herself "infamous," and the daughter alienated from the mother (17) yet doomed to become indistinguishable from her. The diglossia is thus a trap, and part of Antoinette's ultimate confinement and exclusion is foreshadowed in the opening pages and foregrounded by accumulating deictic terms and elements suggestive of spatial separation (" 'Now we are marooned,' my mother said" 16).

The analepses and prolepses that thread the discourse of Antoinette not only link her end and her beginning in an achronal mesh but also give the impression of undermining topic continuity so that the text begins to resemble the ramblings of a shattered mind. So the unity of the discourse is in a sense based on the fragmentation of point of view. Instability of narrator/speaker, shift of focus, suppression of time, and alternation of pronouns all support the metaphor of madness that pervades the novel and forms its major link with *Jane Eyre*. Similarly, the shifts of register that involve code switching from Standard to Creole, from English to French, or even from speech to silence contribute to a fragmentation of language. By reproducing or simply referring to such shifts, Rhys strengthens the impression of the creole woman uprooted, bartered, and denied existence. The unraveling of normal time sequence and the disconnecting of events achieve the suspension of the troubled psyche revisiting the past, haunted by the future.

This shifting of references within the text produces a sense of mental confusion and desperation. Rhys breaks rules and flouts normal maxims of relation, manner and so on to produce a disturbed discourse (see Pratt, *Towards a Speech Act Theory* 163). In this way, the author achieves a shattering of the integrity of the speaker's psyche through manipulation of deixis to convey shifts of memory, disorientation, or dislocation of mind. As the discourse destabilizes into question after question, the I, here, and now of the deictic zero point transform to who/what, where, and when (147).

The alienated narrator is suspended outside of that time frame in which past events are complete, as is suggested in sentence syntax through categories of the verb such as aspect, modality, and voice because these elements reflect duration or completeness, attitudes of certainty or uncertainty, degree of control or agency ("My bed had doors but they have been taken away" 147). Even a swift survey of verbs in *Wide Sargasso Sea* demonstrates the frequency of the imperfective rather than verbs expressing completion in the sentence structure of the discourse, of intransitive verbs and statives, particularly the copula, to focus on states of being (rather than actions), as in "It was sacred to the sun" (109), "I am not a forgetting person" (110).

The dialectic between Caribbean discourse and British literary tradition emerges overtly in confrontation between Creole and Standard dialogue and even between differing types of English discourse or contrasting perceptions such as those of home. More subtly, it is implied in all interactions between the Caribbean text and relevant texts of the British canon.

Wide Sargasso Sea interacts with *Jane Eyre* most subtly by concluding with a final and extraordinary shift in deixis. Just as Rhys entangles the reader in the protagonist's uncertainty by unfastening the normal anchors of the speaker's perspective, she utilizes similar shifts to open the end of a novel that from the outset we would think unalterably fixed. At the end of the novel, tense shifts strangely: "Then I got up, took the keys and unlocked the door. I was outside holding my candle. Now at last I know why I was brought here and what I have to do. There must have been a draught for the flame flickered and I thought it was out. But I shielded it with my hand and it burned up again to light me along the dark passage" (155–56). It is not illogical in a scenario that must end with the death of the speaker that tense should shift to the present just before the close of the novel. But why in such a delicately and deliberately manipulated mesh of tense shifts should we be shifted back to the past in the last two sentences? Strictly speaking, the movement from present back to past could imply continuity of the speaker beyond the end. But this stratagem removes a strut from the certainty of the conclusion with which we began. It undermines a presupposition based on one dimension of the novel's intertextuality, its dependence on *Jane Eyre*.

Intertextuality works both ways, one text providing a context for the next. Not only does *Wide Sargasso Sea* gain depth through its allusions to *Jane Eyre*, not only do presuppositions (based on Brontë) intensify irony and highlight the tragedy of Antoinette's life, but the experience of *Wide Sargasso Sea* creates new conceptions about both Bertha and Jane. The destabilization of discourse in *Wide Sargasso Sea* raises new issues in *Jane Eyre*. Indeed, Helen Nebecker suggests that in writing *Wide Sargasso Sea*, Rhys in a sense rewrites *Jane Eyre*.

A sequel to a well-known text is constrained in many ways to meet reader expectation, and we would expect *Wide Sargasso Sea* to be even more constrained to fit our presuppositions because it is in fact a prequel, with predetermined outcome. The fact that it plays with our presuppositions and questions the foundation of conclusions with which we began makes *Wide Sargasso Sea* in many ways a deconstruction of *Jane Eyre*, for in producing the story of the "white nigger" Rhys relates *Jane Eyre* curiously to the literature of diaspora.

Because *Wide Sargasso Sea* is built on things not in *Jane Eyre*, built around hidden spaces, gaps, and holes in discourse (see Kloepfer 144), *Wide Sargasso Sea* is a novel constructed around silence. And because silence may be a meaningful component of discourse this filling of holes in *Jane Eyre* transmutes it from one literary discourse into another. In this sense, the openness of *Wide Sargasso Sea* denies *Jane Eyre* closure.

The text contains embedded episodes, often discrete discourses of very specific types, such as hearsay. The context of each embedded discourse is itself described in terms of vivid settings flaring against a dark backdrop of uncertainty that is the tortured psyche of the speaker, Antoinette, and the whole discourse is framed by documentation of another text, itself a literary discourse, classical, established, arbitrating our decoding of the message before us. The inexorable thrust in the action of *Wide Sargasso Sea* finds its impetus in *Jane Eyre* and in many ways frames Antoinette's character. As her girlhood in the convent ends, she dreams of a man who will lead her from home into a place she later describes as hell. Declarative clauses in the narrative present give way to a conditional and then to a modal expressing obligation: "I follow him, sick with fear but I make no effort to save myself; if anyone were to try to save me, I would refuse. This must happen" (50).

However, although *Wide Sargasso Sea* receives its impetus from *Jane Eyre*, Rhys not only rewrites but writes. The discourse achieves haunting characterization by inscribing personalities that remain mutually unintelligible, people who will eternally remain illegible texts to each other, and the novel does so by highlighting linguistic distinctions of dialect, culturally defined semantics, and the language attitudes associated with diglossia. Isolated from her own social set, Antoinette has faced throughout her life the difficulties of intercultural communication that make socially determined meaning uncertain and that have framed her in the role of an unreliable persona. Reader involvement in the theme of dispossession is possible through the manipulation of point of view that throws readers into the void with Antoinette, that here from which she has been looking back all along and its endless array of nows. The same manipulation of perspective throws both her husband's rationality and her irrationality under scrutiny, not destroying the link with *Jane Eyre* but forcing us to reexamine it from new angles.

How mad is Antoinette? Does it depend on who defines her? Does it depend on which code of the diglossia we employ? By the end of the novel Antoinette talks almost exclusively to herself, but she may do so because of her physical setting and because, as a Jamaican creole dislocated in time and space, she is only superficially intelligible to British speakers such as Grace Poole. The discourse is internal, and her orientation and distance are psychological, a means by which she recaptures the episodes of her past and their implied logical relationship to her deprived present. "What am I doing in this place," she asks at the end of the novel, "and who am I?" (147).

Where *Jane Eyre*'s Bertha was peripheral to the tale, a silent threat, the protagonist of *Wide Sargasso Sea* is irrepressibly articulate. Moreover, she maintains the narrative stance of an alienated feminine speaker who retrieves the events of her life from deep memory and who reveals her present condition from a perspective that is off center. From this ex-centric locus the speaker replays the disordered past in a narrative voice that is disembodied. She is not only name shifting, but, if her reflection in the mirror at Thornton Hall is to be believed, she is form shifting as well. She inhabits the borders of a reality that she has played no part in defining.

Rhys has constructed a memorable type that entrenches itself in the Caribbean imagination—the woman as outcast. Rhys has also established in the Caribbean canon a relationship between exploited womanhood and marronage. A deficit of semantic components associated with civilization defines Antoinette's exclusion. She lacks centrality, home, conformity, familiarity, material possessions, recognized rationality, (exclusively) codified language, and at last a clear status as definitely living or definitely dead. Excluded from companionship and protection, she searches for definition in memories of a life that is repeatedly stressed as past. Thus, her present is a tortured psychological quest from a locus beyond life. Her discourse is a haunting.

In the end, the inevitability of the speaker's death, the certainty of the conclusion with which we began, remains part of an account in the past of the speaker. And this phenomenon denies *Wide Sargasso Sea* the closure promised by its relationship to *Jane Eyre*. Just as Antoinette is never allowed to live fully in *Wide Sargasso Sea*, her actual death, repeatedly foreshadowed, is never realized.

The inherent ambiguity of a (doomed) first-person narrative contributes to this lack of closure, which is supported by details of sentence structure, such as the grammatical features that accumulate to create static pictures. In the end, whatever readers may believe that Antoinette is about to do, her final leap is not seen. Rhys foreshadows the fiery end of the creole wife only to rewrite the European construct of lunacy.

In the end the disembodied voice of the speaker does not impose closure in meaning, and her end is not shown. Obscurity does not appear to be a flaw of structure or expression but a part of the message. Questions, stated or implied, proliferate as the narrative progresses. Plurality of meaning and resulting ambiguity characterize the message of the disembodied narrator (see Lalla, "Discourse" 69).

For example, in *Wide Sargasso Sea* a sense of injustice kindles anger. In Brontë's novel, the hatred that ignited the fire to destroy her husband's mansion was part of Bertha's madness. Rhys rewrites this hatred, reopens the question of its lunacy, and introduces doubt about its irrationality. Antoinette, who wields a knife by the end of her story, has conveyed her own perspective as a wronged woman. Indeed, persistent, irrational deprivation and confinement have reduced Antoinette to a shadow enlivened only by anger, and she has become extraordinarily dangerous. Her husband intentionally reduces her to "only a ghost" (140), but he cannot put a stop to her; even at the end "she hasn't lost her spirit" (146). Her silence is not consent, and, however meaningless she appears to him, however ruptured are the lines of communication, she is never rendered inarticulate. Her silence in his presence is choice, and like much silence in discourse it speaks of lack of rapport. She compensates for this silence by her monologue in the attic, where she has no participatory listenership aside from the reader (and the unsatisfactory Grace Poole).

Pressed beyond the boundaries of existence and outside of linear time frame, Antoinette produces a narrative of ex-centric locus. As a speaker, Antoinette retains past-tense usage through the conclusion of her story, even as she has injected her endless present into memories of the past. The feminine narrator's ultimate place in space and time is an insoluble mystery from early in the novel, when she reflects that "there are more ways than one of being happy, better perhaps to be peaceful and contented and protected, as I feel now, peaceful for years and long years, and afterwards I may be saved whatever Myra says" (31). Even in her memories of childhood she speaks from beyond her tragedy, dechronologized, disembodied, death disclosed. If the narrator speaks from beyond the attic even at the beginning of *Wide Sargasso Sea*, then how dead is Antoinette in the end? And if neither her death nor her lunacy are absolutes, is mad Bertha rewritten (in subtext) as a construct of her husband's delusions? Thus, the Caribbean postcolonial text indicates what Bill Ashcroft, Gareth Griffiths, and Helen Tiffin refer to as a shifting horizon of possible meanings (187).

The speaker in the attic exists in a vacuum of semantic space, neither civilization nor wilderness, neither life nor death, a vacuum where analepses and prolepses intersect (cf. Hemmerechts 408 and Kristeva, "Women's Time" 16–17) and where circumstances that must involve her death are described by her as in the past. She has looked into the mirror and beheld a stranger, and she has referred to herself as someone. The theme of Caribbean and feminine dispossession has been linguistically driven home by implosion of the deictic zero point as the stabilizing reference point for discourse through continuous rearrangement into "Wh" questions, the replacement of *I*, *here*, and *now* by *who*, *where*, and *when*. The narrator's own uncertainty about events emerges through coordinated alternatives ("As I ran or perhaps floated or flew," 154), the selection of modal verbs such as *seemed*, the negation of experiential verbs and verbs of cognition ("I don't know how long I sat," 155). In the midst of such uncertainty flashes the vision of Coulibri, sharply defined, but it is a certainty and clarity from which she wakes. The writer maintains ambiguity to the end and (by implication) beyond, for the verb *light* may mean "illuminate" or "set ablaze": "I shielded it with my hand to light me along the dark passage" (156).

Antoinette's violent rebellion has the inevitable logic of pure reason. Injustice motivates resistance; imprisonment motivates escape; rejection motivates withdrawal; denial of existence motivates a search for identity. However, each response is frustrated until the end of the novel. *Wide Sargasso Sea* does not portray suicide, and as she throws off the oppression of Thornfield Hall, Antoinette feels her self constructed for the first time, even as mad Bertha of Rochester's vision kindles self-destruction: "Now at last I know why I was brought here and what I have to do" (155–56). The uncertainty of fragmented vision breaks at last in a declaration of certainty and intention. Still, in the end, the alternating points of view preclude closure by constructing parallel and partially contradictory visions of lunacy and marronage in the creole lighting her way, and these conflicting visions superimpose to sear into the mind the parrot's screech: *Qui est là?*

The burning question.

PART TWO

Inside Out

Jamaican Perspectives on Exile and Resistance

4

Leavings

Then you can count yourself lucky . . . or unlucky.
Depending on from where you look at it.
—Elean Thomas, *The Last Room*

IN RECENT FICTION that is unequivocally Jamaican, there reappear many of the dimensions of alienation that Jean Rhys established in the Caribbean canon through her Jamaican character, Antoinette. Characterization of the outcast in twentieth-century Jamaican fiction both reflects and moves beyond Caribbean postcolonial schizophrenia in relating feminine suffering to social passage and to the birth damage of the young nation. Male and female characters alike occur in situations conducive to mental disturbance, and the outcast's persona merges at times with the lunatic's.

There are many instances in earlier novels, such as Roger Mais's *Brother Man*, of alienated and psychotic characters, but in Jamaican novels of the 1980s and early 1990s mind-altering alienation becomes a central theme. This chapter explores both marronage in feminine experience and marronage that is the consequence of separation from the mother. In particular, the chapter examines how both of these dimensions of alienation are encoded in spatial terms and elements of the discourse and how these instances of marronage are themselves metaphors, strategies of discourse for conveying the marronage of a nation. Attention will center on Erna Brodber's *Myal* and Olive Senior's "Country of the One-Eye God" (*Summer Lightning*), but reference to other texts, such as Elean Thomas's *The Last Room*, is crucial to establishing the ubiquity of the theme and of the strategies for its expression.

Room, Womb, and Altered Consciousness

The Last Room explores mind-altering alienation by entering the damaged psyche and looking out of it at the world. This novel therefore shares certain narrative strategies with *Wide Sargasso Sea*.

The alternating perspective achieved by shifting first-person narrators in *The Last Room* is that of mother and daughter confrontation. However, in contrast to the emphasis of *Wide Sargasso Sea*, perceptual and ideological shifts between women from one generation to the next are central to Thomas's novel, whereas female/male relationships are relevant and supportive but subsidiary. The older feminine consciousness (Valerie, or Putus) appears first as a girl deprived of schooling by family circumstances; she is then displaced from her home and mother as a junior domestic, what Jamaican employers termed a *schoolgirl*, and soon burdened by pregnancy. Her mother's rejection isolates her, making her more vulnerable to male exploitation. She in turn lodges her daughter (Icy) with a family in which the girl is vulnerable to male interference, and both physical and emotional distance separate the two women until they meet again in England in a tortured confrontation of guilt and resentment about leaving and being left.

Putus/Valerie and Icy are in many ways mirror images of each other, incomplete and complementary personalities that are interdependent yet repel each other. When Putus is pregnant, her mother reacts, "Look like you going to have to bear yu burden alone" (51). Mothers of the novel continuously struggle to lift their daughters physically and figuratively, and the daughters are heavy, dragging themselves and their mothers down even as they cling frantically. Putus pleads, "Mama, du, help me. Don't leave me alone" (51), but her mother distances her yet further by renaming her coldly: "Valrie, if you don' hurry-up an' come now, A will turn mi back an' lef you right here an' mek Aunt Sisi and Mr Bennett throw you out on the street" (51).

The motif of being turned out and of consequent experiences of homelessness at increasing distances from one's birthplace recurs through the novel. The dialectic of home and foreign, of wilderness and civilization, continues as a central issue. To escape from wilderness to civilization, Putus journeys from Jamaica to London. There, as a displaced colonial, she loses her ideological family (the British) through disillusionment. This ideological marronage, further developed in Icy, parallels a geographical and political marronage. The name change from Putus ("sweet and special," 10) to plain Mrs. Mason accompanies her loss of emotional satisfaction in loving Britain as motherland and adoring the royal family as a source of security. Indeed, it is a policy of the hospital in which she works that the best way to remove confusion from the minds of disturbed patients is to remind them of the royal family, a symbol of certainty and stability (192). In reality, Britain rejects its colonial daughter. *The Last Room* conveys the ideological stance of the postcolonial Caribbean writer who recategorizes past events, codified in nonfiction, by reexamining them through fiction and so exposing history as myth.

The fictional tale of a mother abandoning her daughter (Valerie first abandoned, later abandoning Icy) reflects political separation between Britain and its colony. It also conveys incomplete psychological parturition in a double loss. One is loss by denial, of Jamaica as motherland; the other is loss by disillusionment in Britain as motherland. Icy's recollection of the visit of royalty reduces British power to a legend from the deep past, "come and gone" (181). Valerie discovers that the British royalty only serve as pictures for the hospital wall, placebos for pain, that "can't help . . . against this Man" (193). So Valerie Mason is utterly alone in London, not only unaccepted by Britain but also alienated from both foreigner Jamaicans and "uncivilized" Africans (197). Colonial disillusionment implicitly parallels the explicit and literal disillusionment involved in mother-daughter relations. First, Valerie (Putus) disappoints her own mother by failing in her studies and by becoming pregnant. These events of course repeat and thus intensify her mother's failure. Repeatedly rejected, Valerie finds herself alone in a room in England with her "voices." Her spatial separation indicates psychological marronage.

Icy is anxious that history should not repeat itself. She refuses to become her musician lover's third *babymother*. She leads an unsettled existence that news of her mother (in *foreign*) utterly disrupts. Icy's subsequent arrival in Britain confronts Valerie not only with the daughter she has both abandoned and protected from herself but also with the recollection of her own arrival. Her mind flashes back to her life before arrival, to her life with the two men of her past, to her early life at home with Icy. Since the time of these events, the setting has moved not only from the shore of one island to the shore of another but also from one dwelling place to another, a smaller dwelling in a larger setting and less her own. These increasingly cramped and strange quarters have ended in the boxlike room in Birmingham. By this time she insists, "I am alone in the world" (90).

The setting of the latter part of the book is also psychological, alternating between the minds of both Jamaican women. The narration switches between disembodied voices. No independent narrative comment identifies or distinguishes the speakers, and the text of each speech is embedded with other voices that force the two narrators to interact. For example, the reliable voice of the grandmother instructs Valerie to take up her daughter "before she dead in front yu door" (144). The strenuous efforts at lifting are reported through the confused voice of Valerie's mind (145).

Between Valerie's reports, Icy's mind observes and records, but it does so with disbelief. Her mother's room in England is incredible, "like a little coffin" (149). However, unlike Antoinette's recollections, Valerie's monologue reveals that her own need for material advancement has led to the psychological trap in which she finds herself. Active rather than passive constructions (such as Antoinette's *brought here*) show that the straightened, grave-like confinement to the void of the last room has causal connections in the protagonists' own actions: "I couldn't go home the same way I did come?" (152).

Entrapment and alienation are complementary. The growing distance between mother and daughter is nowhere more poignantly demonstrated than in Icylane's letters. The first is stilted, its polite formality riddled with the pain of feeling "like a motherless child" (155) and pleas to be taken away from "this place" (156). The literal message of the letter, crucial to the plot, has a nonliteral parallel in colonial schizophrenia, where yearning and a sense of abandonment coexist alongside resentment and rebellion. In her next letter, the daughter's response has hardened to rejection: "When I got your reply to my letter, I killed you totally in my heart. . . . I count myself as a motherless child" (159). The change in status that the speaker inscribes on her mother (as dead), changes the status of the speaker herself to that of an orphan. The first letter, already retreating toward formality, is signed, "Your loving daughter Icy (Icylane)." The second ends, "Yours sincerely, Icylane Barton." The distancing in time and space that destroys intimate relationships is here as elsewhere expressed by gaps in communication. Because language is interactive, refusal to respond when communication has been initiated can be interpreted as social aggression. For Icy, ultimate violence is her mother's lack of response: "I am being killed by silence" (165).

An important challenge for the postcolonial Caribbean writer who breaks silence to rechart the past is the obligation to avoid counterdistortion. At times *The Last Room* appears to overbalance in the sheer grimness of Valerie Mason's predicament. Its opening, vivid but somewhat contrived in its connection to the rest of the text, does not prepare us for themes of colonial schizophrenia, motherlessness, and dislocation. It offers to the tourist's curiosity a native vision, but it does not return to the tourist, does not link back the incompletely embedded observation of Putus to the opening expedition. Nor do the crab catchers in any way prepare us for the rather wearisome procession of unsavory men who intensify both Valerie's and Icy's disenchantment. The discourse convincingly mirrors a symmetry of mother-daughter disappointment ("the murder of her dreams" 41) as well as a congruence between the daughter's disillusioned abandonment and the Jamaican's disenchantment with colonialism. Yet Icy's assessment of many of Valerie's connections as "the others who care about you" (197) raises the question of whether the wrongs suffered by Valerie have been exaggerated. If the party that Icy plans to give in the end is justified, then Valerie's isolation is either authorial exaggeration or part of the character's paranoia. At such points it is not clear whether the writer's own ideology intrudes to interfere with thematic unity and logical development of the discourse.

Counterdiscourse can itself inscribe new stereotypes—of the exploited woman, of sordid poverty, of black suffering, and of decadent government. *The Last Room* reinforces such ready-made judgment as "is him that bring me down to this level" (91). Yet parallel to the spawning of our own stereotypes evolve new, independent visions. Mrs. Mason's voices also interject positive direction, rearranging spatial orientation: "Never mind that now. Dat is ole time story. Pick her up" (143).

In Jamaican fiction, a shifting emphasis from exile, loss, and displacement to nationalism is both gradual and ongoing. In discussing Caribbean exile, Jan Carew notes that the journey by sea provides an interlude between home and the Caribbean community that constitutes an island abroad (113), a sort of hiatus between related but distinguishable marronages. He equates the actual exile, the departure from the Caribbean, as a self-willed entry into history and into previously enforced silences. In this sense, the physical displacement becomes a first step to identity and thus to national consciousness, a journey toward a last room that Thomas tracks through geographical, ideological, and psychological marronage. Perhaps this central journey does not quite arrive at the indigeneity or liberation glimpsed in the crab-catching episode with which Thomas's novel opens. Still, here as elsewhere, the marooned women of modern Jamaican texts tend to resist a perspective that excludes them beyond some point of no return.

At the same time, return from physical exile may intensify pain and reveal new dimensions of marronage. In *The Unbelonging*, by Joan Riley, the Jamaican woman abroad (Hyacinth), who is emotionally stirred by recollection and fired by news of progress at home, longs to return. Riley traces a dispossession beyond the loss of kinship and culture, for it extends to a psychological deprivation of memory itself. Mike Alleyne notes the protagonist's psychological and ideological stasis in the period of exile (2). Return to Kingston debunks her romanticized recollections of childhood, for home turns out to be an illusion unmasked as ghetto. Her perspective on the world, presumably fractured by early education, like many Caribbean child characters, has been revised by exile so as to entrench a worldview foreign to Jamaica.

The outsider status of such a returnee allows no scope for reinstatement. In *The Unbelonging*, Hyacinth's romanticized illusions of an idealized independent nation render her blind and deaf to postindependence developments and accompanying political upheavals. She is entirely unprepared for the dichotomy of self, imposed by what Alleyne describes as the "psychosocial encounters of returning," for it must be remembered that this return follows and is expected to heal the initial experience of alienation. Alleyne also notes the degree to which recent Jamaican immigrants have found their exile rendered particularly traumatic by "Thatcherite erosion of immigrant citizen rights in England" (1).

Interestingly, male returnees seem yet more prone to disillusionment and intensified exile. For example, the protagonist of H. Orlando Patterson's *An Absence of Ruins* finds himself beyond the point of no return. His alienation is associated with frustrated relationships with women in general but most significantly with his mother.

Alexander Blackman begins his narrative of emptiness in Kingston with a description of his feelings on return, of vacancy in a stripped landscape. He ends in London, disembodied to a gaunt shadow, a faceless savage haunting the alleys of metropolitan anonymity. Between these points he is increasingly the victim of self-indulgent disillusionment. He finds only social decadence, empty academic and political rhetoric, weary whores, squalid lifestyles, and deadening frivolity; and the text implicates no existing alternative. On the other hand, the text does not suggest that Blackman has expected or sought fulfillment. The vacuum presupposes meaninglessness as a given.

Indeed, Blackman's vision of Jamaican-educated middle-class existence is of dead ends on a "damn' little island" (26). His hypersensitive, almost hallucinatory preoccupation with failure, lonely frustration, and uncreative human intercourse emerges most clearly in the intercepting impressions of his bored episode with the prostitute, his submersion in the "dark, mucous liquid of the ocean" (29), his rejection of his mother's enclosing and prayerful devotion, and the wet dream in which these impressions intermingle. The unifying symbol is that of "lurid transparent slime" (30) as an aftermath of attempts at release. Blackman's revelation on the shore is, of course, that there is no release, that the individual and the globe itself are trapped in "one vast, abysmal circle" reeling in the infinite vacuum of space.

Blackman's cosmic experience confirms the irrelevance of meaning. On the basis of a conclusion that life has found him worthless and caught him naked (155), he yearns for a return to a "dark jungle among whose tangled trees [he] can get [himself] lost for ever." The metaphor leads him back to the vast, "indifferent horde" (155) of the metropolis and a final cross-examination. Internally, he is beset by questions, such as "What of your past? Who are your ancestors? Are you savage or are you civilized? Identify yourself, sir!" (159). And the answer comes back riddled with negations that distance the speaker from meaningful existence: "I come from nowhere worth mentioning. . . . I cannot say whether I am civilized or savage, standing as I do outside of race, outside of culture, outside of history, outside of any value that could make your question meaningful" (160).

This is nihilism rather than resistance. Blackman offers no resistance, seized as he is with the pointlessness of all effort. His alienation is a cosmic joke mirrored in his petty prank of the faked suicide that kills his mother. His postcolonial nihilism thus moves through a passive sort of matricide to settled and unresisting anonymity. As Derek Walcott notes, "To most writers of the archipelago who contemplate only shipwreck, the New World offers not elation but cynicism, a despair at the vices of the Old which they feel must be repeated. That malaise is an oceanic nostalgia for the older culture and a melancholy at the new, and this can go as deep as a rejection of the untamed landscape, a yearning for ruins" ("The Muse" 116).

In *An Absence of Ruins,* as elsewhere (cf. Salkey, *Come Home*), those who have moved out of what they regard as the constricted island society view Jamaica from outside as an irrational, cruel phenomenon, a hard place in the infinitude of space and time.

The return of exiles in literature suggests that reintegration is often impossible. In such circumstances the self may experience hostile rejection. What is familiar may become confusingly "Other." Orientations of insider and outsider and of marginal and central may require reinterpretation. Disillusionment or rejection on return home may transmute the metropolis to home, redefine civilization as more intensely international and modern, and intensify the cultural hegemony of the European or American foreign. Discrepancies between local and foreign urban life grow sharper, as do long-recognized discrepancies between local rural and urban settings.

Apart from transformations of place associated with the experience of return from exile, the returnee may encounter transformations of character. The returnee whose perspective has been adjusted by colonialism may expect to reestablish contact with a familiar character but may instead meet a Caliban, a character dehumanized by colonial negatives. Another characteristic of unsuccessful returnees is that they exchange one type of loss for another. The loss that results from exile gives way to one that results from the substitution of painful reality for rose-colored memory.

Such texts as *The Unbelonging* and *An Absence of Ruins* examine the consequences of marronage by exploring its extension into the unsuccessful return. Other texts are more concerned with the actual urge to leave and site this urge in domestic isolation. Velma Pollard explores feminine reactions to cageness (*Considering Woman* 20), which vary widely from cool withdrawal ("she left, that's what she did," 26) to a chilling arc of children thrown from a high apartment and followed by their mother, a woman shattered by loneliness. In *Considering Woman*, deictic elements and terms encode in the discourse the peculiar tinge of claustrophobia that accompanies some isolation and the impulse outward from the cage (10–11), and she offers glimpses of the distance between minds that might be expected to touch. Understanding of the other's pain comes late in the case of the daughter who expects her mother home from the United States year after year but receives each year only a box of secondhand clothes. Eventually, the year arrives when the mother returns in her own box, the coffin with silver handles, and she returns as a stranger who "was not my mother." Her funeral is a spectacle for strangers, it "couldn't be our funeral" (31). Here a mother-daughter relationship is destroyed not by personal rejection, like Antoinette's by Annette, but by space, by a distance that is first physical, then psychological. The mother's life remains meaningless until the daughter's metropolitan experience, which reveals the orientation of a black working-class woman in a community in which "you live long enough with a face that is always wrong" (28). As in other treatments of dispossession that involve alienation from the mother, this separation mirrors the fractured psyche bequeathed by colonial and neocolonial experience.

Pollard's vision is glancing, subtle. It offers vivid but fleeting glimpses of loneliness and transmits stabs of poignantly conveyed loss. Her ideological stance, more delicately conveyed than Thomas's, reveals sensitivity about a writer's own limitations as a recorder of history: "But I looked back as Lot's wife did and froze into my mind a new last picture of Comfort Hall. . . . After this it would be difficult to see the past with any honesty or truth" (38–39).

In the portrayal of alienation induced by exile, a widening of perspective in Jamaican discourse appears to be prompting new developments. The island psyche ponders its constraints of boundedness and separation but begins in the latter decades of the twentieth century to find new points of departure beyond exploitation and abandonment. The feminine consciousness often moves toward reconciliation with the community. Both Senior and Brodber explore perspectives on the feminine protagonist beyond that of the victim and convey new strength in the returnee.

Brodber's focus, in both *Myal* and *Jane and Louisa Will Soon Come Home*, is one of healing. The theme also emerges in Senior's "The Tenantry of Birds" (*Arrival*), which is a tale of a young woman (Nolene) who passes from the care of a domineering mother to that of an exploitative and deceitful husband. The narrative evokes comparisons between house and island that suggest underlying homelessness of the tenant, the synchronously locked-out and locked-in sensation of the forgotten woman, symbolized in rolled-up car windows and burglar bars. But Senior goes beyond the stereotype by relegating Caribbean clichés on the class interest of the bourgeoisie and worn-out rallying cries of commitment and struggle to a new, local breed of exploiter.

Nolene retains her hold on sanity in a disturbed society to reach beyond dislocation and dispossession and seize control of her home and her self. The narrative concludes with her sitting "thinking for a long long time, getting angrier and angrier, her very anger hardening her, dragging her away from the tree, from the birds, forcing her to focus on her very self. *This* woman sitting alone on *this* veranda now. And finally she came to her decision. She thought, to hell with it! . . . It was *her* tree and *her* house and she was staying. *He* could move out" (61). Spatial reference through deictic terms and elements realigns Nolene's consciousness as central to her life experience. Explicit *there* gives way to implicit *here* as attention is drawn from outer reference points toward the central consciousness by the proximate demonstrative *this*, by the adverb *now*, and by *came*, the directional verb oriented toward the zero point. Similarly, the association of the stative verb *staying* with *her* and the association of the dynamic *move out* with *him* reinforces and stabilizes this newfound centrality of the focal consciousness. Thus, Nolene materializes from the margins of existence.

Shadow-Catching: Retrieving the Half That Has Never Been Told

Simon Gikandi acknowledges a risk "of formulating a theory of Caribbean modernism which is haunted by the shadows of colonial structures" (10). However, this haunting is not a risk or marginal side effect but a central paradox that gives rise to the Caribbean angst. Brodber's *Myal* orchestrates the resurgence of voices that have been pressed beyond the boundaries of existence.

Ella O'Grady, already racially distinct from members of her rural home community, grows up in the home of a similarly mixed clergyman and his white British wife (the Brassingtons). She marries an American (Selwyn Langley) who transforms her to a suitable mate and dramatizes his interpretation of her past on film. Ella becomes incoherent, or "trips out" (84), and must be retrieved by her foster mother, Maydene Brassington. Healing takes place in Jamaica and involves restoration of her identity. The healing of the community is the long-term project of supportive local spirits, whose fellowship Maydene attains.

To speak of a distinctive Jamaican literature is no more to deny its relationship with other literature in English than to deny its closer relationship with English literature of the Caribbean. Jamaican literature can be recognized by stating its relationship to these other literatures in terms of both affinities and contrasts. *Myal* demonstrates how postcolonial writing characteristically reflects power relations in the society of the writer through the literary traditions that colonialism has inscribed on this society. The dismantling of psychological domination takes longer than the dismantling of overt political domination, but to tolerate ongoing psychological domination is to permit covert political domination to continue. Bill Ashcroft, Gareth Griffiths, and Helen Tiffin have persuasively outlined typical postcolonial concerns, for example with place and displacement and with the erosion of self by dislocation and ensuing alienation of vision and crisis of self-image. Their study has distinguished between European monocentricism, which deals inequitably with the complex and culturally varied postcolonial writing, and literatures such as that of the Caribbean that cross boundaries of language, nation, and race (18). These authors treat this literature as regional. As they point out, it is geographically rather than, say, racially defined. They also note that there have been no major studies of Jamaican literature as a discrete tradition.

Like the regional literature as a whole, Jamaican literature is distinguished from the black writing model in that it is less race centered, less hinged to a philosophy of negritude. In *Myal*, whose intersecting stories trace feminine development in black, white, and mixed women, race is a crucial but not all-consuming consideration, as is true of other Jamaican fiction. Like Caribbean literature as a whole, Jamaican writing treats independence of the individual and independence of the community as parallel and related themes. Related and crucial themes are foreign domination, European journeys of exploration or conquest, house building and dismantling, and the confrontation of native and stranger in exotic landscape. Similarly, modern Jamaican texts tend to have discontinuous narrative, a recognized characteristic of postcolonial writing (Ashcroft, Griffiths, and Tiffin 28). All of these familiar features appear in *Myal*.

Curiously, in addition to controlling what postcolonial criticism recognizes as an imperial-colonial dialectic, Jamaican literature resists absorption into regional stereotypes. Apart from deliberately disrupting European notions of history and reordering time, contemporary Jamaican writers appear to tamper even with Caribbean notions and to produce parallel and intercepting perspectives that at times depart from regional vision, moving away from a two-dimensional vision of postcolonial intertextuality (the imperial-colonial dialectic of Ashcroft, Griffiths, and Tiffin).

Myal shows haunting similarities to *Wide Sargasso Sea* but also displays curious differences. The intertextuality of *Wide Sargasso Sea* and *Jane Eyre* is common knowledge, but there has been relatively little attention to the set of affinities and contrasts between *Wide Sargasso Sea* and other Caribbean texts.[1] Again, little comparison has been made between this early Caribbean discourse of feminine marronage and very early texts of feminine marronage in British literature. Elsewhere ("Discourse"), I have explored such affinities and differences, and considerations such as these raise the question of how much British literature should be considered imperial. Comparison of *Wide Sargasso Sea*, *Myal*, and the Old English *Wife's Lament* (Bolton 35–37) throws a curious light on all these works by first defining their central consciousnesses as women dispossessed of life and by then recalling their dispossession, in an achronal discourse, riddled with gaps.

Myal, however, is generically distinct in that it is not complaint, even by implication. Resemblances lie in such themes as betrayal and exile and in the perspective of the alienated wife. In each text a replay of memory retrieves crucial events, and in *Myal* Ella's condition is also associated with a perspective that is off center. However, unlike the speakers of the other two texts, who are nameless or name shifting and formless or form shifting and who inhabit the borders of a reality that they have played no part in defining, Ella shares responsibility for her condition. Selwyn's transformation of her life is achieved with her complicity. Finally, unlike the wives who are dislocated from society with no possibility of reinstatement, Ella's spirit is retrievable.

Both *Myal* and *Wide Sargasso Sea*, like other recent postcolonial works in and beyond the Caribbean (such as Margaret Atwood's *Surfacing*), deconstruct the reader's basic assumptions about power, civilization, reason, and femininity in ways that the Old English text does not. As victims of multiple colonization, both Antoinette and Ella are left adrift in the void between nonwilderness and noncivilization, between nonlife and nondeath, in a locus ultimately unknown. As a victim of neocolonialism, Ella too is pressed to the margins of existence. Ella's cryptic diction (84) indicates that her marronage is verbal as well as social and psychological, and in this sense, too, through multiplicity of meaning and resulting ambiguity, her speech resembles the message of the disembodied narrator. Like a riddle, *Myal* presents a discourse that intentionally highlights gaps and contradictions. The book takes current Caribbean preoccupation with neocolonial trauma beyond binarism (cf. Nelson-McDermott 64); it posits shared responsibility for marronage and graded possibilities for locating the consciousness rather than mutually exclusive loci of margin and center.

Gikandi recognizes in the Caribbean avant-garde a rejection of boundaries and closures, and this rejection enriches old texts with new meanings (41). He also identifies exile as the point of departure for anticolonial discourse that has generated much of Caribbean literature (34). Prospero,

Crusoe, and other castaways all inhabit the paths of exile, but this fact in itself does not make them recognizably Caribbean or even postcolonial. A regional politics and a power imbalance associated with race relations are among the features that imbue *Wide Sargasso Sea* with its Caribbean identity. Thomas's exploration of the damaged psyche has much in common with that of the Anglo-Saxon *The Wife's Lament* because in each case the consciousness is an excluded and disillusioned woman. But Thomas's portrayal (like Brodber's) is closer to that of Rhys because in these novels the politically motivated abandonment of central characters further reflects the Caribbean experience. However, unlike both the Anglo-Saxon wife and Antoinette, Thomas's women promise to regain their hold on reality at the end of perspectival shifts through states of altered consciousness.

This stubborn resilience of Jamaican vision emerges more sharply in *Myal*, where the ex-centric protagonist is reduced to shadow, then assisted in freeing herself to return to a reality that she can assist in recreating. *Myal* comprises several parallel narratives of spirit extraction and replacement, and it explores reconstruction and healing through articulation of the obscure past, the half that has never been told.

In many ways, Ella O'Grady, like Antoinette, is pressed beyond the boundaries of existence and outside of a linear time frame, but more and more the marooned feminine persona of Jamaican literature resists her exclusion or seeks to return aggressively to the place that should be home. The refusal to die becomes a characteristic trait of the alienated feminine character in current Jamaican writing. The persona develops not only by the introduction of new characteristics and the creation of local metaphors but also by intertextuality of a different sort to that observable in *Wide Sargasso Sea* and *Jane Eyre*. Current Jamaican fiction demonstrates an intertextuality that seems to recognize and rewrite both a British and a Caribbean canon.

In Brodber's *Myal*, Ella is excluded from her community. Indeed, like Antoinette, she is doubly excluded, as near-white in a black community and as creole in a foreign culture. Her dislocation is foreshadowed early through the image of osmosis, which she has been taught to define as "the process by which a thin substance pulls a thick substance through a thin cell wall" (11). Ella's cell is no attic but a comfortable house in America. Her husband is no Rochester, in the sense that the writer clearly distinguishes Selwyn Langley from what he would have been like "had he been born in eighteenth or nineteenth century Britain and of upper class parentage. . . . But this chap was American and not even upper class" (42). Langley has none of the angst of the Brontë hero, and he does not suffer the alienation of Antoinette's husband in the Caribbean. Much of Langley's audacity lies in his contriving his stage production without firsthand experience of Jamaica. However, some aspects of the relationship between Ella and Selwyn display enough correspondence to that between Antoinette and her husband for us to ponder the intertextuality that exists between Jamaican texts and those of a developing Caribbean canon.

Langley is "from a long line," although he is not a threatened younger son, so there is "quite a little empire . . . for Selwyn to inherit" (42). His background is complicated by kinship that is ultimately supportive of him and exclusive of his wife. The family is much occupied with the question of "what are we going to do with him" (42). Ultimately, he will be wealthy in his own right, but meanwhile he sets out to make his fortune by exploiting Ella. Selwyn has neither the personality nor the opportunity to do anything so nineteenth century as locking Ella in an attic, but he does transform her into a story of his own making and translate her to an artificial and contrived setting where nothing is real but the absence of her Jamaican landscape, which is expressed by repeated negation. There are "no shiny green banana trees here flat-footed in the ground, brown-trunked windmills and erect. No blue lagoon. No raindrops, fat and thick beating on the tin roof. No black people" (45). Eventually, Selwyn locks her spirit into celluloid (92). As Lemuel A. Johnson notes, the relationship on Selwyn's side is "primarily extractive" (58).

This is the second phase of Ella's marronage, for her exclusion (like Antoinette's) begins in childhood. This second phase does not take place in Britain, for *Myal* conveys instead a Caribbean vision of America. Gikandi recognizes that in the Caribbean view America is full of material advantages. In addition, America is Europe intensified, without Europe's pretense of a civilizing mission. Gikandi notes that modernism (as defined by the metropolis) has produced greater dependence on the powers that dominate current world economics. The theme of multiple colonization thus continues in *Myal*, woven into the mesh of the civilization/wilderness dialectic and the life/death dialectic traced in non-Jamaican texts.

Both of these dialectics are crucial to the familiar theme of colonial exploitation. *Myal* is a system of interlacing texts in which standard narrative is intercepted by interspirit dialogue that defies intervening space and time. These strands of discourse establish by their parallel developments that Langley is a spirit thief to whom Ella has surrendered her soul and that it is "easier to be a zombie. No faith in the people, no faith in themselves" (66). Langley drains Ella's substance until she "felt cold. As she should. There was no heat there in his garret" (82). She is transformed ("Selwyn was her architect") into "the playwright/director's wife" and "the-woman-without-whom-none-of-this-would-have-been-possible" (82). She confronts his distortion of her life/text with the recognition that "it didn't go so" (84). Then she loses touch with those around her. "It is a doll," says Dan (92), when her psychological marronage is complete.

In *Myal*, spirit thievery in Ella's marriage fuses issues of political domination in colonial relationships with those of gender similarly to the fusion of these issues in *Wide Sargasso Sea*. The political implications of the metaphor are brought out in the conclusion through reference to a reading text based on George Orwell's *Animal Farm* and reinterpreted for Caribbean children. Puri points out that the allegory of Mr. Joe's farm would have been reinforced by traditional association of black characters with animal figures (100). In other words, this set of intertextual references has its context in other intertextual references. The allegory that Ella encounters rewrites both history (to suppress the half that has never been told) and the original story of *Animal Farm*. Ella's challenge is that of rewriting the rewrite. Her anger at the version that makes the animals incapable of independent survival takes issue with a perception of the universe in which civilization necessarily involves domination. The link with gender domination is explicit, for "her quarrel was also with a specific writer, a man called Selwyn Langley" (106).

However, the problem with Langley lies not only in his version of being a man but also in his version of being a writer. *Myal* presents a clash of epistemes in which one vision of art as fixed and closed confronts another vision of art as transformative and open. *Myalism* itself, the art of spiritual liberation, is a significant element of Jamaican history.

Myal traditions in Jamaica go back to the eighteenth century. *Myalism* focuses on the present world, refuses to accept (as natural) negative experiences within this world, and thus resists social hardships with religious fervor. Monica Schuler proposes that "the presence of this tradition, a powerful catalyst for African and Afro-Jamaican resistance to European values and control, explains why socio-political protest is often expressed in religious terms in Jamaica, why it is usually millennial" (33). It also explains the coexistence of religious fervor with social violence, such as emerges in Andrew Salkey's *A Quality of Violence*, though Jamaica is by no means unique in this sense. *Myalists* seek to reform society by purifying it of sin, which is conceived of as sorcery, by freeing spirits entrapped by powers of evil and so restoring the living present from disorder, from entrapment in a living death, contrived in the past. In this sense, *myal* is religious, political, and artistic.

Langley's art shares a problem that Ella traces to master texts that present individuals of nondominant civilizations as zombified or, as Reverend Simpson puts it, as "living deads capable only of receiving orders from someone else and carrying them out" (107). Thus, the reference provides also a metaphor for writing within a dominant tradition, in which a canon dictates to the writer. Brodber's text insists on the responsibility of the unzombified reader to rewrite: "Have you been zombified? . . . You have a quarrel with the writer. He wrote, you think without an awareness of certain things. But does he force you to teach without this awareness? Need your voice say what he says?" (107). Metanarrative insistence on rewriting narrative adds a new dimension to meaning in the text—the sense of the text as doctrinal. The discourse falls into a Gilbert-and-Sullivan rhythm to drive home the point even while celebrating Ella's challenge of canonical texts, "a seminar, a seminar, a most ingenious seminar" (109). Parallelism between Brodber's line and Gilbert and Sullivan's, "a paradox, a paradox . . . " underlines the duality of vision at the heart of Caribbean creativity.

Gikandi recognizes Brodber as moving beyond, for example, Michael Thelwell (*The Harder They Come*) in reconnecting with historical reality by breaking up and parodying the master code. Intertextuality thus "short circuits the whole of creation" (*Myal* 110) by enabling the Caribbean writer to recover and release the imprisoned spirits ("Hi thee hither—There was no need to say it," 110). This outpouring not merely subverts the text of the conqueror but affirms fully independent alternatives rather than subtexts: "Different rhymes for different times/Different styles for different climes" (111).

So in *Myal* intertextuality is both specific and general. Specific intertextuality develops the writer's point through links with specific texts such as the colonial pedagogical rewrite of *Animal Farm*, involving systematic networking of references to a particular and identifiable work and even to a certain type of text describable as imperial. However, in addition, a web of other references accumulate, for *myal* also refers to a set of perceptions familiar in the Caribbean, including popular stereotypes, which interrelate structurally to constitute a composite vision, widely enough shared to be approached as a sort of cognitive text. The colonized/zombified woman, the male conqueror exploiter, transshipment, and revision of personality are definitive features in a growing Caribbean canon of postcolonial writing. The Caribbean counterdiscourse itself perhaps waits to be rewritten.

Brodber does not adopt unquestioningly the innocence of the exploited woman, does not absolve Ella of responsibility for her relationship with Selwyn Langley, who does not physically tear her from her motherland or physically confine her in America, the new master country. She goes, surrenders her life and story, permits him to rewrite her, and even (like the animals on the farm) repeats the words he puts in her mouth. He is willing enough to do these things, but, as Brodber points out, this is no nineteenth-century novel. He is merely an opportunist. In truth, Ella acts a part written by Selwyn on her own authority and then collapses in outrage when the part is replayed before her. She is, of course, particularly susceptible to the opportunist because of her isolation, because (like Antoinette) she is not an intrinsic part of her home community. But here again she has from her earliest years deliberately sought refuge in never-never land (11), and perhaps it is not surprising that she should meet someone determined never to let her grow up.[2]

Children of Eastern Caribbean fiction appear to resolve their conflicting worldviews by choosing one above the other, whereas in Jamaican fiction child characters seem excruciatingly aware of vacuum and this growing emptiness seems ultimately more dangerous. The young protagonist of Merle Hodge's *For the Life of Laetitia* clambers out of despair into the normalcy of sunlight, but Olive Senior's acutely lonely, unmothered children in "Tears of the Sea" and "See the Tiki-Tiki Scatter" (both in *Arrival of the Snake-Woman*) float through empty spaces and rooms of dark corners and silences toward desperation and self-destruction. The desperation of some recent child characters in Jamaican literature and the highly variable success of their attempts to return contrast with a growing general tendency toward resilience in adult female characters.

The significance of such developments in personality lies in the fact that personal history, family history, and community history, unfolding as they often do through memory, parallel a growth to political awareness at both individual and political levels. Gikandi's central purpose is to define the ideology and form of Caribbean modernism and the extent to which the writers of this discourse appropriate or reject the hegemonic European idea of the modern as an effect of Western reason and history (4). Walcott has termed this awareness of dichotomy "a gradual loss of innocence about history" (Rowell 11). A simultaneous appropriation and rejection not only of imperial but also of anti-imperial discourse and a thrust toward indigeneity are trends in current Jamaican writing.

Marronage in child protagonists varies extensively in form and degree, and the desperation of children may end tragically or happily in Jamaican fiction. In the case of *Myal*, the feminine protagonist eventually matures and in so doing moves beyond damage to repair and past healing to rebirth. Shalini Puri shows that this coming to consciousness does not proceed in the linear fashion of a traditional bildungsroman but through a complex series of halvings and doublings (99) in a narrative that Joyce Walker-Johnson has recognized as proceeding by a proliferation of homologous stories. In this movement, *Myal* alludes to texts well known through the education system of the Caribbean, and to these texts as they are popularly known. What *Myal* reveals is the submerged half of the story (Walker-Johnson 61).

Brodber's novel represents a Jamaican discourse in that it interlaces the language systems that coexist and intercept each other in Jamaica. Joyce Walker-Johnson recognizes that *Myal* bridges oral and written traditions and mediates between them (48). Orality is not limited to dialogue but equally defines interior monologue and interpenetrates standard narrative. Orality is not synonymous with Creole but synthesizes a number of informal varieties. Within the community, it varies from the informal Standard English of Reverend Simpson (75, 97) to the Creole conversation of Reverend Brassington's parishoners (95). On the individual level, it spans the Creole workings of Amy Holness's mind as well as her polite standard English conversation with white Maydene Brassington, the minister's wife. The text also reflects interference from external dialects that is quite regular in Jamaica. Reverend Brassington's speech reflects his British education ("I say Simpson" 108), and some influence of American black English defines the variety of interspirit exchanges between Willie and Perce (38–39).

Interactions between characters of the novel involve code shifting, as do interactions between thought and speech within particular characters. These include the types of interaction that Reverend Brassington describes as linguistic rituals and game playing in the community and include such unavoidable adjustments of register as those in Amy Holness's conversation with Maydene:

> And the cursing began to circle in her head: . . . "These white people just wan tek people pickney fi practice pon. Want Mary good-good pickney fe pasture out to her two red-face son. Is pumpkin belly dem wan send this one home with too?" But since Amy Holness was the headmaster's wife and Maydene Brassington was the parson's wife, there was no way what was in her head could be expressed in that way. . . . Instead, she said, ... "Why Mrs. Brassington how nice to see you. What a coincidence! Someone just called your name to me. They said you are wanting to take Mary's child into your house. . . . My, your boys will love her." . . . Maydene Brassington was not fooled by the translation. (20–21)

Maydene recognizes her husband's blindness to an important principle of interaction. As she sees it, "There are classes everywhere and . . . those below must hate those above and must devise some way of communicating this without seeming too obviously rude" (21).

Not only translations between codes but conversations such as those that take place in Ella's mind (84) may reflect not merely the linguistic agility necessary for survival but the neocolonial schizophrenia that underlies the split vision and doublespeak of creole characters. In victims of spirit thievery, such as Ella, perception and expression are defective, "and Ella had not told the half. She did not know it" (56). Faced with her own complicity in Selwyn's production, she babbles the tongue twister that summarizes her acceptance (as woman) of the role of a breeder and her acceptance (as crossbreed) of the stigma of sterility ("Mamma Mary's mulatto mule must have maternity wear," 84). Then she becomes "the rigid, silent staring female" whom Mass Cyrus must purge of the effluence that swells her and that is all she can bear from such a marriage. The novel begins with this crisis, and most of the retrospective strands of narrative are anchored to it. The novel moves in the end through recovery and maturation ("Ella. She's been thinking," 108). Only at this point is she in a position to communicate intelligently and consistently, without lapsing into blank staring and silence. Hitherto, her exclusion has been linked with verbal marronage in various forms: "She sang it. She said it in paragraphs. She said it forever. Ella had tripped out indeed" (84).

Neither the study of feminine exclusion by race and class nor the related theme of spirit thievery is limited in focus to the creole woman. Anita's studying is of "the kind that splits the mind from the body and both from the soul and leaves each open to infiltration"; it involves practice of foreign songs such as "Thee I love" (28). But Ella's maturation is most crucially hinged to Maydeen's development. Maydeen contributes to Ella's separation from her mother but also provides her with a father. Ella's initial fatherlessness is a significant aspect of her rootlessness. However, she is never subjected to maternal abandonment or rejection, and Brassington is recognized and recognizes himself as her father by the end of the novel (94, 108). The nativization of Maydeen, the white British resident, complements Ella's growth toward independence.[3]

Maydeen's fascination with the concept of the cusp reflects her role on the margin of her own circle as a "point at which two curves meet" (13). She refuses to let her class or her race deter her from a meeting of minds either in regular conversation or in interspirit exchanges. She resists her husband's colonial obsession with replacing viable, indigenous thought with imperial teaching and does not want to be "the thing with which to fill these sacks which he has emptied" (18–19). She resists the definition of teaching as an exercise in exorcism and replacement.

Maydeen's maturation consists of expansion in communicative skills. Early, she grasps the art of participating successfully in the linguistic rituals of the community and even demonstrates her expertise in local nonverbal communication as she persuades Miss Amy not to resort to obeah (64–65). Within her own home, Maydeen's relationship with her husband strengthens as artificial conversation between them becomes irrelevant, as it is no longer possible for Reverend Brassington to say, "But do what you wish.—And Maydene would do what he wished" (89). By this time, Maydeen too is thinking "her own thoughts. Her spirit was not there at ready waiting to take his orders" (89). She can communicate to Cook in Creole that "Is not all the time is somebody do something; sometimes is you do you own self something" (94). She recognizes the individual's ultimate responsibility for resistance or complicity, and the novel ends with her firmly established as part of a growing "community of resistance" (Puri 104) that manifests itself in her dialogue with spirits.

It is useful to note that Maydeen does not attempt to supplant Mary but to supplement her mothering. Maydeen does not undertake to reeducate Ella in Britain, and, in fact, Maydeen retrieves Ella from the United States and brings her back to Jamaica. The widely used Caribbean metaphor of family for political relations is particularly productive in *Myal*, which, like *Wide Sargasso Sea*, moves the creation of the colonial subject into a mother country or surrogate motherland. (This is a crucial distinction from the journey of the Old English wife.) Both the Anglocentricity of education and economic necessity regularly impelled colonial-born writers to go abroad to pursue literary aspirations. Intertextuality is thus not only a strategy but also a theme of *Myal*, which shows such intertextuality to be endemic to education and creativity. Educational dilemma in childhood is thus linked with political dichotomy and with the rootlessness that results from family fragmentation.

In exploring how a marginalized individual in a local community can retrieve the spirit by taking charge of the life text, *Myal* makes room for interspirit discourse between all classes, races, and religious denominations. Jamaican fiction has advanced well beyond the vision of white obeah in *Hamel* as a twisted discourse between the British missionary and ignorant black rebels. It is also distinct from the canonical Caribbean vision of Antoinette's dispossession and dislocation without hope of return or restitution. The allusions in *Myal* to the imperial canon interrelate topically to develop the concept of spirit thievery—an active metaphor of local currency yet at the same time a metaphor compatible with global symbolism of the undead. However, in *Myal* the spirit is purged and freed, the child and colony grow from zombification to intellectual empowerment. This change is possible only through collective resistance, through recognition of individual responsibility, and through constructive and shared mothering.

The Reject Turned Monster: Olive Senior's "Country of the One-Eye God"[4]

Marronage results from fragmentation internal to the Jamaican setting and from a tension between local and imperial cultures. The growth of a national consciousness sensitizes local writers to separation of communities within the island and to the consequences of abandonment as some Jamaicans select voluntary exile and others are left behind. Moreover, beyond the connection between the dispossessed woman and the deprived child lies a chain effect that links the abandoned child to the violently resentful and demanding youth and eventually to the adult as predator. The gathering hostility of Icy Barton ("I killed you totally in my heart," Thomas 159) diffuses as she reunites with her mother, but this outcome does not hold true for all children whose mothers leave "to go to foreign" (Senior, "Country of the One-Eye God" 21). Senior explores the end result of metamorphosis from such childhood in a consciousness tormented simultaneously by exclusion and claustrophobia.

Through the exploration of altered perspective, current Jamaican fiction reviews entrenched Caribbean visions of alienation by considering the aborted, the miscarried, the dropped-and-left child that strikes back by turning on society or on the family that is society's microcosm.[5] Senior's "Country of the One-Eye God" (*Summer Lightning*) conveys a terrifying vision of the reject turned monster. It is a study in marronage because it is a tale of leaving and being left and consequently of the cold logic behind seemingly irrational violence. In Senior's tale, as in Thomas's, abandonment prompts resentment. In "Country of the One-Eye God" this resentment has social repercussions.

This short story, like any literature in a multicultural context, explores Otherness as a dialectic of interaction and rift between unlikes. Senior presents cultural confrontation with linguistic consequences in a physical context that at first understates cultural distinctions but gradually articulates them as part of the text's meaning. Here, as in other areas of this analysis, meaning is taken as being, at least to some extent, both socially and culturally determined. (David Birch relates culture-dependent meaning to the prioritizing of parole, 131–33.)

Ma B and Jacko are originally of one culture; the links of kinship and village background, the nurture of grandson by grandmother are emphasized. Yet their confrontation reveals profound cultural schism both at the heart of the community and in the bosom of the family. From the context of Ma B's culture, Jacko is a monster who has turned his back on his home community for an essentially unknown way of life.

In addition, Jacko has found himself on the shearing edge of separating communities and is part of a wider social fragmentation. The separating communities are partially defined by semantic variation between cultural groups. It is essential to the argument that follows to recognize that Jamaican society at present is divided not merely into classes that are economically divided but, even among the most deprived, separated by worldview. To distinguish these views as rural versus urban or as young versus old would be to oversimplify the dichotomy, because the rift is produced by several intersecting distinctions likely to vary from one set of individuals to another.

In the multidimensional space of Jamaican society, Jacko has located himself quite differently from Ma Bell. Each of his utterances functions as an act of identity by which he locates himself in this space. One of the clashing cultures is characteristically old, conservative, spiritual, and inward turned in its orientation to the community; the other is young, radical, disillusioned, fragmenting, and out directed. These different orientations produce in Ma Bell and Jacko distinctly different meanings for terms they would seem to have in common. This dichotomy in lexical meaning is important because the semantic drift intensifies the gap between these groups and reflects the alienation of focal characters of the narrative from each other.

Distance

In "Country of the One-Eye God," Senior introduces the theme of ruptured communication from her opening line. Ma Bell is isolated from her family. News of the grandson whom Ma Bell raised comes to her indirectly, incompletely, and disjointedly. An electronic rather than a human medium confirms and completes this news, and the electronic medium is itself of foreign source—the radio originates from the United States. At this point in the narrative most of Ma Bell's dialogue is with the Lord, but it is one-sided; she talks to a God who appears to be deaf. Her links with children and grandchildren abroad are practically nonexistent, consisting of a letter "once in a blue moon." From Jacko himself, since he left home two years before, she "never hear one living word." All communication lines between Jacko and others represented or mentioned in the tale are ruptured. He is distanced from members of the family who have become part of foreign progressive culture and from those that remain in rural conservative culture, and he is out of touch with the urban youth-gang culture with which he has affiliated himself. Ma Bell exists in a closed network that supports little variation in behavior. She is closely constrained by norms and shows a high degree of conformity in her speech (cf. Milroy 155, 178, 184). The break in communication is not to be attributed only to the physical remoteness between her rural location and the urban setting to which her grandson has shifted. The explanation cannot be completed solely by reference to a sort of time warp produced as one community changes faster than another. Her actual encounter with Jacko demonstrates that the rift goes deeper.

The problem with Jacko is in fact a series of cleavages that merge to produce a massive personality flaw. Senior does not present him as a lunatic but as a horrifying mix of desperation and coldly deliberate criminality. She links these characteristics to psychological damage resulting from abandonment. Jacko's departure from normal behavior relates to the rupture of his earliest and most essential links: it begins in the silence of his parents. The magnetic pull of North American culture and the related fragmentation of traditional Jamaican ties is an undertone throughout the text and becomes explicit in Jacko's embittered outcry: "Look how long I wait for them to send for me. . . . Next year never did came for me" (21). Ma Bell's old-fashioned upbringing—talk and chastisement—has only hardened his resentment. Now his needs narrow and crystalize to material survival: "Me no need no more talk any more. Just give me di money" (21).

Communication failure becomes apparent as the turn-taking of normal conversation breaks down in various dialogues. Her muttering of personal needs and commitments for which she has approportioned small sums of money meet with no response. Her threat to bawl to the neighbors is equally meaningless to him, except as grim justice for the discipline she meted out in his earlier years. He ridicules her dialogue with God as useless effort of "rag tag and bobtail" to communicate with "high and mighty" (24). To Jacko, any attempt to cross this gap—the ultimate class barrier—between God and the Jamaican poor is ludicrous. As he raises the gun, her pleadings to him fall on deaf ears even as he dismisses her prayers to God as useless. It is clear that much of the action rests on aborted communication, and the structure of the text is a composite of discourses, almost all broken in some way.

The dialogue between Ma B and Jacko deteriorates to pleading on one side and demanding on the other, and cultural lesion between the speakers limits their mutual intelligibility. Apart from this dialogue, the text contains other embedded discourse such as fragmented news and one-sided dialogue with God. The breakdown in communication between Jacko and Ma Bell is a function of cultural distance. The elderly speaker with expectations of respect and family loyalty, accustomed to being addressed as "Ma Bell" even by her seventy-year-old nephew, is faced first with Jacko's "cold detachment" and absence of greeting and kinship title. She refers to herself as his "old gran"; he never addresses her as such. He calls her "old lady" and eventually "Ma B," but by that time he has also distanced and generalized her with the generic label, "unno old woman."

Nonverbal communication reveals similar breakdowns. Through such gestures as his grasping for the rum, Jacko displays a lack of manners that renders his words meaningless to Ma Bell. His offensive reaction (JC *suckteeth*) at the name of Jesus and sprawling back in her best chair, his searching of her most private garments, his sneering laughter at the notion of Judgment Day, and his obscenity render the gun in her face unsurprising. Seen against the conventions of nonverbal communication normative to Ma Bell's culture, the irrationality of violence is an almost logical development of his incomprehensible rudeness. Maureen Warner-Lewis ("Mask") throws useful light on the relationship of violence and evil to normative values with reference to this text. At the same time, Ma Bell's act of closing her eyes in prayer is empty of significance to Jacko. He is secure in his own isolation by silence that her prayers will be inaudible to God and the gunshot unnoticed by her neighbors.

A gulf yawns between Jacko's concept of civilization as foreign (versus the local experience of those "that turn-down back here," 21) and Ma B's concept of civilization as respectability (versus the revelation of wildness in the kin turned stranger). Ma B perceives civilization as a world of orderly routine, versus a world "all cata-corner and moving off course" (19).

The unbridgeable distance of the youth turned monster emerges in the imagery that dehumanizes him beginning with his initial scratching on the door through his metamorphosis to hairy stranger and dismissal of his comrades in laconic comment, "fren a dawg." This recategorization of Jacko's group from human to bestial has been foreshadowed earlier in the text through such traditional images of evil as the viper. The recategorization to nonhuman becomes overt in the *dawg* metaphor. *Dawg* in Jamaican Creole usage carries overwhelmingly negative associations in contrast to positive connotations of *dog* in usage by metropolitan English-speaking communities. Negative connotations of savagery are compounded by the metaphor of him wolfing down his food (20).

Jacko's stature grows from simply being a strange child, to one who is "bull buck and duppy conqueror" elsewhere but a boy to Ma B, to a huge and threatening presence. Jacko's recategorization from human to nonhuman is a transformation foreshadowed in her early recognition of evil distilled into the boy so that, as she complains to Jacob, they "that dont do no-body nothing bring children into the world and before them old enough to spit, is animal them turn" (18). A field of lexical items thus reduces Jacko's humanity and entails his growing inhumanity. Indeed, by the time Jacko has completed his path of destruction through her house and turned on her per-son, her trust in his common humanity and in their kinship is hopelessly frail: "God, he is my very blood. He wouldn't really kill me? Eh, God?" (25).

Throughout the text, lexical items appear to carry separate meanings for the two consciousnesses that confront each other without understanding. This is particularly true where a word includes the semantic component of affirming or negating distance, for the conflicting cultures in the text differ in their notions of spatial organization. Crucial to meaning is the distance of the deserted boy from his parents. But distance also affects other percep-tions, like that of *foreign*. Ma Bell's orientation to *foreign* is different from Jacko's. She is aware of incoming news or rare letters from loved ones; he is turned outward: "I haffe leave.... Look how long I wait for them to send for me" (21). Unlike Ma B, Jacko sees both her and himself as castoffs, "turn down back here," and he is prepared to murder his way out. He plans for *foreign* with money and passport; Ma Bell plans too, but for a different jour-ney. She looks forward to her flamboyant exit in a splendor of white satin, with the neighbors oohing and aahing. Her ultimate departure is planned in conformity to her community's norms. Between her commitment to respect-ability and his disregard for opinion yawns a fearful distance in values ("Ma Bell shrank away," 20).

The entire action of the narrative spans no more than a day, perhaps even a few hours, from the radio broadcast to the actual encounter with Jacko. However, the narrative expands by implicature through embedded reflec-tions on the past, as in Ma B's family history and Jacko's bitter memories. Senior similarly embeds in the narrative dark hints of the future, implicit in Ma B's premonitions and in the manifold suggestions of burial, particularly in references to the burial money itself, "that is my future" (25). At the same time, the development of Jacko over his nineteen years into a vast physical threat is compressed into a fleeting sensation. Ma B notices that "he had a presence that forced even his grandmother to look away. She shivered and knew that someone had walked over her grave. In the pale light, Ma Bell sud-denly wondered how such a little boy could suddenly grow so huge as to fill all the spaces in the room. She felt shrivelled and light, compressed into the interstices of space by his nearness" (22–23).

Material values dominate Jacko's worldview as spiritual values domi-nate Ma Bell's, and his material presence is an imprisoning nearness like the circle of the kitchen, which tightens around them after the search. The nearness is intensely physical, highlighting their emotional distance. The claustrophobia intensifies through images of entrapment and through the impression of Jacko expanding as the action progresses while Ma Bell shrinks. The relationship between Ma B and Jacko becomes a cord that tightens to strangulation point, so the metaphor of the cord transforms through semantic drift from a binding thread of kinship to a tightening of the heart with fear, eventually becoming a noose that traps and strangles. The encroachment on the grandmother's space is an important feature of Jacko's nonverbal communication of aggression. The closer he moves toward her physically the further he advances toward stripping her of the burial money and sending her out of the world as poor and naked as she came in.

Leaving

The problem of how each will leave is the issue that defines both Ma Bell's and Jacko's thinking and action throughout, and related terms proliferate in the text: *jail breaker, left home, last grandchild had left, tek off, runway, run away, shrank away, a haffe leave, leave? Go where, far, passport, go to foreign, walk way leave me, to run, lef it, never leave this place alive, sent off, leave, leave that way, leave this world, go into the next world.*

Socioculturally separate groups speaking what appears to be the same language may, in certain situations, be unintelligible to each other. What appears to be formally the same word may differ semantically from group to group or may be semantically loaded in one group and practically meaningless in the other. In "Country of the One-Eye God," the word *leave* has different implications for Ma Bell and Jacko.

An essential and shared semantic dimension of the word *leave* is mobility in a direction away from the location of the speaker at the time of utterance. But the ideological orientations of Ma Bell and Jacko are quite differently indicated by deictic terms of spatial reference. Within the narrow and highly specific universe of the short story, the focal characters distinguish *in/out, up/down,* and *far/near* in relation to quite different values. For Ma Bell, for example, *up/down* in a social context has connotations of respectability, economically defined but also strongly bound to notions of morality. For Jacko, *up/down* is socially defined purely in monetary terms, not surprisingly, because his early desertion by his parents has been explained to him as resting squarely on monetary considerations ("They could never afford to send for me," 21).

Similarly, *in/out* has acquired for Jacko, with his different value system, associations of imprisonment and escape that are not apparent in Ma Bell's speech for the greater part of the text. The same value differences affect other terms crucial to the text, such as *family* and *stranger,* in which notions such as *in* or *out* are inherent. The concept of *family* in the conservative culture includes associations of warmth, loyalty, and above all respect, whereas in the underworld youth-gang culture the right to demand monetary support may override all. This mutates Jacko to a stranger in the eyes of Ma Bell and leaves her in a state of bewilderment because, at the same time, she recognizes him as her blood.

With such different perceptions, it is not surprising that other crucial terms, such as *foreign,* should be differently loaded in the usage of the two main characters. To Ma Bell, to have gone foreign and succeeded is a social achievement in its widest sense, one that a breath of scandal may well destroy. However, pride and shame are emotions motivated quite differently in the cultures of "old gran" and "bull buck." For the youth, to go foreign is to escape. For Ma Bell, *foreign* is "over there"; for Jacko, *foreign* is out and (materially) up. For Jacko, the alternative to *foreign* is to be "turn down back here" and to be forever in, buried alive.

Not surprisingly, the different orientations of Ma B and Jacko produce varying understandings of *dead,* as they do of *leave. Dead* for Jacko is final. In his view, Ma Bell will soon "dead and lef" the money; the concept of burial money is not one he can possibly grasp. For Ma Bell, *dead* is not a terminal concept. Apart from her vision of attending her own glorious funeral, Ma Bell's religious convictions include certainty of an afterlife. She advises Jacko to surrender himself to an almost certain death sentence and directs him to Jesus for help with an optimism directed beyond death—"is not too late." But the problem is that, for Jacko, God (if he exists) is located *up* as oppressive authority, as unjust distributor of wealth, and out of the location of the speaker. In this framework, God has not only deserted but also ridicules those who are "poor and turn down." God's *up* is not the same for Jacko as for Ma Bell. Jacko's *up/down* orientation is causally related to secret shame. For Jacko, pride is stimulated by material acquisition and by recognition of physical power, whereas for Ma Bell this type of achievement can produce only "duppy conqueror." Thus, she is proud to have brought up children who could "go foreign" even if they have subsequently forgotten her, provided they retain respectability. Jacko's undying shame is to have been left behind.

Indeed, to Ma Bell and to Jacko, *leaving* can hardly mean the same thing. Ma Bell orders him to "just know you place" from an entirely different spatial organization. Jacko lost his place as a young child, never subsequently found it, and has no concept of Ma Bell's sense of security in place. Other contrasting categorizations (of what is appropriate to *bwoy* as distinct from *big man*, of what constitutes practical help, of the meaning of *talk* itself) are so disparate that the grandmother and grandson speak to each other about leaving from entirely separate perspectives. It is not surprising that his speech is vanity to her and that hers is foolishness to him (20–21). Moreover, an important dichotomy in the text is that between stasis and change, as is reinforced by their contrasting meanings to Ma B and Jacko. To Ma B, stasis is order and calm, whereas change intimates a world "cata-corner and moving off course"; change is dissolution. But to Jacko, escape lies only through change, and stasis is old, empty, and forgotten as the turned-down pot. His present desperation, articulated in "a haffe leave," is indistinguishable from his initial abandonment and unchangeable status as deserted child. The sentence, "a haffe leave," is syntactically ambiguous, for it carries implications of past tense and passive voice as well as nonpast and active meanings. In the Creole, Jacko's resentment at having been left and his desperation to leave fuse in a single output that marks neither tense nor voice.

So for Jacko *leave* is an absolute term, taking the subject permanently away and completely out of a *down* situation. In his expectation, to *leave* (active meaning) is to escape; in his tragic experience, to *leave* (Creole unmarked passive sense, "be left") is to be deserted. His alienation and thus his character as outcast are defined both by passive suffering (rejection, having been left) and by active intention (escape, need to leave). For Ma Bell the term raises questions of where, of how far. It does not automatically imply *foreign*. Her grandson had left the neighborhood but not the island, and she plans for the time when she too will leave, but in style—the memorable exit in satin and polished wood with silver handles. Of course, she can only leave through an agency outside of herself, at God's summons and borne by twelve strong men. Jacko takes the business of leaving into his own hands. He rejects stasis. This urgency and this disregard for others are aspects of his badness to Ma Bell, for whom leaving must be orderly and must not incur inconvenience or injury to others. Because Jacko considers himself to have been dumped by family, society, and God, he feels justified in leaving at his own convenience.

These differences are tied to their varying perceptions of material security. For Jacko, the money is a way out, the way to foreign. For Ma Bell, it is a provision for respectability when the time comes for her to "leave this world." Jacko says she "soon dead and lef" the money anyway, not recognizing that where for him it is a means of leaving, for her it is a means of leaving respectably. Of course, he turns out to be right in a grim sense because his intervention will separate her from the hope of this respectable departure.

The money thus becomes a snare for Ma Bell. It will bring her death without providing the stylish exit. Physically and emotionally stripped, she will leave as poor and naked as she came. Jacko will leave her as "poor and turn down" as he himself was left. The strange child with the "right hand of falsehood," the child "whose mouth speaketh vanity," does not "lift up his head" like the others she has raised. He lifts up his hand, with the gun. By this time the ruptured dialogue has fragmented completely. Her pleading is meaningless to Jacko, her threats empty, and her prayers useless. His demand has placed her in an impossible dilemma, to relinquish the burial money which is her future or to cling to it, die, and be stripped.

The gun does not go off in the text, and what is not in the text can be semantically as important as what is. The gaps define for the reader the boundaries of Ma Bell's experience. Thus, although readers have information hidden from characters other than Ma Bell (such as the location of the money), they cannot be audience to the gunshot because they are tied to her perspective, subject to her capacity to report. There is no certainty of the gunshot; there can be no such closure. And readers must to some extent be bounded by Ma Bell's experience to experience adequately the Otherness of Jacko. In any case, real history is open ended, and closure is a strategy of traditional fiction and so vulnerable to exposure as a lie. Senior's open-ended tale conveys two tragedies. One is Jacko's failed search for identity through escape to *foreign*; the other is Ma B's tragic underestimation of the repercussions associated with betrayal and abandonment. The composite tragedy hinges on a mutual misunderstanding. Neither comprehends what *leaving* means to the other.

Although the reader's perspective is tied to Ma Bell's, the reader shares with the writer experiences external to the text. This is social information associated with the individual's total network of linguistic categorizations. Readers make judgments unconfined by the horizons of the particular character whose point of view defines the discourse. At least to some extent, linguistic orientation independently defines judgments of the focal character. In analyzing the differences between Ma Bell's language and Jacko's, it is almost impossible to avoid imposing values implied by use of language, by categorizations. Readers' analyses are thus a weighing and balancing of ideologically loaded structures and meanings that may vary in the different cultures that interact in the text and in their own idiolects. This choice between ideologically loaded meanings, informed by matters extrinsic to the text (for example, other comparable texts or social situations) renders reading a political act. The evolving background of experience means that readers provide the sequel to the action, but they do so only while recognizing that from Ma Bell's point of view, the gun is the end of the story.

The reader is thus not autonomous, not free to a degree suggestive of bardicide (brilliantly dissected by Levin), but integrated into the communication process by the writer to complete the speaker/message/hearer requirements of discourse. The writer manipulates reader interpretation through the placement of gaps, through the exploitation of semantic drift in the usage of words by different characters. The writer also manipulates the reader by intertextuality through which the reader's attention is drawn to relevant extrinsic experiences, which include clearly identifiable allusions such as biblical references as well as more universal, archetypal imagery, such as that of blood. Ma Bell's usage early associates blood with kinship and closeness, but her later usage destabilizes this positive sense of the term. She uses it with her earlier meaning (that is, the speaker/character's meaning remains unchanged) but in a context of impending violence that evokes in the reader a consciousness of the negative associations of blood. Thus, there is plurality of textual meaning as distinct from the character's meaning. The semantic drift of the evolving metaphor introduces blood, like the cord image earlier discussed, as a kinship bond, but in the end the image of the raised gun and her identification of her assailant as her "very blood" cumulatively suggest murder.

Figurative language is ideologically loaded in "Country of the One-Eye God." In the text, culturally defined metaphors convey socially determined meaning, as in the recurrent *turned-down* reference. The turned-down pot with its implications of emptiness and disuse is made more poignant in Jacko's speech by the fact that the term *pot* itself is never articulated, leaving the reader open to other implications of the phrase *turned-down* and reinforcing reader sensitivity to Jacko's sense of rejection and desertion.

Ma Bell's rural cottage reflects Jamaica in microcosm, and events in the story parallel patterns of history. Generations of discipline by preaching and chastisement on the one hand and marginalization on the other conclude in colonial schizophrenia. Colonial disappointment at being left hardens into a desperation to leave; yearning sharpens into demand and pain into violence. Parallel to the continuing attraction of the foreign metropolis runs a gravitational pull of Kingston that lures rural youth to urban homelessness, frustration, and crime. Shattered family ties thus recall not only the unraveling imperial-colonial relationship but the torn fabric of Jamaica's internal history. Society's inability to support all its children forces some into a dehumanizing struggle for survival that unleashes almost apocalyptic chaos.

"Country of the One-Eye God" lends itself to current critical interpretation of the literary text as inherently political, as a revision of a history yet in progress and so as a network of unfinished meanings. The text denies closure not only because of all that is left unstated in its ending but also because tensions between contrasting cultures and culture-defined meanings interfere on surface with the coherence of the text. So do unanswered questions in the dialogue, responses that appear not to fit the comments that triggered them, lexis shifting semantically with context. But this apparent incoherence is itself profoundly meaningful, highlighting through the communication gaps rifts widening in a society of disintegrating values, a society drawn by the relentless attraction of *foreign* even as it increasingly entraps the "poor one that turn down back here." Thus, semantic inconsistency within the society of conflicting cultures produces a surface incoherence, but this surface incoherence, through semantic drift, actually reinforces through congruence the deeper coherence of the text, the paradigmatic relations between consistent webs of meaning in each of the conflicting cultures, of Ma B and Jacko. In these conflicting cultures, the flaws of different generations intersect in a fragmentation of society that is intensified by social conditions.

Senior articulates her characters' sense of a widespread social malaise through biblical apocalyptic imagery to convey a traditional Jamaican insistence that there is "evil, evil, evil in the land" (18). This is not a native evil, inherent in the land, but a new savagery induced by economic hardship ("is the hard times breeding them tough pickney," 18). Indeed, economic considerations underlie Jacko's motherlessness and influence his denial of the old gran's authority and of all other authority. The end, foreshadowed in the beginning, demonstrates that the gun is Jacko's tragedy as well as Ma Bell's, an ambiguity conveyed in the phrase *their destruction:* "It predick you know Ma B. As the Good Book say Job Thirtieth Verse Twelve upon my right hand rise the youth they push away my feet and raise up against me the ways of their destruction" (19). The text conveys fragmentation of values and dissolution of communication lines in a situation where a culture has split and where its conventional and radical offshoots intersect again tragically.

Where *Myal* portrayed marronage in the indigenous consciousness confronted with colonial or neocolonial power, "Country of the One-Eye God" demonstrates the growing rift between radical and conservative consciousnesses within Jamaican society. This plural perspective propels the reader beyond Ma Bell's limited point of view to an understanding of what it means to be the leavings of a society.

5

Naked into the Storm

Winkler and the Wilderness Within

Lemme outta dis damn madhouse.
—Anthony Winkler, *The Lunatic*

To VARYING EXTENTS, Anthony Winkler explores psychological marronage in three novels that have appeared during the past decade. Whether this alienation takes the form of a withdrawal into madness or whether it demands resistance to mental breakdown, the solitary struggle for selfhood is physically located outside of civilization and is, importantly, a mental as well as a physical struggle. The isolated character suffers as much from exposure as from confinement.

Winkler's most recent novel, *The Great Yacht Race*, focuses on the hypocrisy of a social group on the brink of extinction—the well-to-do colonials of Jamaica's Montego Bay. In doing so, the book touches on alienation in a variety of forms and questions the sanity of a society out of touch with reality. However, Winkler's first two novels concentrate on the marronage of the individual psyche.

The Great Yacht Race opens by juxtaposing a brutal murder with the harsh conversation of the mourners and the sudden fear and bewilderment of the deceased's brother after the wake (" 'Island life,' he muttered speculatively," 9). Familiar Caribbean metaphors of colonial schizophrenia define the life of the murderer. He begins as an unloved waif, abandoned by his mother, exploited by his guardians, and at eighteen, "afire with resentment" (18). Unlike Winkler's other dispossessed characters, who drift from loss to loss into the countryside, the deprived youth who becomes Bowen's murderer drifts into the Kingston slums, where he survives by crime and so becomes familiar with imprisonment. "One broiling day," we are told, "as he broke rocks with a sledgehammer in the prison quarry, he heaved a sigh and went mad" (18).

Winkler summarizes this losing battle in *The Great Yacht Race* but adopts the perspective of the alienated consciousness in his first two novels, which differ in that *The Painted Canoe* traces a struggle against such resigned withdrawal into madness whereas *The Lunatic* begins after this part of the battle has been lost and relates a madman's refusal to resign himself to a life of crime. Both of these earlier novels present wilderness experiences of psychological conflict, but they encode the psychological dimensions of marronage differently. Meaning will be approached in *The Painted Canoe* through word meaning and metaphor, but it will be examined in *The Lunatic* by concentrating on rule-flouting in the discourse.

Meaning in *The Painted Canoe:* Mind Versus the Deep

Winkler's first novel explores isolation and resistance through the perspective of a protagonist who refuses to go mad and who avoids insanity by redefining himself. The narrative traces the experiences of a fisherman (Zachariah) whose face is hideously deformed. Ridiculed by passersby, he is unable to sleep on the night before a challenging voyage, and he falls asleep at sea and goes adrift. Over the ensuing weeks he retains his sanity despite his solitude and the hostility of the elements. On return to land he is ecstatically welcomed by his wife (Carina) and the rest of the community but soon learns that he has been diagnosed as terminally ill. The English doctor resident in the area is infuriated by Zachariah's stubborn hold on a life of suffering. The doctor's efforts to convince others of the inevitable and logical supremacy of death confirm among his acquaintances the widely held view that he is mad. Eventually, the doctor ends his frustration in suicide, but Zachariah sets out to sea to pray for assistance. The community regards his healing, shortly thereafter, as a miracle, but the brown Jamaican doctor who has replaced the Englishman contemptuously distinguishes superstition from science and identifies the fisherman's healing as remission.

Gerald Moore noticed early in the history of Caribbean criticism that the fisherman, although sentimentalized in some Caribbean writing, "emerges with an undiminished primal force in the best writing. He alone, it seems, escapes a mentality still deeply marked by slavery and colonialism. . . . He alone does not appear marooned by time on a shore that does not yet belong to him. And he is master of the element which defines, if nothing else, the status of the Caribbean islander" (45). Moore identifies this "oceanic sensibility" as preeminently that of the "small islander." *The Painted Canoe* offers a rare view of the fisherman in Jamaican fiction, and Zachariah's resistance not only demonstrates the currency of the fisherman image to the larger island but also shrinks the spatial setting of Caribbean marronage further, from the island to the canoe.

The world of *The Painted Canoe* is one of circling horizons, and its shifting perspectives are those of souls at sea in various senses. The perspective of a center of consciousness that has been set adrift dominates the structure of the text, which follows this drifting perspective rather than strict chronological sequence. Causal relationships link crucial events.

The course of events falls into two clearly distinct phases, the fisherman's struggle with the sea and his struggle with cancer. Both are studies of resistance. The first can be explained implicitly and explicitly by definable causes, a chain—or perhaps more properly a mesh—of cause and effect. Through medical incompetence and parental ignorance, a medical disorder in the protagonist's childhood remains untreated, resulting in the ugliness about which he is so sensitive as to be unable to rest adequately on the night before the voyage. A crucial factor in this first phase, Zachariah's loss at sea, is therefore his preoccupation with his ugliness. This acromegaly caused by pituitary malfunction incites the first phase of the action, just as cancer incites the second. Disease thus topically links both phases of the novel.

The Painted Canoe questions the rationality of existence as currently defined by modern science. It struggles to redefine the meaning of life to elemental humanity. Natural and social causes set in motion a return to elemental chaos or wilderness and the stripping of isolated humanity to its essentials. From the point of view of the fisherman, his second predicament is inexplicable suffering. Medical science can account for suffering coldly or arrogantly as entirely logical, but to ordinary common sense it seems quite unreasonable.

The central consciousness and most important perspective is that of a character regularly referred to as "old negar." Zachariah faces overwhelmingly hostile forces that attack him externally and internally, and to confront them he must marshal qualities that are inherent. The sources of his suffering are physical, social, and psychological and compose a universe whose raging forces of disorder he chooses to resist. At least in part, this vision of disorder is cumulatively suggested by lexical semantics, and it is indigenous to the extent that this mesh of meaning is specifically Jamaican.

The lexis of *The Painted Canoe* is distinctively Jamaican even though most of its words are derived from English. Code shifting between Standard English and Jamaican Creole reinforces a perspectival shift from universally shared vision to an indigenous one. This shift must be achieved without losing those readers who are dependent on written Standard English. Indeed, it must reinforce for such readers, without loss of comprehension, the distance between the creole consciousness and that of the noncreole.

One process of lexical development in Jamaican speech (Lalla, "Word Mesh") has been a phonological reinterpretation that distinguishes Creole lexicon from Standard English sufficiently to make Creole words of English origin unrecognizable to the noncreole hearer. Conversely, both a Standard and a Creole reading of the same word can occur because by rendering a Creole sentence in Standard English orthography, a writer returns most of the Creole terms to their source for the convenience of the non-Creole reader. The reader uninitiated in Creole encounters an easily digestible Standard-looking vocabulary and so deals more easily with the unfamiliar syntax. But the Creole speaker naturally retains oral (Creole) pronunciation, as in the cases of *dirty (negar)* and *worthless*.

The discourse also exemplifies an ability of Creole words to shift word class and to function in a wider variety of ways than in Standard English. This multifunctionality is closely linked to the flexionless patterns of characteristically analytic Creole sentence structure, and it also contributes to the expansion of the Jamaican lexicon by freeing words to operate in sentence positions and with syntactic functions that are closed to them in the international language. Again, Winkler draws on this characteristically Creole process to reinforce his theme of disordered vision: "Dem short me pay, sah. . . . Three months now and me tell dem me pay short, dem don't do nothing yet. How man can live on short pay?" (134). This redeployment of words familiar in Standard English and their recategorization to new functions further distinguishes Jamaican literary discourse from international English without rendering the novel unintelligible to those who do not speak Creole (see Lalla, "Word-Mesh").

Jamaican discourse includes far more than Jamaican Creole, as it includes the Jamaican variety of Standard English and automatically appropriates all items of the international language when and as necessary. Yet it is easy to overlook the degree to which this shared lexicon is nativized, and most discussions of Caribbean language as used in Caribbean literature focus almost exclusively on Creole inclusions.

To overlook the reinterpretation of the English lexicon in Jamaican language is to miss nuances of meaning in which much of the creativity of Jamaican literature is rooted. This is true of *The Painted Canoe*, where, as in his later novels, Winkler is deeply occupied with the problem of a nation that is out of order (in the preferred Jamaican sense of improper, rude, or unruly as well as the sense more general in Standard English, not in proper working condition). The global meaning of any text emerges partly through accumulated word meanings, and meaning in *The Painted Canoe* is vested in a lexis that has evolved through processes of development characteristic of Jamaican discourse.

This text shows a relatively lower proportion of overt Creole than much other Jamaican writing, but its discourse is identifiably Jamaican, partly because some Jamaican derivational processes of word formation that are native to English (such as compounding) are reinforced in Creole by their prominence in other contributing languages. Winkler draws on word derivations of the sort that utilize English morphemes and join English words regularly but that produce in Jamaica terms such as *boastiness* and *johncrow,* which are non-English although they do not violate any identifiable rule of English. Simple iteratives such as *fool-fool,* used in the text both for people and for arguments, achieve emphasis by stressing through reduplication both the degree and the spread of the essential quality (foolishness) that the term conveys.

The Painted Canoe conveys meaning through words and phrases such as *out of order, old negar, worthless,* and *ignorant,* which differ semantically from their Standard English counterparts in ways that accumulate to have thematic significance. The derogatory usage of *negro* in Yorkshire (*neeagur,* "negro or contemptible fellow," recorded by Ross and Holderness 99) resembles the semantic significance of the term *negar* when prefixed, in Jamaica, to indicate derogation (Lalla, "Word-Mesh" 131). The European component both in Standard and in non-Standard form thus brings its own inherent biases to the Creole. In addition, Creole combines *negar* with *old* in a phrase or compound that is more than the sum of its parts. In the Jamaican discourse of *The Painted Canoe, old negar* begins by being even more worthless than *negar* and certainly more contemptible than a *negar* who happens to be old. The term conveys an ideological perspective in which *old negar* is conceptually low and therefore excluded from civilized community.

The thematically related term *worthless occurs in all its Standard senses and is used with a distribution similar to that of old negar.* In addition, the Jamaican reader associates *worthless,* in its Creole pronunciation, with a stereotype— the feckless ne'er-do-well who does not live by his own effort. In other words *worthless* in *The Painted Canoe* well describes some essential features of the character suggested by *old negar* in all its derogatory usages.

This lexis of obvious English origin but distinct Jamaican semantics offers an indigenous perspective on the out of order world in which the fisherman is cast adrift. A non-English apport, *butu,* extends Winkler's field of terms that share a common semantic component of worthlessness. Frederic G. Cassidy and Robert LePage show that probable sources of the term in Twi and Ewe signify inversion, stooping, and squatting, and the Jamaican noun refers contemptuously to a person of low social status, of little value in terms of class and refinement. Because the term now carries attitudinal implications in addition to its original implications of spatial/directional orientation, *butu* partakes of the pejoration of African terms that is a general trend in the lexical history of Jamaica. More frequently, African influence comes through convergence. Winkler uses *dirty* in its Standard English senses but also in contexts where Jamaicans would understand *dutty* not only as an adjective but as a noun. The Jamaican noun *dutty* retains its Twi meaning, "earth, ground," whereas the adjective preserves the English meaning together with an added Creole meaning of low. Not surprisingly, *old negar* is at times dismissed as *dirty negar,* with aspersions of low social level rather than of physical uncleanliness. The connotations of low social level readily mesh with those of moral corruption.

The Painted Canoe conveys its Jamaican perspective not only through local rather than Standard English meaning in individual words but also in semantic relationships that link groups of words rather differently to their semantic linkage in International English. Like any text, *The Painted Canoe* provides sets of words, each associated with a domain that is unified by the same content. Areas of content are specifiable conceptual ground, and these areas are covered by terms that bear clear relations of affinity and contrast with each other. These semantically linked terms compose lexical fields, and, given semantic distinctions between identical terms in Jamaican and International English, lexical fields in Jamaican discourse are not necessarily identical to those in International English. So not only is *old negar* Jamaican, with no corresponding Standard English term (although both *old* and *negro* are English words), but the semantic field that relates *old negar, dirty negar, butu,* and *worthless* is Jamaican rather than International.

Worthlessness, in its Creole sense and pronunciation, is a concept central to a crucial semantic field in this novel, and it relates thematically to ideas of disorder, incompetence, and lunacy. Semantic fields comprise contrast sets under a covering term, and some terms refer to basic concepts (such as *worthless*) whereas other terms are peripheral. Mixed contrast sets also occur, so terms peripheral to one set may be basic to another, or terms may be peripheral to more than one set. Thus, sets may overlap. For example, *ignorant* and *fool-fool* belong to the same field as the basic concept *stupid,* but *ignorant* in Creole more often means angry, frequently unreasonably angry. Lexical fields in *The Painted Canoe* overlap in ways that reflect a composite Jamaican rather than an exclusively English semantic composition, extending the dimensions of disorder and worthlessness traditionally associated with *old negar.* From this traditional point of view, the semantic universe of *old negar* is one of multidimensional disorder. That is, to apply the epithet *old negar* is to posit not only race (and not necessarily age) but also to posit disorderliness of several dimensions—mental, physical, behavioral, moral, and so on.

However, the semantic reinterpretation of terms is open-ended. As the plot unfolds, the text reflects amelioration of the term *old negar,* which is traditionally abusive. It becomes a slogan of solidarity. Zachariah embraces it in an effort to establish identity by affirming self-worth. The phrase becomes a watchword and at last a recurrent battle cry, "Old negar not easy to kill."

The amelioration of *old negar* comes about through sociohistorical forces. Users of Jamaican discourse have habitually encountered choices that are situationally constrained because of the coexistence in the lexicon of socially unequal pairs in which one term is acceptable (usually Standard) and one unacceptable (usually non-Standard or Creole, possibly West African). Most recently, boundaries of acceptability have blurred not only with growing nationalism but also with the widening attraction of black youth culture, which has focused on the ghetto experience. This phenomenon is true not only of Jamaica and the wider Caribbean. In specific contexts, American Black English *nigger* has become an address for signifying intimacy or at least common ground, providing that part of this commonality is racial. (*Nigger* is not a form of address likely to be appreciated by a black addressee from a white policeman.) This semantic transformation is by no means complete or universal in Black English or in Creole. The choice between acceptance and non-acceptance is situationally constrained. In *The Painted Canoe* Zachariah accepts the designation of *old negar* when he returns to land, but Carina resents it. Their situations differ in the separate experiences that constitute different contexts and impose separate meanings on the term for different characters.

Language attitudes in *The Painted Canoe,* as in other Jamaican texts, are thus important to the underlying propositions of the text that together compose the Jamaican setting. Winkler frequently highlights language attitudes that are central features of his setting and that affect meaning.

The text systematically ridicules inappropriate language usage, as in the treatment of political addresses on radio. These embeddings of political discourse are always fragmentary. Offered out of context they are irrelevant and thus blatantly meaningless. In Winkler's full discourse they link syntagmatically only with each other and only as bits of an interminable flow of meaningless rhetoric. Paradigmatically, they link with Winkler's larger themes of disorder and madness.

Not only does the writer repeatedly highlight the irrelevance of political outbursts to any obvious context and so emphasize their consequent meaninglessness, but he implicitly proposes their impropriety. The emphasis on correct address and naming throughout the novel (21, 89, 259, 270) parallels an important distinction between appropriate and inappropriate selection of linguistic codes and signals the importance of pragmatic rules in the social order. The disconnected present tense in political outbursts on the airwaves interjects a comical antinarrative. The text ridicules meaningless exploitation of Creole by educated speakers whose intention is to dupe or to patronize the public. On a parallel track runs incorrect use of the Standard, as in the promise of "electrification" for the village. The stridency of political address clearly distinguishes the political use and abuse of Creole from legitimate, interactive use by "real" Creole speakers. Whether Jamaican discourse selects the Jamaican variant of international English or it selects Jamaican Creole depends on social constraints. Observance or nonobservance of these constraints contributes to the meaning of the discourse by revealing the capabilities of speakers or by raising questions about their motives.

Meaning in *The Painted Canoe* is thus profoundly shaped both by the lexical semantics of Jamaican discourse and by its pragmatic constraints. Zachariah's struggle against absorption and domination by hostile forces is defined in terms that have characteristically Jamaican meaning and patterns of usage. The creole protagonist retains his integrity by reevaluating *old negar* and recognizing that the forces beyond himself rather than intrinsic worthlessness threaten to overpower him. This redefinition becomes a source of strength.

In addition to the meaning locked in a lexis obviously similar but subtly distinct from international English, meaning in *The Painted Canoe* is conveyed by metaphor presented through this Jamaican lexis. The most far-reaching metaphor is that of the encircling sea as the elementally hostile context of life.

Through *The Painted Canoe*, Winkler restructures the world to ensure that items are no longer taken at face value. In truth, the novel attacks on every front what is generally taken to be common sense, and it forces the reader out of a universe in which meaning can be resolved through binarism in terms of features present or absent. Terry Eagleton notes that "common sense holds that things generally have only one meaning and that this meaning is usually obvious, inscribed in the faces of the objects we encounter" (108). However, the reader's own politics play an important enough part in determining meaning to make difficult the monolithic expectations of an ideal reader or super reader such as is usually posited by structuralism. Such a reader, as Eagleton points out, is in effect "a transcendental subject absolved from all social determinants" (121). *The Painted Canoe* presupposes such monolithic expectations and presents apparent polarities only to reveal that this expected order is skewed.

The Painted Canoe is a study of truth versus folly in Jamaican society. It exposes the flaws of apparently rational but (in fact) illogical arguments (such as those of the doctor) that undermine life, and it explodes false propositions that produce a revulsion for life rather than death. It attacks assumptions about the intrinsic worthlessness of "insignificant" people as well as doctrines about the inevitability of suffering as an inheritance of ethnicity ("negar must suffer because he is negar," 122). The text proposes a reason for certain types of suffering in Jamaica ("Wrongful doctrine sick me," 8), and it distinguishes unjustified suffering rooted in social foolishness from pain that is external and part of the natural struggle for existence (169). It refutes the proposal that interpersonal relationships must be based on dominance and oppression by ridiculing the vertical dimension of Zachariah's relationship with Carina. The whole matter of who should be on top is "a fool-fool argument" (11).

In many senses, Zachariah's survival hinges on his obsession with truth, but his is not an easy truth or one universally perceived. One dimension of this truth is the passionless and elemental hostility faced by the common man in a simple effort to survive, even without human interference ("the sea gnashing its teeth at him," 182); another dimension is the added damage that human foolishness imposes. The text interweaves these two dimensions, and they mirror each other to reflect the truth from an unusual angle. The fisherman must be almost mad to see through the trickery of life, and he must at the same time consciously ward off madness that is imminent and waiting on the fringes of his mind to invade and destroy him. These terrors are elemental, but he confronts them rationally, for "as long as he could stay awake, none of these could drift into his mind" (179). The sea prowls around his mind constantly, close and threatening or distant but equally threatening in empty circling horizons, and he survives by calculatedly filling his mind with the values that maintain sanity. He purposely excludes madness by filling the emptiness of his mind with dreams and memories of personal relationships (179).

The challenge of living is an enormity that Zachariah views squarely and perceives through the metaphor of the sea ("eyeball shattered against it," 166). The English doctor also perceives clearly the inimical forces that crowd life and continually decompose it, but for the doctor the destruction is overwhelming, denying life of meaning. *The Painted Canoe* offers to impose a new structure on thought, the strength to resist both elemental hostility and social foolishness: "He leaned over the canoe and stared down into the fathomless depths of the ocean, and it was like staring into the eyes of the enemy. Then he scornfully dipped his hands into the water and washed his face. 'Negar not easy to kill,' he whispered to the sea, and returned to sailing the canoe" (132). Zachariah articulates a counterchallenge. Under the heavy burden of his ugliness he maintains dignity and compassion, unlike the alewife, a worthless bawling fish, and the hammerhead, which is evil in its persistence.

Zachariah clings to life and sanity even as the doctor, maddened by the enormity of the challenge, aligns himself with the forces of destruction and urges, " 'Eat him, sea! Eat him!' Until he was sitting on the car fender and hissing malevolently the same words in Jamaican patois, 'Nyam him, sea!' " (151). The doctor adopts an indigenous discourse unauthorized by European and thus by Caribbean education, but he adopts this discourse destructively. In selecting Jamaican *nyam,* an African term for "eat," the doctor infuses into the command an added venom, because *nyam* (pejorated from its original West African meanings of "food" and "eat") carries connotations of ravenous greed that are not intrinsic to the English *eat.* Carina's parallel story supports the fisherman's and presents a counterdiscourse to the doctor's as she screams encouragement to her husband over the voice of the sea and despite the logical impossibility of communication imposed by distance: " 'Fight him, Zach,' she hissed again, this time louder and with murder in her voice" (74).

Characters from different sectors of society fail or refuse to comprehend or accept each other, and this social polarization is an inescapable fact of Jamaican life. At the same time, the character of the brown Jamaican doctor who replaces the Englishman reduces the polarity between black (folk) and white (technologically progressive) standards and introduces a separate and crucial issue—the distinctive position of the Jamaican brown. Winkler exaggerates the definitive aspects of each character to the point of sharpening these portraits to caricatures, poignantly conveying not only the black and the white but also the brown angst that complicates the tensions of Jamaican society.

Like other Jamaican texts, *The Painted Canoe* purges from the mind of the reader tidy oppositions between civilization and wilderness. Civilization is opposed to wild indiscipline (286, 289), which characterizes *old negar* in the eyes of white, brown, and in some cases black characters of the novel. Yet Zachariah imposes on his mind a discipline that protects him from twisted vision, and even as he wards off madness, he recognizes that the wild-eyed earnestness of the mad must be approached with caution and gentleness (174). The metaphors of madness and blindness intersect each other, and, as the fury of the sea becomes an encompassing metaphor for the inimical forces of life, the fisherman strikes through the eye of the monster that rises against him out of the deep ("I blind you pickney today. . . . Negar not so easy to kill," 183). Thus, he engages the monstrous forces that, in the white doctor's twisted logic, make existence ridiculous, even revolting, and at last pointless.

In affirming the rationality of even Zachariah's irrational existence, *The Painted Canoe* states a seeming impossibility or at least offers an alternative to the logical, scientific view. The text achieves this revision largely through metaphor. The cognitive significance of any metaphor arises from its capacity to restructure or induce a new structure on a given content domain, that area of experience defined by the terms of a particular semantic field (see Kittay 37). Metaphor transforms our perspective on the world and is a natural cognitive process in the evolution of an indigenous vision (cf. Mac Cormac 136).[1] *The Painted Canoe* captures new perspectives through metaphor by reordering content domains, such as life experience, in accordance with the relations governing semantic fields that cover other content domains, such as the sea. Moreover, the sea can *swallow, eat*, or *nyam*; there are layers of interrelating content domains. At base, this process is no more than a normal cognitive one because, as Mac Cormac points out, without metaphor the extension of knowledge from the known to the unknown would be difficult, and language itself would be largely static (50).

Winkler demonstrates a special ability for the process that Mac Cormac describes (136), the ability to step outside of the normal way of conceiving of things and of reconceiving them in a new conceptual system. Winkler achieves this by reaching into the long-term semantic meanings of associated terms and activating widely separated parts of the network, reassembling concepts in an innovative way that startlingly illuminates Jamaican experience. The struggle for existence recurs as a resistance against loss of integrity, a fight against being swallowed up by the deep: " 'Man eat fish,' one dour, obese higgler declared, flashing her eyes darkly over the harbor, 'and fish eat man. So it go' " (70).

A semantic field consists of contrast sets, some in ordered sequences (Kittay 248). Winkler's semantic field of the sea includes such sets as *sea, ocean, deep, waves; turbulent, squall, breakwater; seafarer, fisherman; canoe, boat, craft*, and so on. Within any set are subsets, the *boat* group, for example, including *sail, hull, gunwale, prow, paddle*, and *oarlocks*. One term, such as *fish*, may cover many others, of which one, such as *shark* (as distinct from *goatfish* or *alewife*) may itself cover a further subset, such as *hammerhead, nurse*, and so on. Fish contrast in appearance, monetary value, or character, as do Winkler's human characters. Terms in the semantic field of the sea are so structured as to add up gradually to the reader's vision of what Zachariah is up against, and this information is crucial for the reader to assess accurately the enormity of the fisherman's isolation and resistance.

By confronting the reader with ordered contrast sets, the text unfolds its meaning through the metaphor of the sea, which represents the enormity of Zachariah's situation. The reader encounters items in this semantic field not only in an ordered sequence (or syntagm) but also within a system of paradigmatic contrast sets. Sets contrast not only in terms of the rules that govern their sequential relationships but also in terms of those that cover their membership in classes. Such classes may be defined by grammatical roles in the discourse. That is, each set occupies a given place defined by its grammatical role, for example as patient, agent, instrument, or location of the action or process that the verb represents (see Kittay 247). Some of these contrasts are essential to interpretation of the novel.

One such crucial contrast is that between the canoe and the water. In the system of contrast sets within the semantic field of the *sea*, the canoe contrasts with the water as a vehicle does to its medium. When the sea becomes a metaphor for life experience, Zachariah's mind becomes the frail craft that navigates this deep. For the Jamaican fisherman, the canoe is not only a craft that he possesses but one that he has fashioned with his own hands and refuses to relinquish for any money. It is also a minute and fragile vehicle in which to confront the wild, engulfing void. Consistent paradigmatic relationships preserve intact the thematic roles of medium and vehicle on the content plane (the nonliteral meaning) as on the expression plane.

An unlimited chain of connotation is possible because of the conflation of multiple content domains. As a result, metaphor produces seeming anomaly by transgressing redundancy rules or meaning postulates. Thus, the text conveys meaning by transgressing constraints that designate the sea as inanimate. Similarly, it alternately confers emotion on the hammerhead or deprives it of emotion by implicitly reassigning human or nonhuman features to the shark. To clarify how metaphor conveys meaning in *The Painted Canoe*, one can adopt a view of semantic descriptions, such as animate/inanimate, as coordinates of a map rather than as building blocks of meaning. For Kittay, such semantic descriptors are points of interconnection through semantic fields (256). The shift from nonhuman to human is associated with the hammerhead's relocation from the semantic field of the sea to a new semantic field, that of battle.

Although Winkler, like any writer, utilizes both dead and standard metaphors, he also introduces active, novel metaphors in conveying his characters' search for meaning. The active and novel metaphor employs two or more fields "rarely brought together or rarely brought together in such a way as to effect the particular relations we find in that distinct case" (Kittay 299). Winkler brings together the semantic field of the sea, applied to the enormity of human experience, but he further superimposes a field of hostile opposition by both nature and society of forces striving for domination.

A crucial development in Zachariah's battle with the sea and with life itself is the shift in power relations between his mind and the deep. His situation is at once one of entrapment and exposure. The circling conspiracy of sky and sea at first constrains and threatens his mind, crowding and seeking to penetrate his sanity (179). But when the ski and sea force their way in, he takes charge of them and recognizes that in conceiving them his mind is greater than they are (180). Then he identifies the hammerhead as a nightmare passing through the mind of the ocean, and he whispers his challenge, "Come, you rass, you" (182). The blinding of the hammerhead is the turning point in this confrontation of the fisherman's will with the brooding deep. The outraged sea retaliates, for "in reply, the water fanged white, and the stinging spray blinded him. The sky howled with a ravenous hunger for the canoe. The waves attacked her with white teeth, trying to tear her hull" (185–86). Zach responds with screams of encouragement to the canoe and threats to the ocean. The downpour that follows is a cosmic joke on the ocean that in trying to kill him it has provided him with water. At this point the text throws up an ambiguity: "The darkness paraded its own mysteries. The domination of night began" (188).

The ostensible meaning is an introduction of a new phase in the fisherman's experience on the ocean—the sea under the regulation of darkness rather than the assault of the sun. At the same time, these sentences conclude the account of a major triumph over death, and the next section of the novel reveals the darkness of the doctor's vision—one of intrinsic death as the essential goal and guiding principle of life. Furthermore, a lexical ambiguity compounds plurality of meaning, raising the issue of whether the darkness is physical, natural, and independent of man or metaphysical and psychological—depending on whether the word is understood in its basic sense or according to a standard metaphorical extension that has hardened into an alternative meaning of the term in the official language. Moreover, Jamaicans commonly use *dark* to attribute ignorance and backwardness to human referents.[2]

In addition, a syntactic ambiguity in "the domination of night" foreshadows the eventual triumph of the fisherman, who is to survive both the physical night and the darkness of the doctor's despair. Zachariah will also emerge from the obscurity of superstition, ignorance, and disease. The abstract noun *domination* enables the writer to suppress the subject of the verb *dominate*. Underlying the output sentence, at the level of concept, are alternative subjects: the night that covers (dominates) all and the human subject that rises above (dominates) darkness. These alternative subjects are associated with varying metaphorical sentences and thus with different meanings.

Departing from a position in which linguistic units are viewed as endowed with intrinsic meaning, this book argues that meaning without context is meaningless. From a similar stance and as a backdrop to what H. P. Grice would call "timeless meaning," Kittay argues for the notion of the default assumption. In contending that all meaning (including literal meaning) is context dependent, Kittay agrees with J. R. Searle that the truth conditions of the sentence depend on contextual background assumptions (Kittay 104). The features of the world that are taken to be normal serve as an implicit context (the default frame) determining interpretation. Kittay defines default assumptions as "those assumptions on which speakers rely, in both verbal and non-verbal behavior, in the absence of any contextual evidence cancelling or questioning such assumptions. . . . They are default assumptions because they are what we assume in the absence of any contradictory evidence" (55).

The default frame of alternating light and darkness in the natural world provides the ostensible meaning of Winkler's sentence, "The domination of night had begun." However, alternative meanings are possible because of the context (provided by the text) in which these sentences offer both lexical and syntactic ambiguities. In other words, each alternative meaning coheres with similar meanings presented elsewhere in the text.

Because much language is polysemous (as in *darkness*, above) context dependence is crucial to understanding. Sets of alternatives, like the contrastive relations provided by semantic fields, are crucial to information because all information relates to additional or distinctive content. Information is never isolated but includes or is included in other information. In other words, all information is nested. Different pieces of nested information may be spoken of as information shells (see Kittay 128–30). The meaning of any literary text is accumulated linguistic content, and because linguistic content is potentially informative, textual meaning has an information-theoretic basis. Kittay aligns her definition of metaphor with a Saussurean position that meaning emerges from the apposition of two differential systems. The labels in the lexical field may have contrastive relations, such as *alive* or *dead*, or some may show a graded antonymity, such as *calm* versus *troubled* and *wild* versus *frenzied*. Indeed, quite apart from structural approaches to semantics, it is clear from polysemy and from the information-theoretic basis of content that words have meanings because they contrast with other terms in the language.

The Painted Canoe exploits this contrastive dimension of meaning, specifically in the form of graded antonymity, in certain extended metaphors, such as that of the fisherman's separation from his community. Zachariah is blown away and isolated at first rather than rejected by his community, although the elements of rejection have been incipient all along in sporadic references to his ugliness and to rifts between the classes. The community systematically avoids him only later when his illness seems to mark him as unlucky. He moves by degrees through increasing isolation.

Similarly, civilization and wilderness do not oppose each other by neat presence and absence of binary features. Both civilization and wilderness lie in the eye of the beholder, and observers vary in their reliability throughout the text. The brown Jamaican doctor places Zachariah well outside of civilization. From the fisherman, whom he views as a beast from the wilderness, the doctor distinguishes himself as a learned and gifted man, "risen out of the same abyss of superstition in which that monstrous-looking brute now wallowed" (296). His description echoes the fisherman's view of the hammerhead, and indeed perhaps Zachariah is this doctor's "hammerhead," haunting the brown man from the deep of a despised past. The same doctor is careful to care nothing for the worthless lives of his patients and views his service to them as a bargain that he must pay off to the government (286). What saves the situation in his view is that "He did not have to pretend that they were civilized" (286).

To repudiate the position of the brown doctor is not to embrace verbiage that romanticizes negritude for political mileage. Winkler ridicules the rhetoric of politically correct visions of nationalism. Michael Thelwell earlier demonstrated the difficulty of mobilizing a people to become a nation (*The Harder They Come*), and indeed the irony of this fact is widely recognized. Frantz Fanon laments the inadequacy of such superficial nationalism as a "crude and fragile travesty of what it might have been" (148). Current Jamaican nationalism retains that schizophrenia between cultural traditions that fosters marronage. Thus, in addition to the Caribbean limbo recognized by Simon Gikandi (14, 15), current Jamaican writing reflects such inner and intersecting dichotomies as the opposition between the village and the town, between the country and the local metropole, between black and brown. The dialectic of civilization and wilderness is complicated by the many different perceptions of civilization, each entrenched in its own community.

The brown doctor's concept of civilization as a system for commercial exchange of commodities makes his perception of medical attention purely mechanical, a patching up and mending of "miserable bodies" (286). It replaces the English doctor's perception of the ultimate meaninglessness of life as random distribution of matter causelessly connected (265), of human identity as fragmented by inherent death. The river paws the doctor like a lover, and he embraces death as a logical choice. This frustrated English doctor presents an inner wilderness that Zachariah recognizes in the doctor's eye as the malignant intensity of the sea. The constable recognizes this inner wilderness as a vast empty dreariness inside the doctor's heart comparable to Folly House, a relic of ruined (imperial) civilization (270).

It does not follow that there is in this novel no positive construct of civilized social relationships. The civilization from which the ocean sunders Zachariah is destructively superstitious, but it includes a close-knit system of family bonds and friendship. Through contemplation of these connections, Zachariah's mind first resists the engulfing emptiness outside and eventually expands to absorb, contain, and master it.

Thus, *The Painted Canoe* does not lack identifiable concepts of civilization or wilderness; it merely juxtaposes conflicting constructs of varying truth value. Similarly, some terms (such as *civilized*) display appreciable semantic drift even from group to group within a speech community. In *The Painted Canoe*, human identity founded on compassionate interpersonal relations and spiritual strength provides a structured existence that renders Zachariah civilized and keeps him sane even as the lack of this perspective caricatures the expatriate doctor as wild and mad and the local doctor as brutal.

By reordering one content domain, such as human suffering, in accordance with the relations governing the semantic field of another content domain, such as that of the sea, metaphor effects a perspectival shift and in a sense establishes new categories. In Kittay's words, "metaphor provides epistemic access" (326). It hooks up to the world to allow a chain of ideas to interconnect sentences of the discourse anaphorically. Just as the meaning of the metaphor can be understood only through context, metaphor refashions regular and rigidly conceived orders of thought, including the factual, by transferring relations across domains and inducing the structure of one field on another to reveal new categories of thought. In this sense, metaphor is thus not so much the assertion of falsehood (controversion theory) as an instance of the fluidity of truth.

The Painted Canoe presents two major conflicting value systems in exploring the fluidity of truth regarding marronage in Jamaica.

Each perspective is that of an isolated psyche. The expatriate doctor is spiritually lost on the island, alone and comfortless in a community in which he is an alien. He escapes his original place in society, but his mind brings no support to him: it offers only scientific fact. His vision of truth proposes the worthlessness of man; he sees Zach as Zach sees the alewife. To the doctor, human life is random and corrupt (265), and his own life's work is motiveless benignity (267). The cultural values that define his view of civilization and wilderness reduce the value of the isolated, independent individual to nothing. The text reveals this "truth" as folly by demonstrating that Zachariah, physically lost at sea, triumphs through a rage for life and a raging resistance of death. His perspective reverses the wrong values of scientific absolutism, of ignorant superstition, and of insincere religious cant. His more flexible mind enables him to shift perspective between the infinity of the deep and the infinite potential of his own mind.

In contemplating his place in the cosmos, Zachariah's mind moves from opposition to containment. He preserves his identity first by resistance, and Winkler expresses this content by superimposing on it not only the semantic field of the sea but also that of mortal conflict. Expressions pertaining to conflict abound outside of actual physical struggles such as that with the hammerhead. Beyond resistance, Zachariah achieves mastery of his own life. In other words, the metaphorical treatment of conflict provides an expression plane for one level of content, which is his effort to survive at sea, but together they provide a combined expression plane for another level of content, the struggle for identity or selfhood (compare Kittay 290). Between and within the semantic fields involved there occur transfers of meaning. The survival must be mental as well as physical. He must emerge sane. Zach (and by metonymy Zach's mind) engages with the sea and with mind-bending life experience in deadly combat.

Beyond this conflict Zachariah glimpses a greater truth—that his mind is invincible not because it resists but because it can conceive and thus contain the vastness of the universe. This realization strengthens him not only to confront experience but also to invite it on and deal with it.

Zachariah's mind rejects "wrongful doctrine" but retains its hold on known and trusted supports. He rises from his deathbed during Easter week while the boys outside play "bounce back" marbles (279), and he pushes his canoe out to sea even as the doctor's self-revulsion ends in suicide. True independence begins for Zachariah when he decides to avoid asking for help except in extremis, and he progresses toward taking control of his life through infinitesimal stages, such as recognizing that in his relationship with Carina it does not matter who is on top. Power dynamics in interpersonal relationships become meaningless, and true civilization emerges as a balance of selfhood and human compassion. An important stage in the fisherman's maturation is his recognition that there comes a point beyond which sheer independence can take him no further, a point at which it is both practical and proper to request and accept assistance.

In *The Painted Canoe*, the island psyche, which is isolated, exposed, and yet physically constrained, contemplates the deep, first with resistance to avoid loss of identity and then with resilience to discover inner strength and a mastery that is nonpolitical. *The Painted Canoe* takes the theme of marronage beyond a perspective on resistance of the imperial by the oppressed and beyond obsession with injustices of the past. It locates the Jamaican struggle for identity as internal to the island, as present and as psychological—problematical at every social level and for every race. It posits the continuing importance of the community to the individual and demonstrates that selfhood is compatible with selflessness.

The adjustment of perspective that facilitates self-preservation and reconstruction in the face of seemingly invincible odds and aggressively gathers these odds to synthesize a new and stronger self may be the "ignorance" of *old negar*, or it may be the fundamental heroism of essential humanity. The constable shrugs it off as simply a Jamaican character trait: "But this is how these people are. So they born, so they die. Rockstone not tougher" (199).

Renegotiating the Parameters of Reality: Winkler's *Lunatic*

The Lunatic pursues the familiar postcolonial theme of the mind-altering effects of motherlessness and homelessness, but this text produces a perspective from which to evaluate absolute and unmistakable insanity within new parameters. A vagrant lunatic (Aloysius) encounters a German tourist (Inga) in the Jamaican countryside. Inga wields her sexual power over Aloysius mercilessly, but, starved of human relationships, he grows genuinely to love her. The relationship offends not only the rural community but the surrounding countryside itself, especially the flame-heart tree (Aloysius's confidante) and the prudish bushes. To make matters worse, Inga extends the relationship to include a local butcher (Service). As money runs short, Inga and Service plan to rob the house of a prominent member of the community, Busha (a term derived from English *overseer*), and they insist on Aloysius's complicity. Busha interrupts the robbery, and Service attacks him savagely, but largely as a result of Aloysius's intervention, Busha survives. On the basis of a defense by a solicitor (Linstrom), Aloysius is eventually freed. In the end, he moves in with a widow who is as determined to rehabilitate him as to recover vigorous male companionship.

Winkler reconsiders the sanity of our current civilization by viewing it from the point of view of the ultimate Jamaican outcast (the vagrant madman) and by introducing into the Jamaican countryside new and dangerous exploitative forces. *The Lunatic* imposes a present of deviant family relationships on a past of disrupted family ties. Escape and resistance, essential components of marronage in Jamaica, are first associated with Aloysius's companions rather than with the lunatic himself. Indeed, in the end he must depart from their schemes and resist their violence, but meanwhile they constitute an aberrant colony in the wilderness. The results are outrageous.

Disordered Nature: Tradition and the Politics of Lunacy

Winkler's scandalous comedy is perhaps the most unorthodox novel to have emerged in the history of Jamaican literature. Flaunting its disregard for taboos, flouting maxims of appropriateness to literary discourse, screaming obscenities, *The Lunatic*'s initial shock value lies in its flagrant unorthodoxy and irreverence. Yet its setting of psychological and moral disorder implies the normative values against which to measure its deviance.

The literature of the hitherto British colony continues to exist in a historical frame of British literary tradition. Orthodox interpretation of traditional literature enshrines normative values, and most Jamaicans of general education encounter these orthodox interpretations. The Jamaican novel, like some traditional literature, deals with the politics of lunacy, where the individual (as outcast) finds himself thrust naked into the storm.

Like Shakespeare's *King Lear*, *The Lunatic* is an extended study of social and political disorder and of its relationship to the disordered mind. Prior to recent critical approaches such as Marxist analysis or feminist or postcolonial recovery of subtexts, traditional interpretation of British classics offered a frame of normative values. From such traditional readings of this canon, widespread and shared concepts of order continue to precondition most Caribbean readers.

In a sense, the settings of both *King Lear* and *The Lunatic* are pastoral, although William F. Zak designates *King Lear* as antipastoral on the basis that ultimate evil in the text is not cosmic but human (58). Both works implicitly contrast civilization to wilderness and thus prompt the reader to reassess notions of civilization continuously. In *The Lunatic* as in *King Lear*, the dialectic of court (legitimate versus illegitimate government) and country (ordered versus violent or outraged nature) presents nature as harsh rather than healing. But this dialectic also demonstrates that evil is a product of human society rather than of nature. Similarly, Aloysius opposes Inga's rejection of

God for entertaining himself with the sufferings of man (cf. *King Lear* 4.1.36–37.) The problem of suffering is human and social, with conflicts in the physical setting that reflect those in the psychological landscape.

Action in *The Lunatic* ultimately unfolds from family disorder, even as *King Lear* explores natural and unnatural relationships and shows how even natural and legitimate relationships can become disordered. Winkler adopts the recurrent postcolonial metaphor of the broken family but subverts it to that of the deviant family to convey social disorder. Aloysius's deprived background begins with a lack or a curtailment of proper parenting, yet he recalls guidance and has learned compassion and respect. Inga, on the other hand, views her father as a source of material support. She flouts his authority and affords him no respect. Service boasts of having murdered his father. Aloysius's association with Inga, however physically and (at times) emotionally satisfying, raises innumerable moral issues for the dutiful lunatic. The extension of this relationship to a so-called family that includes Service is a travesty. Here, as in *King Lear*, order in the individual, the family, and the wider society is intertwined. Beneath the glaring unorthodoxy of *The Lunatic* lie epistemic correlates to traditional texts.

Such comparison by no means proposes that Winkler rewrites Shakespeare or was even conscious of a particular British work in creating his text. The intertextuality of Jamaican and British texts reaches beyond intentional counterdiscourse and indeed predates and perhaps supersedes it. The affinities between these widely dissimilar works suggest that Winkler reintroduces certain traditional values hitherto entrenched in the most established texts of the colonial education system and that he does so in the most outrageous terms.

In *The Lunatic* as in traditional works, individual lunacy metaphorically parallels social and national chaos. There are repeated references to disordered government, but Aloysius is not responsible for introducing divided or invalid rule and bears no responsibility for sociopolitical disorder. On the contrary, his personal lunacy, a microcosm of social madness, is the result rather than the cause of wider chaos. However, no interpretation of *The Lunatic* can ignore its ribald commentary on disordered rule in Jamaica or its parody of power relations between local and expatriate, black and white, rich and poor, male and female—oppositions against which the apparent polarization of sanity and lunacy are first suggested, then deconstructed.

Aloysius is indeed, according to generally shared social meaning, the archetypal madman, the epitome of disordered nature. Nature in *The Lunatic* is a crucial concept and mirrors traditional concepts of nature in imperial discourse quite closely. By portraying a disturbed consciousness as exposed to the wilderness and rejected by civilized society, *The Lunatic* prompts the assessment of human nature on the basis of socially agreed on notions of order and the weighing of civilized man against essential man.

The Lunatic is concerned with natural reactions as opposed to cold calculation and with the honesty of plainness versus opulence. Inga and Service between them demonstrate much of the malignant nature of Shakespeare's Edmund—unorthodox, antisocial, reasoning in a purely regulative way to twist things to their purpose. Each is a schemer and careerist and applies Machiavellian justification for outrageous strategy. Aloysius's morality transcends maxims of expediency, but his interpretation of nature is denied by plainly evil characters (such as Service) and unrecognized by those of imperfect vision (such as the barrister, Linstrom). The lunatic represents values (truth and charity) that transcend time, even though the Machiavellian may succeed in the temporal world.

In *The Lunatic*, much irony lies in the confrontation between types of mental disorder that are immediately identifiable as lunacy and other (perhaps more far-reaching) types of mental disorder that society masks and tolerates. Mental and social stability require ordered vision as distinct from disordered vision, but this contrast too is graded. "De darkness cover me mind and me eye," sobs Aloysius (71); he is at least clear-sighted enough to recognize his deficiency. In his relationship with Inga, he is blinded by love into participating in crime. Only nature sees clearly enough to scream the truth at him: " 'Go 'way, you damn thief!' the tree hollared [*sic*]" (161).

The structure of *The Lunatic* follows the unraveling of moral order in the community that has produced and rejected the mad vagrant, and the action swings between blindness and insight as Aloysius progresses from principle, through lapse, to moral recovery. Throughout this process, Aloysius's vision of himself is never inflated, except once when a bush corrects him for assuming the title of "Lord," and here Aloysius acquiesces at once, revealing inherent self-knowledge and humility.

The stature of a protagonist is one indicator of genre, quite apart from the happy or grievous outcome of the action. Traditional definitions of both comedy and tragedy turn on the theme of disorder and its relationship to responsibility, but the protagonist's lack of stature contributes to comedy in *The Lunatic*. Aloysius's nakedness in the storm seems unrelated to any sin or misjudgment on his own part. His very insignificance makes him a casualty of social callousness. However, even in the midst of his mental confusion, he assumes responsibility for his actions.

Grim comedy through incongruity and grotesque symbolism exploits the cruelty that underlies much humor, and in *The Lunatic* the mixing of discordant elements is exaggerated to outrageous proportions. As in earlier British literature, the grotesque humor reflected in disorder at the level of the individual elicits guilty laughter. Implied ridicule of the choleric old man in *King Lear* and physical abuse as spectacle parallel trends in other art forms of the time, such as the gargoyle as decoration. Similar attitudes have their place in *The Lunatic,* which ridicules Busha's choleric obsession with his own interment and humorously dissects Inga's and Service's fascination with violence. The current preponderance of modern horror comedies in cinema suggest that weird and cruel comic elements are again finding social acceptability. Indeed, the growing perception of the butcher as artist[3] is one aspect of Jamaican society that *The Lunatic* penetrates and unmasks as distorted vision.

Winkler takes no apocalyptic view of social disorder but explicitly ridicules local politics and implicitly compares Inga's outlandish rule with the mad government of the nation. The ribald narrative commentary on the rise and fall of governments, on the succession of equally meaninglessness types of rule, and on the ensuing inversion of social values tracks the undercurrent of political lunacy. At the same time, the postcolonial vision provides a contrasting point of departure regarding power relations: " 'Let me make one thing clear,' she said, standing up. 'I am the boss. You understand? Otherwise this cannot be. You understand?' 'Vhy must one person be boss, Inga?' Aloysius asked" (116). The alternative perspective of the lunatic disrupts the binarism of both imperial and local (party-polarized) concepts of government.

In the raucous Jamaican drama that lampoons local disorder through strutting villains and histrionic bushes, there is no vista of tragedy looming through references to apocalypse or foreshadowing of final chaos through images of demonology, curses, flame, lightning, and thunder. There is also no solemnity of fallen greatness. Instead, there is incisive detail that punctures rather than expands inflated stature.

The Lunatic accumulates a profusion of minute and individual oddities to portray an era of social madness. Tragedy emerges at the individual level as a personal one of isolation and rejection (cf. *King Lear* 3.6.107). Aloysius's loss of tie after tie precedes the action of the novel but is part of an ongoing chain reaction in which a storm of fortunes has stripped him to essential man and seems eventually to have unmanned him by undermining his reason. *The Lunatic* presents to the reader an outcast in rags that are inadequate to cover his nakedness, a mind tattered by deprivation, but nevertheless a character of intrinsic dignity.

Aloysius journeys through madness toward self-knowledge, his experiences raising again the age-old question: "Is man no more than this?" (*King Lear* 3.4.105). Aloysius retrieves his integrity by recognizing at last that whatever might be the truth about Busha's dishonesty, "He, Aloysius, was not a thief" (155). In the end, beyond grief and amusement at human frailty and wonder at undeserved suffering, readers recognize Aloysius as humane and moral. The madman decides in favor of compassion in a sudden stand that is clearheaded and tough. The integrity with which he earlier objected, "Ve can't thief from Busha! Dat not right!" (150), resurfaces and strengthens him to defend Busha. Aloysius reconciles opposites—passion and order, innocence and maturity, defenselessness and strength. He endures every turn of fate and experiences regeneration after error. His characterization does not pretend to Promethean torment of the mind, but he is riven by the disappointments of life and eventually by guilt. His little tragedy is that complete restoration is impossible. He moves into a personal hell and emerges from it. Still, in *The Lunatic*, disordered nature is a rack on which the personality is stretched out to demonstrate human vulnerability and endurance, and although there is increased self-knowledge, wholeness of mind is never quite attained.

Aloysius takes in the reactions of the rational world and cannot square his values with them. He concludes, "Me brain confuse" (147). However, by confronting the values of rational society with those of the lunatic, Winkler gradually balances the testimony of Aloysius's outer lunacy with testimony of his inner sanity, while the outer sanity of the status quo (landowner, tradesman, tourist, professional) is gradually undermined by testimony of inner disorder, the morbidity of Busha, the homicidal violence of the butcher, the sexual excess and political anarchy of the tourist, the nihilistic disillusionment of the lawyer. While Aloysius moves from vagrancy through prison and the lunatic asylum to a home, other characters of the novel move in the direction of institutionalization—in a mausoleum, in jail, or in "bumpkin heaven," all dimensions of their out-of-order civilization.

The possibilities for comparative and contrastive analyses of texts are limitless. Such comparison confirms that current Jamaican texts continue to relate intimately in broad areas of theme and value system to other traditional literature in English. However, these local texts may substantially alter orthodox perspectives. They may also challenge dicta entrenched in Caribbean counterdiscourse, however much the national literature continues to relate to the regional literature in broad areas of theme.

Comparison to traditional texts demonstrates that *The Lunatic* subverts some familiar postcolonial metaphors. For example, it presents scheming and exploitative femininity as a disruption of nature and portrays the abandoned child and social reject as capable of compassion and reconciliation. It substitutes personal responsibility and interpersonal concern for angry nationalism based on historical injustice, and it hinges social order on a distinction between imperial domination and traditional respect for authority— divine, legal, and parental. As the wilderness speaks through the madman, the text posits an essential sympathy between inner and outer landscapes by linking Aloysius's conscience with his sensitivity to the physical environment. At the same time, in opposing the histrionics of bush morality with the decadent, morbid, and grasping fixations of a threatened (propertied) class, the text conveys the vulnerability of all levels of society to error rather than denying hierarchy as inherent to social structure. In portraying cruelty as spectacle and positing society's toleration of violence, it unmasks the integration of brutality with artistry.

In parodying the political ideology of the mini-state, *The Lunatic* suggests varieties of struggle that the individual must resist and proposes causes to lay down. But the text conveys its orthodox message by exaggerating character into caricature, by storming the sensibilities of the reader, and by adopting the perspective of insanity to reveal the disordered kingdom as a travesty of nature: " 'Tis the times plague, when madmen lead the blind" (*King Lear* 4.1.46).

Deviance and Discourse[4]

The Lunatic establishes its characters' perspectives on the world by manipulating and frequently deviating from linguistic norms; it conveys mental and social imbalance by departing from conventions of discourse. Through these strategies, Winkler relates individual alienation from society to the distorted judgment or warped values of that society.

In creating a reliable or unreliable consciousness, a writer may adhere to or depart from a logical thread of narrative discourse. The writer may also choose to depart from conventional spatial or temporal frameworks or from traditional mores of literary narrative. Both as a social phenomenon and as rule-governed behavior, language communicates individual or social deviance, and the language of a text may communicate such behavioral deviance through linguistic deviance. *The Lunatic* conveys violent distortion in both individual perspective and in social values by flouting conventions of narrative discourse.

The most obvious manifestation of deviance in the language of *The Lunatic* is the departure from conventional restraints regarding verbal taboos that are both social and literary. These conventions are international in the sense that the prohibition of several words in the novel's lexis is widespread among speakers of international English. At the same time, Winkler appears to target Jamaican conventions specifically by highlighting local obscenities. Moreover, in addition to flouting both local and international conventions of acceptable language usage, the writer departs from other conventions of literary discourse by interfering with norms that usually define the reliability of the speaker.

To refer to norms of literary discourse is not necessarily to adopt a view that literary discourse is linguistically autonomous. Discourse analysts now increasingly question assumptions about literary discourse being governed by laws for poetic versus prosaic (i.e., everyday) language. Thus, Mary Louise Pratt compares what W. Labov describes as "natural narrative" with the narrative of literary discourse, undercutting monolithic approaches to literary versus nonliterary discourse. At the same time, contextual information regarding a speech act raises expectations, and Pratt points out that as in any situation, readers adopt a speech posture in picking up a novel (*Towards a Speech Act Theory* 149). The text of *The Lunatic* presents a verbal display, a rule flouting crucial to interpretation. Even in the context of what David Saunders describes as a global historical movement toward the decriminalization of obscenity in literature, *The Lunatic* is conspicuous in its open disregard for taboos. Deviance in language is here more than a support for theme. Linguistic deviance, which is often a message that there is something to discover in the content, in this novel constitutes part of the message itself. Rule breaking is not only a strategy but also an important point of the utterance.

Verbal jeopardy carries the quality of game or ritual in some parts of *The Lunatic* (43, 76). This phenomenon presents no threat to intelligibility, and so it leaves the cooperative principle of discourse unassailed, although it is still an interference with the norms of discourse and so must be taken seriously. Pratt notes that because the protection of cooperative principle is crucial to understanding, linguistic rule breaking as a whole carries social weight (*Towards a Speech Act Theory* 161, 165, 215). In *The Lunatic,* rule flouting occurs at so outrageous a level that it assists in what Pratt might term a deconditioning of the reader (222).

Readers of *The Lunatic* can only redefine norms as the novel progresses. Obscenity and the articulation of that which is taboo challenge the power structure of a society because such articulation is often an expression of nonconformity or of aggression against those who define the norms of that society. Language being both cognitive and social, the defiance of normative style by willful flouting of taboos in the text implies both mental and social unstructuring.

At the same time, the rule flouting in this narrative takes other and more important forms than obscenity. At one level the narrative follows a chain of episodes that are temporally linked visions of a lunatic. A parallel chain reveals the busha's morbid anxieties and the consequences of these anxieties. Both chains eventually link. Like any narrative, the whole discourse operates in a speaker/audience situation, but within it are episodes in which characters (the German tourist, Busha, the lawyer) are in turn audience to a lunatic. Moreover, the lunatic is so alienated from normal society as to be himself an audience of peculiar sensitivity, and the novel's point of view is largely his. None of these situations in itself necessarily suggests rule flouting, but the establishment of the lunatic as a reliable consciousness, or as near to reliable as is available, produces conflicts with our social knowledge about lunatics. Leslie Clark offers a helpful explanation of the relationship between social knowledge and stereotyping for readers, who process information provided by the experience of other texts. Because readers' social knowledge provides a context for information in the text, readers of *The Lunatic* work within an apparent disjuncture between text and context.

The opening of the novel establishes Aloysius's individual deviance beyond question by drawing on social knowledge about insanity and accumulating evidence necessary for stereotyping. With alarming speed, however, readers enter Aloysius's psyche enough to accept such peculiarities as talking trees and animals. The lunatic's (relative) reliability is gradually established. Feeling overburdened by his own sensitivity, he wonders aloud "why every rass thing on this island" must chat with him. The answer is clear: " 'Is because you is de only sensible man in dese parts, who have ears dat listen,' said a green lizard sunning itself on a rock" (28). In no time at all, Aloysius himself raises the question as to "which one is de madder one"—the German tourist or himself (38). The question of the comparative lunacy of characters in the novel will be raised repeatedly. By implication, the narrative questions the sanity of the society itself as the lunatic's view increasingly emerges as reliable.

Speaker reliability in *The Lunatic* is not an absolute, present or absent. In Winkler's redefinition of reality, semantic features are not binary so much as graded and relative to each other. First of all, the madman's vision is deviant but orderly. The language of the trees and bushes shows convincing social variation. The bushes, early identified as babblers, are empty, ignorant, and abusive; the trees are generally more informed and dignified unless mistreated. Aloysius shows a strongly developed sense of propriety. He insists on respect, reproves Inga when she flouts social mores, and corrects and disciplines the bushes, who "like unruly schoolboys, needed to be occasionally reminded of their place in the world" (25). He respects authority, particularly that of God, whom he refers to as his daddy. He denounces everything that is "out of order" and resists Inga's efforts to draw him into what he considers abnormal or improper behavior ("Me modder don't raise me to grind under stop sign! Dat is slackness!" 80).

The reliability of the lunatic's vision becomes most important in the novel's treatment of violence. The butcher, Service, demonstrates a chilling delight in the art of killing:

> The goat screamed—a falsetto wail filled with terror and helplessness. It fought vainly against the rope; it jerked and danced on its end like a hanged man. The young man chuckled at its antics.
>
> He showed the goat the knife, holding it up so that the animal could see its silver grin, resting the icy flat side of the blade against its throat. The goat shuddered and shrank from the chill of the blade, wailing in the shrill voice of a terrified virgin. (110)

The text presents two perspectives on the goat's head as it rests on its "rubble of bone and meat." Text cohesion through sentence parallelism in the dialogue highlights stark contrast between the visitor's vision and the lunatic's:

| [English] | "He is | an artist," Inga breathed. |
| [Creole] | "Him | a butcher," Aloysius muttered. (111) |

Inga romanticizes death, but she does so with the interest of the predator, "stalking around it like a hunter." Aloysius shrinks from it "and would not meet the piercing stare of the decapitated head mounted on the ruins of bone and flesh" (111).

The obsession with violence is a recurrent motif. To Inga, the essence of the goat is its dismembered remains, and violence and hatred constitute a philosophy of life to be injected into a backward nation. Even when Aloysius has begun to love her so much as to speak like her, the lunatic cannot comprehend this philosophy, and nature itself is outraged into obscenity:

> "I think I know vhat is wrong with this island," she said softly.
> "Vhat's wrong?"
> "Too many lies. Not enough hate."
> "Vat dat?"

"There is reason for hate. Poor people everywhere you look. A few rich people. There should be hate. But there is no hate. That is vhat is wrong with this place. It needs more hate."

"Hate?"

"In Europe, ve have lots of hate. That is why Europe is strong and rich. This is vhy Jamaica is poor."

"Bumbo," whispered the tree. "Listen dis now." (108)

Similarly, Busha is obsessed with death, occupied with plans for his interment. His neurosis transforms grazing animals in a cemetery to a looming horror of annihilation. Service actually revels in the work of killing: " 'Him love death too much,' Aloysius grumbled" (121).

The sane characters are, in a very real way, madder than the lunatic, and both the morbidly insane and the violently insane exist in a society devoid of guidance and vulnerable to predatory external forces. First, the rapacious expatriate searches for spectacle through the metal eye of the camera. "What is dis, O Lawd, that Jamaica come to?" the bushes bawl (37). She is a new, inexplicable tourist studying the country through ganja-distorted vision, and her camera gnaws the land. The vision from within the country is little better. From the perspective of reliable lunacy, it becomes easy to dismiss politicians as empty babblers and to ridicule the senseless ebb and flow of governments. This process culminates in the expatriate's declaration of herself as boss on the basis of her ability to offer immediate physical gratification. A bush, vulgar but perceptive, screeches, "From Socialism to Capitalism to Pum-pumism. . . . Lawd Jesus God, what now on de head of poor Jamaica?" (117).

Under this rule, despite apparent civic improvements, Inga establishes a new slavery, promotes violence against the Busha, and burns with a hatred intense and passionate enough to be indistinct from her obsession with sex. When Service butchers the goat, an explicit comparison between the gaping wound and the harlot's lips introduces an image recollective of the whore of Babylon (110). The image will echo throughout the novel, especially in lurid references to Inga's exhibitionism. This image of the insatiable maw fuses a vision of ravening greed with a vision of violent death. Through the linguistic rule breaking that contributes to the characterization of Inga and through lexical cohesion (*gaping* 183, 184), the novel reduces to absurdity the legitimization and institutionalization of colonial/neocolonial greed.

Winkler presents a society of distorted values in which Inga's contacts enable her to escape through bribery. She leaves the indigent lunatic to satisfy the law and make his peace with this society. The professionals who should protect the society by upholding laws of various kinds are ambiguous in their values. The lawyer, Linstrom, does not truly distinguish for the reader between his concept of socialism and what he conceives as "bumpkin heaven." The doctors smack of immorality and the parsons of shallowness. The ethical supports have crumbled, and directionless and hollow administration compound the social disintegration that is manifest in irrational violence ("A form in the hands of a socialist was as bad as a gun," 68).

Violence in this society is not restricted to the obviously disordered consciousness. For some, violence is part of aimless reaction; for others, it is a normal way of life or even a profession. In this setting it takes a lunatic to be consistently repelled by it. Indeed, violence in *The Lunatic* does not erupt as the supreme expression of social deviance. In the surface structure of the text, it is the most obviously deviant character, the ragged madman, who rejects violence. At a deeper level, of course, violence remains a signal of extreme disturbance in this society whose outcast madman is its strongest link with moral truth.

As in any other novel, the social information with which the reader begins constrains that reader's interpretation. However, a critical theoretical stance that is exclusively reader/analyst centered not only deemphasizes the speaker/writer but conceals an essential message of this text. A reader preoccupied with personal ideology and preconceived views on Jamaican society may resist the deconditioning offered by rule flouting and produce a sterile interpretation in which all that is unmasked is the reader's own politics (see Birch 29), overriding the message, circumventing its encoding or artistry. In fact, *The Lunatic* restructures the social information of the reader.

Consequently, of course, social information must be present before the text can restructure it, and social information remains an essential basis for critical inference. Isolated formalism in textual interpretation divorced from sociohistorical information is unlikely to provide a complete reading of *The Lunatic*. In fact, solid social information and traditional expectations in the reader are a starting point for the decoding of the discourse, even where the ultimate purpose is to decondition the reader. After all, there can be no clear sense of deviance without a clear perception of norms.

Leslie Clark emphasizes shared social knowledge as the basis of inference processing in text comprehension and notes that many of these inferences are inherited from world knowledge structures associated with different classes of people (102). *The Lunatic* works first by stereotyping—vagrant lunatic, *busha*, tourist, middle-class professional, bumpkin—and then by deconstructing the types that have been inferred from shared social knowledge. *The Lunatic* is certainly a text to approach "open to ideas from whatever source, hostage to no system" (Hassan 5–6) for, apart from the insights that text-centered and reader-centered approaches may offer, traditional criteria remain crucial. It has already been noted that the link between social disorganization and disordered consciousness is as classic as *King Lear*. Such a connection may be expected to form part of what Clark might call world knowledge in any moderately well-read reader. Traditional literature is in fact part of the sociohistorical information for decoding modern literary narrative and provides a norm against which to measure deviation.

Through stylistic deviance from the norms of traditional literary discourse, Winkler deconditions his readers in preparation for new inferences about social deviance. By inverting notions of reliable perspective or by lexical foregrounding (through the flouting of verbal taboos), the writer unmasks social insanity. Texts normally maintain the cooperative principle, postulated by H. P. Grice, by observing such maxims as the one of relevance. Conversely, a writer may convey mental instability by flouting this maxim, creating gaps in logical connection. In violating the normal rules of discourse, writers also call attention to differences between the way their subjects order their experience and the way in which readers may be expected to do so.

Aloysius's susceptibility to the advice of the flame-heart tree cannot be supported on rational grounds. But readers are more likely to align themselves with these values than with those held by other characters in the text. Yet these are sane characters from the perspective of the civilization that excludes Aloysius. Deviation in language promotes, in a roughly Whorfian way, a change in thought or attitude, and *The Lunatic* goes beyond the social knowledge with which readers begin by creating a new field of reference. The novel does so by forcing readers to question and eventually discard original assumptions that what has been accepted as civilization is sane and that what has been accepted as lunacy is, by contrast, barbaric.

It may seem at first glance that traditional comic treatment of Creole language continues in *The Lunatic*, perhaps as a screen for taboo material. However, in truth, language usage in this discourse is not a screening device but a tool for unmasking. Specifically, language usage in the novel highlights conflicting perceptions of a society in which the sane have lost all illusions and reorganized their values and ideals and ethical principles have come to be viewed as delusions. This unmasks elements of savagery in civilization and invests the outcast who clings to rejected values with a dignity that is as tragic as it is comic. The text reveals the absurdity of such reverse progress (of civilization to wilderness) through semantically anomalous sentences so short and simple as to seem matter of fact: "One day the cemetery would eat the Busha" (65). Absurdity is frequently a function of verbal incongruity, and incongruity in *The Lunatic* triggers laughter. However, this is often hysterical laughter, born of shock. *The Lunatic* not only links words semantically anomalous, such as *cemetery* (inanimate) and *eat* (used with animate subjects), but also connects words that are semantically synonymous but pragmatically distinct, for example when the lunatic refers to God as his "Daddy." The text also highlights clashes between individual terms and the passages into which they fit.

Rule breaking arrests the reader in the discovery that within the novel those who define the norms are themselves distorted. Within this new field of reference the reader must reevaluate the assumption that sane, civilized society views violence as an extreme in deviant behavior: " 'You know, sometimes I believe dat de worse thing you ever did,' the barrister said in disgust, 'is to spare dat dam white man's bumpkin life. . . . You really mad to rass' " (220–21). The sane view that rejects the vagrant as mad evaluates violence as a practical means of problem solving: "Dey need chopping" (129). For Service, death is a way of life. For Busha, interment is an obsession around which life is organized. For the successful Syrian proprietor, the graveyard is big business. For the expatriate, butchery is spectacle or local color. *The Lunatic* is a comedy of social death in a community where violence is becoming normative. A thoughtful tree ponders whether "all Jamaica is like one rass big graveyard" (73). The reader's reality, in which the tree is just a tree and the lunatic protagonist is unquestionably mad, comes to coexist with the reader's observation of the tree's sensitivity and the lunatic's reliability. Such instability of textual meaning is a device for tearing away society's mask of sanity and normalcy and, through absurdity, for revealing madness.

Winkler goes out of his way to assault the sensibilities of conservative readers and to outrage proprieties, and it is to be hoped that even a permissive society will never consider *The Lunatic* as a school text. But perhaps Winkler most disturbs, amuses, or offends because he exaggerates flaws out of proportion to reality. This strategy of distortion may evoke hysterical laughter or gross insult, but it captures current Jamaican preoccupation with an out-of-order world through outlandishly out-of-order discourse and conveys the peculiar mixture of strain, derision, and endurance that characterizes the response of many Jamaicans to the troubled present.

Such radical deviance from the norms of discourse is a recent development in Jamaican literature, as is the portrayal of violence as routine and almost normative. In contrast, the earliest literature set in Jamaica represents nineteenth-century Jamaican society conventionally even where this literature records social values that seem grossly distorted to modern readers. *Marly* supports the values of its society in the end—logically when one considers the novel's social context, illogically in terms of its textual structure.

The lacunae in the logical component of the narrative itself reflect the split vision of its author. Apart from this apparently unintentional peculiarity of discourse, the language usage of *Marly* is traditional, departing from literary norms of the time only in recording Creole speech. In the same way that this Creole is used to demonstrate the deviation of blacks and creole whites from normative European behavior, *Marly* equates the established social order with sanity. Deviation from this will unleash insane violence. More recently, in *Brother Man*, Roger Mais conveys his recognition of social distortion, but the text shows little stylistic deviance. Although even the earliest novels in Jamaican settings suggest violent disorder as built into the social framework, this violence remains latent, exploding only sporadically from individual trauma.

More recently, this message of inherent violence has gathered force, adjusting the code itself. Violence becomes a means to an end and is consciously selected and rationally worked out. In *The Lunatic*, where greed has assumed grotesque and even obscene proportions, violence comes to be routine, working its way into the norm. *The Lunatic* uncovers the institutionalization of violence in a society where insatiable greed ravages life itself ("It was like death, this thing that had come among them," 150).

The text frustrates analysis of the type that fastens on polarities. In the end, it is impossible to distinguish civilization from savagery on the basis of presence or absence of such absolutes as sanity, order, or propriety. The text also tampers with stereotypes to invert meanings entrenched in Caribbean literature. We have already noted that *The Lunatic* subverts the theme of gender exploitation. It also exposes stupidity, greed, and brutality at all social levels and in a variety of ethnic possibilities without romanticizing ignorance among the poor. The text upholds human compassion as the basis of human reason and of life itself, and it portrays a society departing from this basic blueprint.

It is in this sense that recent Jamaican literature writes back not only to imperial discourse but also to some aspects of counterdiscourse now familiar in the postcolonial Caribbean. The current literature of Jamaica not only reexamines the alienation as an experience of the expatriate in Jamaica, of Jamaicans in the metropolis, or of Jamaicans caught in a clash of cultures, but also it looks at the alienation of Jamaicans in their own fragmenting society. This altered vision of marronage at home penetrates rhetoric about past imperial responsibility for current Caribbean alienation. A deflected perspective incisively attacks local mismanagement and inhumanity and reveals it as cohabiting with foreign greed.

This shifting perspective distinguishes but does not divorce the national literature from the regional literature. In portraying a damaged man and ridiculing an exploitative woman, the Jamaican writer expands the symbolic relationship between gender exploitation and neocolonial damage. This change does not mean that the type of the exploitative woman is absent from the literature of the region but that the portrayal of extreme sexual exploitation supported by capricious violence is unusual in characterizations of women, while the dismemberment of women by men is relatively common in the literature. The fact that Inga's fascist rule is followed by the more subtle but equally forceful government by the black widow entangles issues of race and gender inextricably.

Similarly, motherlessness warrants reconsideration as an issue in masculine as well as feminine development. The themes of abandonment and homelessness entangle with that of madness, as rejection by civilization traumatizes the developing mind. Yet it is not the old, imperial civilization or the newer lure of the American metropolis; it is not foreign at all. It is the Caribbean construct of orderly existence—a synthesis of inherited elements, perhaps, like other Caribbean epistemes, but all the more creole as a result of synthesis. Winkler playfully scrutinizes this civilization and redefines it as madness.

A Play-Play Reality

In *The Lunatic* the social exiles mask themselves in disguises and playacting. Aloysius unwillingly assumes the part of a criminal. His abandonment, isolation, and exposure unfold from a past that is irredeemable, and this outcast status unites him with a cast that his loneliness makes it impossible to resist. This emotional trap draws him to what seems an inexorable finale in the human condition that *King Lear* laments as a "great stage of fools" (4.6.185). Aloysius finds himself trapped in a part that horrifies him, rehearsed and drilled in the role of a criminal until he breaks out of this drama that outrages nature.

The Lunatic is set in a wilderness that imitates civilization. Trees talk and bushes preach even as the outcasts parody civilized life in their house building and government. The acting of parts by wanderers in the wilderness provides information about the civilization from which these outcasts are excluded. Winkler reveals this civilization through the games his characters play. The element of game underlies social interaction throughout the text. Sex games substitute for love; cohabitation (of lunacy, violence, and sexual excess) substitutes for homemaking; random violence as well as rehearsals for housebreaking substitute for art; crime substitutes for profession. The constructive, reconciling influence of teamwork in the cricket match contrasts with these destructive games even as, interspersed with all of these, Service indulges in the "fun" of butchery.

The cricket match brings Aloysius onto the team and welds him to the community through recognition and admiration from all walks of life precisely at the point at which he is scheduled to become an accomplice to crime. C. L. R. James has envisioned cricket as a means of reentering history through play (99), and in the cricket match Aloysius develops from a removed spectator to a participant in human life. Simon Gikandi discusses James's appropriation of cricket as a synecdoche of colonial culture. Village cricket adapts to the Caribbean a symbol of British upper-class leisure and inverts this symbol to an expression of popular will. Gikandi describes the game as a mode of communicating emerging national consciousness in the midst of white middle-class control of colonial space and of a continuity of English culture at the periphery of the empire (164). Yet Gikandi's perspective is regional rather than national. In *The Lunatic*, the cricket match enables the individual consciousness to emerge from that of the gang and the outcast consciousness to reunite with the team, the local community.

Winkler's characterization of the outcast madman who enters the community through the cricket match presents an ideological shift from the imperial/(post)colonial dialectic to one that is internal to Jamaica, that of the marginalized individual and local society. The cricket match and the experience of belonging that it entails come at a crucial point in Aloysius's history. They enable him to claim an identity that repudiates crime against a teammate and to recognize an integrity that separates him from Inga and Service.

Prior to this event, Aloysius's alienation is structured on an alternation between playing at homemaking in the wilderness and rehearsing for housebreaking in the civilization that denies him a home. The uncaring civilization masks its own barbarity and lunacy. The play-play nature of civilization is suggested by the fact that even the propertied Busha has no sense of belonging in his own community. The local metropolis does not even provide a satisfactory home for the living. Busha decides that Kingston is Sodom and Gomorrah as well as Babylon "all wrapped into one" but longs for it as a good place "to dead" (165). Jamaica itself is not a real nation to the stones around Aloysius, which cry out, "Dis is Jamaica for you! Where man treat man like dirt! God strike me down dead if I don't migrate to America next year!" (154). Nakedness in the storm is a theme of universal currency that Winkler delivers in unorthodox terms, but he implies conclusions that correlate in many ways to orthodox values. Yet in reviving these values he challenges assumptions that compose Caribbean stereotypical concepts of civilization, for he ridicules the rhetoric of social reform, balances blame on the landowner with parodies of political resistance and economic want, contentiously replaces the woman as victim with the exploited man, and in general refuses to absolve anyone of responsibility, whatever their history of suffering.

Winkler recognizes and challenges a binarism in the relationship between the imperial status quo and a developing Caribbean one. Aloysius does not run away from civilization; he is rejected. He eventually escapes and resists a travesty of family life and government instituted by Inga but made more repulsive by the local butcher. He joins the village community when it is prepared to accept him, not because it is truly civilized but because it is the only option. Indeed, he does not actively return any more than he actively escaped; he is reabsorbed.

Winkler provides a new perspective on marronage by continuously shifting information to unexpected and incongruous contexts. Because literary content is information and is thus nested in other information, innovative literary content, as new information, nests in outer shells of information that are known and shared. The developing indigenous literary discourse of Jamaica reexamines the same world as before, but it does so from a different perspective. The literature reveals additional truths through alternative content, but it is nested in shells that include old information. Literary indigeneity is constrained by a context that includes canonical texts of both British and Caribbean origin.

Jan Carew has described the Caribbean writer today as "a creature balanced between limbo and nothingness, exile abroad and homelessness at home" (453). But the themes of Jamaican writing suggest that even this asymmetrical opposition is graded. Something like an indigenous construct of home begins with Aloysius's adoption by the widow, though this too is fraught with domination and exploitation. It is a gentler, more orderly rule than Inga's but just as determined and just as one-sided in the distribution of power. The man of a thousand names consigns all but the one approved by the widow to the toilet. In her presence he must pretend that the wilderness is silent, and he must answer his customary companions, such as the flame-heart tree, only in secret. How well the new game of playing house is to work will depend on how adroit Aloysius becomes at playing sane.

Aloysius exists to bring into question the sanity of the civilization from which he is outcast, and his partial absorption into the community at the end of the novel is possible through surface changes (physical cleansing, acceptable dress, and edited speech) rather than deeper psychological rehabilitation. He retains mentally, although he must no longer articulate them, the same multitude of names by which his barrister has established his madness to the satisfaction of a jury. What enables the writer to jolt his readers' expectations is the persona of the confirmed madman who is innately seized of a distinction between right and wrong based on simple human compassion.

In producing an indigenous vision, *The Lunatic* most wildly distorts the theme of deviant family relationships versus normal households. The text sets its vision of abortive and then more gently skewed family relationships against a background of ineffectual government. In other words, Winkler, like many Caribbean writers, adopts the metaphor of family relationships for his political commentary. This strategy works particularly well because literal and nonliteral connections exist between the family and society. There are causal links between fragmented family life and the characters' confused loyalties, contempt for authority, rising resentments, and eventual explosive violence. In the end, Aloysius averts this violence and moves from the wilderness into the community. Although his rehabilitation is assumed, readers have no doubt that he will continue to fit, provided he maintains the mask of sanity, because the civilization in question is itself only playing at sanity.

The altered perspectives of characters distanced from civilization by mind-bending alienation yield alternative glimpses of truth. Winkler's ordered wilderness survives outside a society of directionless political rhetoric and the life-denying materialism that compose some perceptions of civilization. By adopting the perspective of madness for countering some familiar Caribbean discourse, Winkler reveals that nationalism, however apotheosized, does not produce paradise. Stephen Slemon argues in favor of preserving for post-colonialism "a specifically anti-colonial discursive energy" (6). However, Winkler's writing suggests that national developments within the regional literature may well react to postcolonial counterdiscourse because this counterdiscourse has become entrenched enough to exert pressure on margins of its own making.

Winkler unmasks reality by deconstructing it. Subverting even Caribbean expectations, he forces readers to revisit old values, some hauntingly orthodox. Aloysius has much in common with the noble savage celebrated in imperial discourse of the British romantics. Here is a persona decent by nature versus nurture, a character that the materialism of a demented society has bypassed and left unspoiled. Aloysius, who is compassionate, honest, sensitive, moral, godly, and romantic, is also outcast, incomprehensible, and therefore mad. He is the (admittedly absurd) extreme of a man of feeling rather than of reason. Inga, who recognizes only instant physical gratification, cannot understand his love. Busha cannot bear the notion of his compassion. Service threatens to chop him when he becomes emotional. In the midst of it all, Aloysius resists recolonization by Inga despite his devotion to her, even as he resists dehumanization by the butcher and refuses to become a psychopathic killer like the lunatic of *The Great Yacht Race.*

Thus, Aloysius escapes and resists absorption into the microcosmic state founded on greed, and thus he maintains integrity. For what Winkler has suggested through the hypersensitive vision of lunacy is a deranged concept of civilization versus wilderness. Busha's vision is decadent but recognizably representative of well-to-do rural Jamaica rather than of *foreign.* The widow, too, has a distinct but locally influential vision. These views demonstrate affinities to and contrasts with each other and with traditional imperial and more current metropolitan epistemes. Against this many-faceted and contradictory vision, social outcasts in the wilderness construct their own revolutionary civilization, a mini-state founded on greed and violence. Eventually, the lunatic refuses to be absorbed in this entity, but meanwhile his experience of marronage within marronage locks him into a profound psychological dilemma.

To reintroduce bygone truths, *The Lunatic* deconstructs some current perceptions and in their place constructs a contradictory reliable madness. Through deviance in discourse Winkler conveys distortions in the perspectives both of individuals and of the wider fragmenting society. Current Jamaican fiction employs the altered perspective of the disturbed psyche to reconsider the relationship between home and self, to extend the definition of marronage, and to question the sanity of a composite vision of civilization that is, to borrow a favorite phrase from *The Lunatic,* "damn out of order."

6

The Trackless Past of
Hearne's *Sure Salvation*

Ghosts without consolation, unable to communicate
with the living or with each other. Each doomed to
circle the place of death, in silence, forever.
—John Hearne, *The Sure Salvation*

THERE IS LITTLE mention of Jamaica in John Hearne's *Sure Salvation*. It is neither a source nor a destination for any character, and it is not a remembered or fantasized setting. Kingston is merely a source of reliable stores laid aboard (161) and later traded profitably in Cuba. The ostensible connection between Jamaica and the text is its author, and what seems to be implied is a Jamaican fictional perspective on history—a history that is not only Caribbean but global. Hearne looks out at the world and back at the past from a Jamaican present to reconstruct points of view other than those of traditional history but also other than those that are politically correct in the Caribbean.

The sea drama set in the horror of the Middle Passage has elements of charade. It plays out the riddle of responsibility for history by highlighting the roles of participants in the action. It demonstrates that the personal consequence of such responsibility is isolation and the social consequence is fragmentation. Unstated but inescapably reflected by the circumstances of the ship are the circumstances of an island and of minds at sea. By interfering with temporal sequence and reshuffling events, the writer reveals alternative possibilities in the causal links between these events.

A Community of Outcasts

The structure of the discourse exposes the polemic. To ask who is responsible for the ship is, in a sense, to ask who is responsible for history and for the composite creole psyche. The command of the ship rests on lines of communication that entangle discourse with power. Communication takes place within strictly defined pragmatic constraints. The link between responsibility and power emerges through patterns of discourse.

Communication is first limited by rank. Hogarth communicates officially with his officers, Bullen and Reynolds, essentially through elocutionary acts of the command type. He answers necessary questions but discourages conversation likely to disturb the vertical orientation between himself and those below him. Conversational turn-taking is limited, reducing the likelihood of patterns that might reorient the relationship to a horizontal one. Hogarth firmly squashes persistent efforts at "chattiness" by Bullen. The captain directs commands to sailors through officers and never, at any time, addresses cargo (the slaves), thereby maintaining the implied distinction between cargo and crew. Beyond such distinctions as those of ethnicity, bondage, and language differences lie implied perceptions of the cargo as nonhuman, which reduces the possibility of verbal communication between crew and cargo. Hogarth's rank relieves him of the need for any communication whatever with cargo.

The officers similarly address seamen who rank beneath them. Actual conversation between seamen takes place horizontally. Calder, Dunn, and Dolan talk with each other but clearly distinguish themselves from the Portuguese seamen ("ignorant dagoes"). No discourse of the conversation type takes place between any of these groups and the cargo. Reynolds's addresses to slaves in the hold are entirely manipulative, commanding, or cajoling through tone and gesture; his verbal language is unintelligible to them. In his cabin, his addresses to the girl whom he keeps naked and chained to his bed impose obscenity by placing his own chosen words in her mouth.

The ambivalent status of Alex conflicts with established patterns of rank because extensive horizontal discourse of the conversational type takes place between Alex and Reynolds and between Alex and Hogarth. This disruption in the normal network based on status discloses by implicature the deceptive nature of Alex's status as cook. The seamen note the discrepancy, and Dunn resents commands from Alex. Alex systematically establishes horizontal (conversational) communication lines where vertical lines would normally be expected in the social context of his discourse—that is, where his address would normally be directed upward. Once these horizontal lines are established, a further tilt establishes his status as upper. The vertical line of discourse that assumes or maintains power is reestablished but with the positions of speakers reversed.

Class is of course a conditioning factor of rank but has distinctions that are important in the tale. Hogarth's class makes his command of such a vessel a social degradation. In his class lies the potential for aristocracy by movement through the upper echelons of a company with the power to impact on the wealth of Europe. Class prompts his initial hesitation about an unsuitable marriage that ruins his potential for legitimate wealth. Hearne inscribes class distinctions in the text through social variation in language.

Hogarth's language is separated from Eliza's and from Bullen's by an elaborated code distinct from the standard but moderately educated usage of the latter two. Hogarth's vocabulary is further separated from Eliza's by her farmyard comparisons, those references to the content domain most readily available for explaining herself. Hogarth's language also separates him from Reynolds, whose own social acceptability and considerable education emerge in both fluency and diction. Reynolds not only stuns others with his volubility but also bewilders them with his vocabulary. But Hogarth expresses himself with a yet more upper-class restraint that is lacking in Reynolds, who, however acceptable in family, is naturally vulgar. Reynolds's speech, thought, and nonverbal communication expose this vulgarity through exaggeration, expression of the serious as comic, and violation of taboos. Hogarth rigidly observes linguistic inhibitions, distinguishing himself as socially superior to Reynolds through this conformity.

The most obvious constraints on communication are those linguistic differences associated with national and ethnic boundaries. This phenomenon fractures even the Europeans into two groups, for differences in worldview effectively separate the British and the Portuguese. Continuous chatter and insensitivity to lines of rank render the Portuguese a cohesive but unintelligible group to the British. The Portuguese fail to observe nonverbal conventions relating to proxemics—the physical distance between speakers that, among the British, should relate to social distance. Hogarth must control variables of distance where infringement of these variables is meaningful. Bullen, for example, might like to disturb variables of distance to establish power solidarity. English speech on the ship intensifies the impression of a fragmented community because it also varies somewhat according to regional dialect. The Irishman is separated from Calder and Dunn yet is closer to them than to the Louisiana black. The extreme in linguistic diversity is squeezed most tightly in the hold, where the slaves command languages of entirely separate families from that of the Europeans and speak tongues unintelligible to each other.

The linguistic complexity recurrently produces the need to speak through intermediaries, and this need is both linguistic and social. It widens gaps in the already complex speech community, even as the common language of seafaring superficially binds the crew together.

In addition to the distinctions of class, traditionally perceived gender distinctions separate Eliza's speech from that of Hogarth. Eliza's letter informs Hogarth of her pregnancy and pleads for his support. She attempts to justify herself while absolving him of all responsibility; the missive offers devotion and demands nothing, affirms his power and her helplessness, confirms his morality and her worthlessness; it pleads for him to command her and offers obedience on any terms:

> I beg you to marry me, William. . . .
> I will be a good wife to you, William. . . .
> Send for me, William! . . .
> Oh please write to me, William, and advise me, and tell me what you would wish me to do. . . .
> Even if there can be no immediate marriage, I will join you wherever you say (I have money for passage). (178)

Her letter is, most of all, persistent discourse in the face of stony silence, a tenaciousness underlined in the parallelism of sentence structure. Her greatest injury is his lack of response, and this too persists through parallel constructions during her nightmare loneliness in childbirth:

> Had he replied to my letter. Had he told me of his return. . . .
> Had he but answered that letter. . . .
> Had he but come to me on the instant of his return. . . .
> Had he but come to me before the pain. (178–81)

A final major constraint on communication aboard the *Sure Salvation* is innate ability. To some extent, amount and fluency of speech are situationally constrained, but the degree of fluency is also an essential aspect of characterization. Dolan, who feels the inactivity of the calm more than other sailors, jokingly alludes to their emerging from their danger with crippled tongues. Bullen stammers into halting and inappropriate conversation with Hogarth. Eliza's pleading cannot break Hogarth's silence, and she later injures him with her own prolonged silences, broken with rebuke. Reynolds directs his undeniable verbal ability to warping information; his lessons to the slave girl distort reality and deny her humanity. Reynolds's volubility produces deceit.

In contrast, Alex is a virtuoso speaker. First, he is a master of many voices. He commands varieties of black English varying from near-Standard to a more distant and socially unacceptable variety, and he slips along this continuum, at will, motivated by his own convenience. He exaggerates his own Black American dialect, choosing "I'se" when it suits him to assume a "deficit," for example, when addressing Honeyball.

In addition to English, he speaks French and presumably the French Creole of Louisiana, negotiates as successfully in Spanish as in English, and shifts into Portuguese when operations on board require it. His distribution of *bhang* in the drinking water hints at other possible language contacts and media of negotiation and control. He quickly and naturally identifies those paths of communication by which, through possible intermediaries, he can network his command of the ship, and he becomes an intermediary himself to retain some hold on power when Honeyball takes command. His natural linguistic ability, apparently unrelated to class or education, enables him to manipulate a variety of speakers who cannot or do not communicate with each other. This natural ability is thus directly proportional to the speed with which he reverses vertical lines of communication and is an index of power.

The Sure Salvation is a fragile speech community partially unified by a shared content domain that is nautical but fissured by multidimensional communication gaps. Massive linguistic variation cramped within rigid physical and social boundaries defines who speaks to whom as well as who speaks when, how, and what. The roles of participants in the action are encoded in the discourse through thematic rearrangements of sentence structure. Some role reversals are explicit ("Thus I recruited him. Or, rather, thus he recruited me," 154). But role adjustments are also conveyed through adjustments of voice ("as if I had been carried bound to this time and this place," 146) or of transitivity ("for he must have perceived in me the instrument—no, let me call it by its true title, the slave," 147). In addition, responsibility for action is encoded in the temporal structure of the narrative through arrangement of the plot to highlight causality rather than to deliver events of the story in chronological order.

The relative importance of Hogarth and Alex and thus the power structure on board the ship define the narrative structure of the novel. Within the linguistic setting described above, the total discourse takes the structural form of a narrative containing several embedded discourses. Many of these inner discourses are themselves narratives that have causal links with the major discourse. The inner narratives are linear sequences of events, but the text delivers these sets of sequenced events in nonlinear order. The effect is not merely one of postcolonial discontinuity for its own sake. The combinational pattern of sets of events embedded into each other slows action and delays the outcome of the central discourse, which is appropriate to the encompassing situation, essentially one of stasis.

Suzanne Fleischman's scheme for the global structure of narrative (136) is based on W. Labov's and takes into account the perspectival shifts associated with the move from the speaker's now to the story's now in the abstract and from the story's now back to the speaker's now in the coda. *The Sure Salvation* has neither abstract nor coda in its major discourse, but these elements of narrative may be traced as different speakers move in and out of individual embedded narratives. Indeed, the embedded narratives demonstrate the characteristic structure of abstract, orientation, complication, peak, resolution, and coda.

For example, in one internal monologue Hogarth shifts from the time of his speech, in which he evaluates his relationship to Alex, to the (embedded) story time in which he recalls his meeting with Alex, and in doing so he indicates his topic (abstract) even as he establishes time, place, characters, and situation (orientation). Hogarth recalls that Alex interrupts the unloading of the ship, assists in negotiating for supplies, and offers himself as cook. This complication reaches its peak when Hogarth attempts to tip Alex and sees his guineas tossed to the black Cuban children diving from the wharf. It is characteristic of Hogarth's speech that evaluation takes place at every stage of the narrative, but it is after the peak that Hogarth pauses to evaluate in detail the impact of Alex's dismissiveness. The captain relives the affront to his sensibilities brought about by Alex's disregard for the gold and for wealth as an index of power. The resolution is an understanding between them; Hogarth employs Alex as cook. The coda is lost in further shifts of topic, and the resolution itself reveals a parallel and more accurate arrangement of events ("Thus he rebuked me for daring to treat him less than one of my rank, and thus I recruited him. Or, rather, thus he recruited me," 154).

Alex's recruitment of Hogarth is part of a related but distinct narrative, that of Alex's career. This narrative is distributed through others in sets of events that the text does not present sequentially any more than it presents them continuously. The abstract to Alex's story, as he recounts it in first person, establishes at once the paradigmatic link between his and other bids for power in the context of race relations of the age: "As Louis Delfosse used to say, *Two of us could take and hold that country, Alex, if you were only a white man*" (53). The major narrative—of a prolonged calm at sea, of welcome progress again, and of mutiny and arrest—proceeds through a number of intercepting discourses by various speakers, discourses themselves discontinuous and delivered in parts that are not necessarily ordered in temporal sequence.

An event is essentially a hermeneutic construct for converting undifferentiated experience into a unit of narrative (cf. Fleischman 95), and the definition of sets of events, the sequencing of these sets, and the causal links that such sequencing may imply are matters of choice. Hearne chooses to arrange the sea story as parallel and intercepting narratives of Hogarth's and Alex's careers in such a way as to challenge the perspective of traditional history.

In this traditional perspective, Hogarth's career is maritime adventure, and Alex has no career. In addition, Hearne's narrative challenges the perspective of Caribbean counterdiscourse, in which Hogarth's career is exploitation and Alex's career is a struggle for freedom. Hearne appears to propose that there comes a point at which all free participants in an event share equal responsibility. From this perspective, the focal event is a contest for power. Hogarth locates this contest as "between the true gentlemen of history" (159).

The logical component of the narrative that accounts for its propositional content is what maintains cohesion between the events of *The Sure Salvation*. For example, its sets of implied arguments have some features in common. One such recurrent feature is the testimony of Alex's unprecedented power, which is repeatedly linked to his own understanding of power relations and his ability to transmute them for his own empowerment. The reader meets Louis Delfosse in what appear to be random recollections, but they actually summarize Alex's early life in the wild company of a white adventurer. Alex's enigmatic character is the result of an overlay of cultures. He is as obscure to the slaves in the hold as to the crew on deck. He is an entirely new product of cultural fusion, the black man in white man's clothes (87).

The recurrent features of different narrative threads in the discourse are linked through events that are logically related rather than encountered in temporal sequence. Causal links ensure that events lead up to and proceed from each other. A flashback explains Eliza's behavior as the result of Hogarth's earlier treatment of her, and her behavior explains the tension in their cabin and accounts in part for Hogarth's involvement in so inferior an enterprise. Discontinuity enables the reader to encounter together events that come from different areas of the time frame but are topically or causally related. This temporal nonlinearity highlights such causal links as those between materialism and betrayals of trust.

Not only logical relationships but also strategies of expression weld the intercepting narratives, for example by exploiting overlapping semantic fields or by punning. The theme of commerce in human flesh emerges both in Hogarth's participation in the slave trade and in his treatment of Eliza and their unborn child, a connection implied by the homonyms *birth* and *berth*. The metaphorical connection between these terms emerges in Hogarth's mental reconstruction of a tasteless joke between his business associates, Llewellyn and Oates, who imagine him "dropping anchor" in his "rightful berth" (175). This event precedes Eliza's letter, which informs him of the impending birth of their child and begs his support.

In employing fiction to rechart history, the Jamaican writer reconstructs events and redefines causal links in innovative terms. An element of predetermination in this process produces an effect described by Gerald Prince, a sort of teleological determination in which "the narrative displays itself in terms of an end which functions as its (partial) condition, its magnetizing force, its organizing principle. Reading a narrative is waiting for the end and the quality of that waiting is the quality of the narrative" (*Narratology* 157). Because many of the embedded narratives are flashbacks, they seem teleologically determined. But in addition to analepses, prolepses such as Hogarth's vision of his own hanging reinforce the atmosphere of waiting, as does the whole tension-fraught stasis of the ship.

The entire fiction is structured on perspectival shifts within and among characters arrested in time and space. The novel opens with stasis, which convulses into movement only near the end. Before this definitive movement begins, the novel shifts locus between different areas of the ship. In each setting occur embedded discourses of various types—commands, conversations, recollections, anecdotes, and letters. The context of stasis sets time in abeyance; actual events are played out chronologically but so slowly that the otherwise unoccupied minds on board relieve monotony by wandering backward and forward between the nonpresent and the present. Similarly, the narrative integrates spatial shifts (there/here/there) associated with shifts of person. In presenting the experience of individual characters, sometimes in third person, sometimes in first person, sometimes shifting from one first-person narrator to another, the narrative alternates between an account of situations and events in which the narrator is a character (homodiegetic) and an account in which the narrator is not a character (heterodiegetic).

Such shifts from one wandering mind to the next facilitate adjustments of time reference that move the reader between situations then/now/then. The message that "time itself must have been tricked, frozen by violence" (47) is as much encoded in narrative structuring and in tense manipulation as in actual wording.

Time, both in its sequence and in the duration of events, is repeatedly stressed. The opening of the novel marks the eternity of the crew's stagnation over days and then over weeks ("the ship was the still centre of a huge stillness," 7). Existential verbs hold action in abeyance and convey situation rather than process. Passive voice undermines the agency of the ship by shifting it, with its crew, to the role of patient of the action ("The barque was ringed. . . . Labor was invented. . . . Bursts of activity were succeeded. . . . They were tantalised," 7).

The present of *The Sure Salvation* is a trap to which they have sailed and a future that awaited them. This phenomenon is frequently expressed through aspectual constructions such as the perfect, which marks the persistent rele-

vance of a past situation to the present or of a past within the past to the
simple past. As Hogarth sees it, "Failure had been waiting for him like an
uncharted sargasso here in the open ocean, and he had sailed his life into
the clutch of its invisible tendrils" (17). As he walks across the deck of his
present command, he sees his own body jerking at the end of the rope that
foreshadows his future (25). The conjoined sections of the unfolding action
contain embedded units drawn from various time layers of past and future,
composing a discourse of dependencies within dependencies. The reshuffling and superimposing of events from different times has the effect
of dechronologizing action, of decomposing the total time frame. This
timelessness emphasizes the stillness to which Hogarth's mind has been
brought (146).

The narrative thus encodes stasis both into sentence structure and into
the global structure of the discourse. Narrative perspective moves from character to character and, even within the perspectives of individual characters,
shifts between perception, surface memory, shallow memory, and deep memory, with rapid adjustments of tense and aspect (cf. Fleischman 62). Although
Reynolds retrieves some events from the distant past, for the most part he
observes and represents what he sees as he sees it. In contrast, Calder evokes
personal experiences for comparison with his present. His incidents are auto-
biographical, from surface memory. Hogarth narrates his inner struggle regarding marriage to Eliza in the distanced and objective tone of the historian,
with the detached recall of what Fleischman defines as shallow memory.
Eliza retrieves from deep memory and with pictorial clarity portions of an
experience that she has internalized and that have become part of her self.
Her account stuns in a way that Hogarth's does not because in her "the 'existential ego' has replaced the 'observing ego' " (see Fleischman 62).

Memory is thus central to the unfolding of the narrative and to the sup-
plying of causal links, and much of the setting is psychological. The physical
setting of the slave ship on a motionless ocean implies temporal as well as
spatial stagnation. There is no way out, nowhere to go, nowhere forward;
physical and temporal imprisonment mirrors the psychological trap: "In this
prison of unyielding silence and immobility their only proofs of being were
the writhing edge of the sun and the nightly fattening of the moon" (7).
Hogarth's intelligence and sensitivity tragically lock him into a prison of the
mind from which there is no escape along any dimension. Even the lines of
his face define his lips as "in parenthesis" (15).

Within this framework of profound psychological disturbance, the narrative shifts suddenly from past tense to narrative present, for example as
Hogarth discusses with Alex such horrible contingencies as the need to

throw slaves overboard to stretch food supplies should the calm continue. The narrative present, used with third person, obviously refers to past events. However, present-tense narration implies simultaneity of the events described when narration shifts from third to first person. Reynolds's mind is entered through a monologue embedded in the larger discourse, a monologue that comprises recollections and obscure threats conveying even greater vileness than is explicit in the encompassing narrative. "The world shall learn," Reynolds seethes (83), and indeed discovery of his character comes through shift after shift. One further change offers a new perspective on Reynolds's distorted personality, as the narrative reverts to third-person reference in the reflections of the naked slave whom Reynolds imprisons in his cabin. In her vision, "he was *Elegwa;* evil without purpose . . . a thing outside the decent order" (83). Such fluid shifts of person as well as tense reveal a decomposition of spatial dimensions that parallels the decomposition of time frame described above.

The structure of the novel therefore results from manipulations of deixis and shufflings of reference and of those pointers in discourse that traditional narratives keep stable to preserve the orientation of both narrator and audience in relation to events. It is common enough in traditional literature to encounter in an external point of view shifts from mind to mind by an omniscient narrator whose third-person account is independent of any one character's limitations. However, in *The Sure Salvation,* the internal point of view is equally unlimited. It not only offers different perspectives on varying events but also shifts perspective within the same series of events. The writer thus imposes on the reader the need to find out what account of the narrated is closest to the truth (cf. Prince 54).

Through alternative perspectives, the characters continuously redefine themselves and each other, each with imperfect vision and shifting or warped perceptions but contributing eventually to accumulating information. When all the information comes in, there is nothing left to do, nowhere left to go along any dimension. In the end and in his frozen present, Old Calder "peels and chews and digests the last artichoke leaf of his experience. . . . What Calder contemplated in the blue furnace of sky above him is his future and the dead. . . . Old Calder jumps" (216–18). By departing from the past-tense usage that narrative employs in its prototypically retrospective orientation, Hearne unfastens the expected temporal framework, integrating grammar with metaphor.

Only to the maddest of all these characters does time appear important and definitive. Eliza Hogarth's derangement begins long before the voyage, in childbirth, as she lies listening to her own agony (181). For her, even as spatial reference decomposes, time is at the root of everything: "Had he but come to me before the pain" (181). This portion of her past remains forever embedded in the stagnant present of the voyage, even as, for the other characters on board, time becomes irrelevant:

> For a ship is a world and who can tell how long it takes to witness a world refashioned?
> So when Eliza Hogarth came from the cabin and stood beside her husband, the men on the deck were still held in a curious rigidity—almost as if they tranquilly contemplated something of enormous significance being created in a space and time that had nothing to do with the trivial ticking of a watch. (195)

By reorienting temporal and spatial dimensions, the writer displaces experience outside of normal civilized life patterns. Similarly, thematic rearrangements in the sentence, such as passivization, highlight subjects to whom things happen by agencies that are external to them and often unspecified. The personae on board find themselves trapped in a ship of the damned, deprived of the "breath of God" and thus waterlocked, haunted by their own filth. Yet helplessness does not absolve participants in the action of responsibility that is inferred in implied causal relationships. The crew's common exclusion from ordered existence, from propriety, has come about through the pursuit of material gain. The unhealthiness and the unnaturalness of exclusion from the orderliness that constitutes life and reality permeate the novel through the image of filth. The disruption of decency involved in the commerce in human flesh inverts life values so as to unstructure reality, to deny existence, and to substitute a living death. The slave girl whom Reynolds violates understands herself mated to "a thing outside the decent order" (83). The text conveys how she perceives the ambivalence of her situation, through epistemic modality (*possible even*) and elliptical constructions suppressing agency (*left on the ground*): "Anything was possible among people who had no sense of order and ceremony. . . . It was possible even that she had died. . . . She could not remember very much of that journey except that many of her town had died. She had seen them left on the ground, impiously, without ceremony, so that they would become ghosts without consolation, unable to communicate with the living or with each other. Each doomed to circle the place of death, in silence, forever" (84–85).

After Berth

Feminist criticism in the Caribbean has pointed to a tendency for male writers to preserve stereotypical visions of women even as they depart radically from other stereotypes of imperial discourse. In *The Sure Salvation,* Hearne presents three women, Eliza, Mtishta, and Tadene, who to varying degrees further the action of the novel in presenting the self in marronage as exploited woman.

There are other women who are not met directly. Eliza's mother is part of the rural household of Eliza'a past and appears only through recollection. She mothers, comforts, assists at childbirth, and prepares and buries the dead. She offers herself as confidante to a daughter in trouble. She forgives and embraces. Yet even as she performs these most traditional of roles she betrays subtle resistance to male power, offering an alternative approach to Eliza's problem, distancing her husband from the body of the child he has viewed only as a blot on family respectability. Still, her support is so low key, almost secret, as to be barely noticeable among louder, deeper voices that command and negotiate Eliza's future.

Rather similarly, the servant, old Jessie, exists only in relation to the physical functions of mating and birth. She assists in the communication of lovers, presides over childbirth, and has insight into reproductive capacities and foresight regarding marital relations. Her parting discourse is an implicit curse on Eliza for the unnatural union with Hogarth that she contemplates. The crone, like the mother, is an identifiable type, but again Hearne's character displays a subtle difference. Her wisdom is pitted against the judgment of men—Eliza's father and Hogarth on the subject of the marriage and the doctor on the subject of Eliza's capacity to bear other children. The fact that Dr. Tulloch's view is supported by a midwife and that Eliza trusts Jessie on the basis of Jessie's experience in the delivery of calves renders Jessie's judgment ambiguous. In any case, her sphere of action is traditional.

Both Eliza's mother and old Jessie move among the shadows that people Eliza's mind. They exist only as relevant to a traumatic experience of her past, and this relevance constrains their roles regardless of the presence or absence of authorial male prejudice. Similarly, women in the dark recesses of Reynolds's mind are types—the hypocritical prude, the governess with covert (and implicitly perverted) sexuality, the obvious slut. All of these types and others are interpretations by characters within the book, and their stereotyping is, at least in part, a strategy for characterizing those personae whose minds they inhabit.

The three women whom the reader actually encounters on the voyage are confined in various ways and with varying consequences. The African women are physically bound in the hold, and Mtishta is later confined (in naked readiness) to Reynolds's cabin. Tadene retains her integrity by maintaining her grasp on physical reality, however revolting, and she eventually exits the hold with a prize so gruesome that Hearne can hardly be accused of concentrating on feminine dismemberment. Mtishta displays classic features of the woman as victim—stasis, virtue, and innocence deflowered. Reynolds undertakes to violate her spiritually and mentally as well as physically and emotionally, but he has limited success. She is the victim of Reynolds's sick humor, a practical joke that he perpetrates through discourse, as he instills in her a twisted version of his language. However, that Reynolds enjoys a vision of femininity as obscenity is a crucial dimension of his brutality. Still, Mtishta does not display physical activity; she does not even emerge from the cabin in the action of the novel. She is simply found. She is, on surface, a stereotypical woman as victim.

Mtishta begins and remains a child, clinging to her certainties of right and wrong, her faith in the wisdom of elders, and her belief that sin and crime result from ignorance. She never relinquishes the security of ancestral teachings and communal belief; for her, Reynolds remains an external and irrational evil. That Mtishta never dissolves into useless pleading, complaint, or sacrificial self-pity but plans the future, interprets the present, and reaches for support into the past indicates that her vulnerability is only flesh deep. In a sense she resists his violation by remaining incorruptible and indivisible.

Frozen in her preoccupation with her own betrayed virtue, Eliza remains loudly silent on the issue of the hold. This one fact is enough to ensure that she never obtains the unqualified sympathy of the reader who is alert to gaps in discourse. Another distancing feature of her personality emerges in her tutoring of Joshua, the ship's boy. This repressive and ascetic schooling not only reflects nineteenth-century British culture but also conveys the strictures of rather more recent Caribbean education, to which writers in the region frequently refer. George Lamming's *In the Castle of My Skin* portrays school as a slave ship, and the boy characters yearn to "make history." Eliza's situation thus repeatedly affirms her connection with the dominant culture, so that she can never be accepted uncritically.

Indeed, the rapid perspectival shifts of the discourse produce a sequence of restricted visions of Eliza, each qualifying the preceding vision, all ultimately cumulative. The full picture contains gaps that are themselves informative. Eliza has neither the lightning mind of Tadene nor the spirituality of Mtishta and is insensible to the moral significance of the voyage. However, her treatment of Hogarth, as explained by her treatment by Hogarth, establishes a pattern of causation that rationalizes the personal history of the madwoman in the cabin. The revelation of Eliza's perspective through flashes of memory and especially the memory of childbirth comes late in the action and contributes to her complexity as a character rather than fixing her as a type.

Indeed, the perception of Eliza in terms of woman as vessel accumulates from such resonances as the *birth/berth* homophones, but this perception exists in Hogarth's mind. When she reveals less receptive qualities, following his eventual proposal, he regards her with disbelief. Indeed, as a vessel, she slips, like the ship itself, increasingly out of his control, and their marriage reflects the intractable stasis of the becalmed ship. The mutiny restores her to sexual activity; Hogarth feels forced to respond to this activity, and it adds to his increasing helplessness rather than restoring his control.

Hearne characterizes Eliza as a changing personality, formed by her country upbringing and the cultural repressions of her time. Her father warns her not to be seen among too many thick books but to appear to read only poetry so as not to put off admiring young men. He tightens around her the constraints of male-defined "women's duties" (132). Even Eliza's reading of femininity is necessarily learned. Because of her peculiar mix of social and cultural conditioning and her own innate sense of independence, she assumes full responsibility for her pregnancy and waits for Hogarth to give of himself as unselfishly as she has given of herself. Her refusal to name the father is stubbornness because she is a woman, "pride, I suppose, for which I have been justly and mercifully punished. . . . But there was something more I cannot properly name. Were I a man and not only a woman, I suppose I would call it honour" (180).

Eliza's inability to find words for qualities expected of a man but inexplicable in "only a woman" is one of the factors that prevent her from reading her own life as a complete text. No one in her circle can assist her in integrating fragmented episodes, and such assistance is a psychoanalytic necessity for a subject suffering from dissociation. Because she can never integrate the painful fragments in her consciousness, Eliza can never be healed, and her own attempts at resistance remain inadequate. Eliza's dissociation is a psychological marronage of increasing intensity.

Eliza's dissociation begins in her abandonment by her lover at childbirth. At this time she separates herself from the woman in pain. The child's death and its disfigurement by her own birth canal induces guilt, which she had not previously felt, for her religious instruction produces in her a sense that she has borne a child into damnation. Coming as it does after all of these events, Hogarth's arrival at the berth/birth is too late. Eliza accepts his offer of marriage even as she refuses to be his wife. In this qualified resistance she exacts a terrible vengeance camouflaged as (somewhat belated) Christian purity. She reinterprets herself as a willing vessel of the Lord, and this piety together with the physical cabin insulate her both from inner feeling and from the outer reality of the slave ship.

This reality breaks in when she emerges from the cabin in the midst of the mutiny and into the full horror surfacing from the depths of the hold and from all the pasts that have led to this point in time and space. This birth from the hold, with its comparable context of betrayal and mutilation, triggers further dissociation. Eliza drops the frozen posture of wronged Mrs. Hogarth in favor of carefree country girlhood. Hogarth, for whom Eliza's mind has never had any reality whatever, is incapable of ministering to her except in agonizingly dutiful sexuality. When the ship berths and its crew and cargo disembark, Eliza has blotted out both past and future, disconnected immediate experience from formative events and their consequences, and so broken the causal links between these events, fragmenting her personality completely.

Eliza's dissociation metaphorically reflects a current social disorder, a dissociation from past pain—modern society's inability to integrate all its formative fragments into coherence. Such integration requires attention to marginal voices whose very expression has, until recently, been deemed improper, but integration also requires the voicing of views that in modern society may not be deemed politically correct. Eliza's separation is not only from the woman in pain but from the woman's voicing of her pain, which is impropriety. The context of such restricted discourse in the white woman informs our interpretation of the possibilities for discourse in the black woman. Mtishta's introduction to English is from a rapist who teaches her *bitch* as the word for woman. Tadene, who is central to the mutiny that overthrows white dominance of the ship, is nevertheless also termed by the new black regime (that Alex reflects) as bitch. Alex reveals himself as substituting one racially defined variety of imperialism for another and as perpetuating male dominance when he reflects, "that dried-up old bitch is the luck I was waiting for" (142).

The outer (third-person) narration orchestrates the manifold voices of the novel and enables each of the repressed voices to disturb the world, first singly and at last (for the blacks) in disharmonious unison. After the berthing, the black women have nowhere to go back to; the white woman has nowhere to go but back.

Hearne's achievement may not be a feminist reading of history, but he does admit readers to an experience—the childbirth trauma—restricted to women. Perhaps it is possible for him to do so precisely because of the first-person narrator's dissociation, which admits Otherness as an aspect of the experience. The extraordinary accuracy of this portrayal by a male author of an exclusively feminine experience can properly be evaluated only by women and indeed only by certain women, those (relatively) few who have experienced prolonged and severe childbirth. That he can do this must give us pause before we reject the birthing/berthing metaphor as just one more example of male stereotyping of women.

Leonie Harris has aptly described *Natives of My Person* as Lamming's testimony of the birth of colonial man (Baugh and Morris 207). Lamming has little to say of the birth of colonial woman or of feminine European miscarriage, although he does present brutal violation of the European woman in *Water with Berries*. Lamming also presents the European woman as sexually exploitative, troubled by glimpses of the horror on which imperial wealth is founded, but appeased with trinkets. The Lady of the House, in *Natives of My Person*, has her price. Hearne's Eliza differs from the Lady of the House in that she cannot be bought off.

In portraying the lady of the ship and her surroundings, Hearne selects realism instead of allegory. He creates complex rather than stereotypical characters and constructs a functioning ship on a sea of which readers are continuously aware, not a nominal vessel. Hearne's commander, Hogarth, is riven by his guilt/gilt dilemma, as are other members of his crew, unlike Lamming's characters, who tend to deny their guilt. By opening the individual pasts of each character, Hearne achieves multidimensional characterization. Hogarth, for example, is by no means an archetypal commandant. His conscience, although inadequate to deter him from exploiting others, at least ensures that he does not rest comfortably in his actions. In a sense this is a lip-service morality that distinguishes wrong from right, does wrong, laments, and continues in wrongdoing. This con(man)science satisfies him that he is doing the honorable thing in making an honest woman of Eliza. Similarly, it enables him to partake in the moral corruption of the flesh trade. In depriving him of his marital "rights" (he is too honorable to rape her), she disrupts traditional power relationships.

Eliza's complexity distinguishes her from the woman whom Lamming identifies as the Lady of the House—woman as whore. Eliza's personal history enlarges the understanding of repression not only by but also within imperial culture without absolving her of responsibility. It admits another voice, requiring attention as critical and unbiased as any other, intersecting ideological moulds with new epistemes.

Holes in Time and the Waste of History

The perspective of simultaneous entrapment and exclusion is facilitated by a system of concentric circles that is *The Sure Salvation*'s universe of the damned. On a vast and motionless ocean circled by the horizon spreads the effluence surrounding the ship, and the ship itself encases within its outer loci of stern, helm, and deck the central and secret horror of its hold. The hold of the *Sure Salvation* extends the dimensions of the composite room/ womb/tomb image that recurs in the rest of the literature.

The hold does more than contain and trap. This *hold* (substantive) is even a separate lexeme to the substantive derived from the verb *hold*. Etymologically, the hold of a ship is an independent development, actually from *hole,* and indeed the hold of the *Sure Salvation* relates paradigmatically to other (thematic) holes—the disruption of natural order, the final innermost abyss of guilt, the black hole in the psyche, and the orifice of a passage that bears death rather than birth. The hold is also the central point in the commerce in flesh, the point at which wealth becomes filth. The narrative mirrors this perspective of global history in a personal history, that of Hogarth's traffic with Eliza and the tormented stillbirth of their child, "laid beyond resurrection in unconsecrated ground, strangled by its own mother's cord and broken in the breach" (185–86). The relationship of cabin/hold/hole is variously reflected in the captain's quarters and Reynolds's cabin.

The concentric circles that reinforce stasis and circularity of action both entrap and exclude. They are related to the central question of responsibility through the image of defilement, both in the surrounding circle of effluence and in the waste (multiple meanings) of the central hold. The pervasiveness of the image is at once apparent when the lexical terms in the semantic field are collected. Terms semantically associated with waste abound in *The Sure Salvation.* Terms associated with refuse, filth, and corruption are associated with sustenance through polysemy in such terms as *mess* and *swill* and through metaphors for waste such as "small pudding of shit" (44). Waste and corruption are associated with trade in the phrase *dirty trade* but also in longer expressions: "it's your fortune you're sniffing" (40); "the one you and I have just disposed of over the side" (56); "they're the leavin's and scrapin's of the world" (118); "only the final dismissal by men who had looked on me as a friend who would enhance their fortunes, the refused flesh of a woman who has once offered herself to me . . . and now a cargo that I would have repudiated ten years ago" (167). Waste and corruption are further associated with deterioration of character in those involved in such an enterprise: "If he's correct my life has been a waste" (146).

The cumulative effect of the items in this field and the unpleasant incidents and situations that are their contexts are offensive yet understate reality. Indeed, unmitigated realism might have been unbearable, and Hearne frequently sidesteps the grossness of reality through the alternative shock of the surreal, a Bosch-like misshaping of figures or exaggerated comparisons that suggest the outrageous without portraying it in extended detail. Thus we glimpse Reynolds's personality: "When they laid Christ on the cross, he was the one laughing as the nails went in" (57). Against the inhibitions of Hogarth and the narrative restraint associated with his point of view and even with Alex's, the documentation of Reynolds's mind is harrowing. Yet the grotesque inversion of values that he exposes and even flaunts before the reader demonstrates intelligence, brutalized by sheer greed and spiritual decomposition. The slave girl's thoughts, in confrontation with his, testify to a value system that she has managed to preserve intact, and her ordered and civilized consciousness highlights his moral degradation.

In a number of content domains various polarities seem inherent—polarities between, say, savagery and civilization, order and disorder, life and death. It might be expected that these opposites should mesh into an orderly semantic matrix with such constructions as value and valuelessness, broken down perhaps into wealth and poverty, worth and worthlessness, food and excrement. In *The Sure Salvation* such oppositions collapse, as is especially obvious in the horrible intertwining of symbolism for food and excrement. Once again binarism oversimplifies the distinction between value and worthlessness, between civilization and savagery. For example, the text proposes quite early that only the barbaric mind demands and accepts human sacrifice (9). But the captain recognizes this fact even as the slaves moan below deck, so Hogarth's definition of his civilization is from the first grounded on savagery, and his intellectual attempt to redefine himself from outcast to civilized man is as unsuccessful "as though he were salvaging a fragile artifact from the chaos of a midden" (12).

Both the captain and the crew repeatedly meditate on the issue of responsibility for the passage of events. The accounts of the British seamen express varying views on the command of their superiors, and Old Calder takes security in reminiscences about the experienced control of ships, past and present, by their captains. Shifts in responsibility, with sudden reversals of power, produce the incongruities that contribute to cruel humor and the occasional rictus of pleasure superimposed on horror. Such grim comedy reinforces the theme of impropriety. Certainly Hogarth is officially in charge of directing the boat—if only he can get it to move. Within the period of stasis, Reynolds's exaggeratedly frolicsome movements contrast with the terror of immobility and with the ensuing lethargy of the crew. He contrives, he manipulates, he moves others whom no one else can move—until he is decapitated and his head borne from hold to deck.

Of course, the real maneuverer is Alex. More and more it emerges that it is his command, his ship. Indeed, it is his initiative that chose Hogarth. The revelation of paradox in status, the cook's selection of a captain, barely precedes the reversal in rank inscribed by the mutiny and by Alex's performative speech acts at that time. The role reversal revealed by Hogarth's recollections and its associated shifts in pronoun reference parallel the change that takes place in possessive pronouns shortly afterward when Hogarth, in addressing Alex, makes the adjustment from *my ship* to *your ship.*

At the same time, even as Alex seizes power, he denies ultimate responsibility. In his evaluation, events are preassembled and await approach from whatever direction "brought here," as Hogarth perceives it. Indeed, in the end, Alex does not execute the conclusion to his plan. Having intersected Hogarth's intentions with his own and having seized command, Alex finds his ship boarded, seized by Lieutenant Honeyball, who takes it relatively close to where Alex had wanted it to go in any case.

At this point the surviving characters move from varying degrees of power toward helplessness. Eliza, for example, lays belated claim to her husband's sexual attentions, but she is thus restored to good humor by collapse into the total irresponsibility of insanity. In a sense, even this insanity has been prepared beforehand in the interchange between herself and Hogarth about responsible and irresponsible actions.

Conflicting perspectives in the claustrophobic setting of the ship intersect to produce a glimpse of the grotesque in history, a horror made more excruciating by its comic dimensions. The novel conveys mental and social imbalance by departing from conventions. Hearne establishes his shifting outcast perspectives by manipulating and at times deviating from linguistic norms. In this way he highlights both individual and group alienation from society and associates them with distorted personal judgment as well as with warped social values.

Thus, Hearne continuously raises new issues regarding the responsibility of each narrative consciousness for the events that take place. The writer alternatively adheres to or departs from what might traditionally be conceived of as a logical thread of narrative discourse, from conventional spatial and temporal frameworks (indicated by such linguistic features as tense and person), or from traditional mores of literary narrative. Because language is both a social phenomenon and rule-governed behavior, individual or social deviance is clearly communicated through deviance in language. Like *The Lunatic, The Sure Salvation* conveys violent distortion in individual perspective and in social values by flouting rules of narrative discourse. Hearne's novel throws history into question by revealing alternative causal relations. The effect is similar to that aptly described by Simon Gikandi, in which "history, instead of being the crucible of fixed meanings, is a source of disorder and neurosis" (178).

Hearne merges the physical setting with the psychological and portrays social and individual distortion through unorthodox manipulation of those features of discourse that normally anchor the point of view of a narrative. Hearne links physical and emotional isolation both naturally and metaphorically. Among the crew becalmed are souls that went adrift long before boarding. This book lacks the straight linkage of kernel narratives as in *Marly* and the parallel interlocking episodes of *Brother Man*. Hearne provides a present of stagnant calm circled with the filth of the past. The present is built on shame, a structure of secret within secret, betrayal within betrayal, violation within violation. The narrative movement is as much inward (psychological) as forward (temporal and spatial). Fastened together in nonrelationships, the characters can only pull outward, away from each other. Yet physically there is nowhere to go. Physical and psychological settings imply this interlock between alienation and claustrophobia. The text conveys the theme of entrapment through a lexical field of terms for imprisonment.

In this setting of exaggerated physical and social constraints and collapsed or skewed moral constraints, violence is not only structurally inherent but also a logical option for survival and self-advancement. The relationship among altered perceptions, skewed dimensions, and violence is explicit (47).

Rule breaking in the form of sudden shifts of reference (as in tense or person) affects legibility of the text at surface level. However, at greater depth such rule breaking increasingly reveals the mental decomposition that takes place within the inescapable social warp of the slave ship. Similarly, the flouting of pragmatic norms signals psychological disturbance. Eliza's sexuality below deck reawakens ludicrously, out of the shock of mutiny and gruesome dismemberment on deck. These syntagmatically as well as paradigmatically linked developments place a strain on Hogarth that creates a fusion of humor and horror incongruous enough to thwart the natural expectations of the reader: " 'God send me strength,' he said to himself as he rose from the chair" (203). This too is rule breaking. It flouts the cooperative principle that links speaker and hearer in a maintenance of rules (in this case pragmatic rules) that ensure intelligibility. The reader shares the inversions of experience and reversals of perspective that disturb Hogarth, "as though forcing him to make an adjustment of his imagination and understanding to the reflections cast on the wall of a *camera obscura* across which his now unpossessable expectations passed, in image, upside down" (202).

Eventually, as Eliza parts with her husband, she not only is insensitive to his fate but also has lost touch with those episodes of the past that have brought her to the unthinkable present: " 'Now remember, William,' Eliza Hogarth said gaily as she hugged and kissed her handcuffed husband, 'we must be back in England before the end of August. Father'll be needing help with the harvest, and I don't know how we will manage without you to keep an eye on things. He just cannot *command* prompt obedience as you can, my dear' " (221). Yet here text coherence becomes most apparent, weaving the levels of their past to present and future and highlighting contrasts between disordered perception (*command*) and reality (*handcuffed*), between expectation and inevitability. Lexical foregrounding highlights incongruity (*gaily*) as does phonological cohesion such as /g/ in *gaily* and *hugged* or /h/ in *hugged* and *handcuffed*.

The Sure Salvation is a study of the different faces of insanity that alienation can produce. Reynolds's mind (filth heaving upward) establishes his distance from civilized behavior in terms of moral depravity. Eliza's mind (barricading her emotions until every support disintegrates) defines her exclusion from normal intercourse as a sterile obsession with past wrongs, as entrapment in the role of the victim. Hogarth's persistently rational mind is nevertheless bruised by his moral and social decline and stagnated by guilt. Indeed, as the parameters between sanity and insanity collapse, who is to determine that Hogarth is sane merely because he is rational? The ship is at the same time a world, a society, an island, and a mind whose pathological deviance is unmasked through rule flouting in discourse.

Hearne flouts other rules when he replaces stereotypes of the creole black with a politically incorrect or at least questionable creation. Alex, the opportunist, seizes power wherever he finds it—though not with Hogarth's sense of birthright or with Reynolds's maniacal irresponsibility. Alex is exploitative but relatively humane, ruthless without "unnecessary" cruelty. As the product of exploitation, he is that totally unpredictable factor of a joint venture, the man without obligations. From his creole perspective, the blacks are no more his people than the whites. Both Africans and Europeans traded in his past. He identifies no society to appease, no culture to cling to, no family to live up to, no loyalty of class or race, and no constraint but choice.

Another curious figure in this meshwork of outsiders is the brown clerk in the Abari town. Weddington, whose name Honeyball cannot remember, falls outside of the group for which anyone has responsibility and outside of the group that has power. He is to wait for the return of "the *sahibs*," the "real people" (222–23), as Honeyball describes the governor and "every white man, woman and child" (220). Pronouns establish possession as the base for maintaining order. Honeyball addresses Weddington in these terms referring to the *sahibs* as "your . . . your . . . your real people" and the blacks as "all yours now" (223). To the end, possession remains associated with evaluative terms that suggest material worth. Honeyball recommends Alex as Weddington's aide, a role in which Alex promises to be "invaluable." Weddington completes the web of social and ethnic variation in the novel.

The landfall itself completes spatial and temporal variables, constituting the third point of the triangle and the locus for an emergent society. This conclusion to the passage constitutes a beginning by abandonment on a new shore and fuses past and present.

In *The Sure Salvation*, as in other recent Jamaican novels, is that touch of the avant-garde that defeats expectations, that invites enemies through rule flouting, that forces a fight through implied overstatement of negatives. These novels represent reality by slashing the canvas and by attacking the discourse itself (see Gass 91). Current Jamaican writers interfere with those features of discourse that anchor it in a single, stable perspective of one reliable speaker. Where *Marly* was deviant only in its internal fractured logic, Hearne logically redisperses dimensions of space and time and disrupts orthodox narrative structure. Anthony Winkler logically dispenses with pragmatic rules and unravels normal processes of characterization to substitute new and outlandish ones. Thus, he plays with notions of speaker reliability to invert values through antithesis between text and context. Hearne, too, unmasks reality by deconstructing it. He ends with a composite view of exploitation and counterexploitation (racial and sexual) as ultimately destructive. The self-sacrifice of Hogarth's parents, his own dangling body, and the ledger in which greed balances human life in monetary terms all come together to compose his perpetual, soiled, and tortured now of a vessel becalmed.

To step outside of a time and space that is thought of as Jamaican is not to abandon the search for its history. Pouchet Paquet shows how, in *The Emigrants*, Lamming reproduces a colonial mentality that begins to disintegrate as it encounters the metropolis (32), and Gikandi indicates how this disintegration "raises the possibility of a pan-Caribbean identity" (95). Recent Jamaican literature reasserts nationalist and individualist identities, even as it reaffirms shared experience of dispossession. In addition, Hearne proposes a global responsibility for pan-exploitation and diaspora. To do so, he moves beyond an increasingly common Caribbean deconstruction of colonial vision, and he revises Western black consciousness, of which the Jamaican consciousness is a microcosm. Edouard Glissant emphasizes the "real discontinuity beneath the apparent continuity" of Caribbean history (91), and

Hearne (like Derek Walcott, Wilson Harris, and others) resists the European model of history as anchored on notions of progress and temporal closure. However, in countering European history, Caribbean ideologies have provided their own blockades that must also be navigated by Jamaican writers (cf. Glissant 62).

Some Caribbean stereotypes constrain critical expectations. Frank Birbalsingh views Hearne as essentially escapist and describes his Cayuna novels as failing to deal with real and provocative issues in Jamaican society, especially in the treatment of political issues of race and color consciousness. He asserts that Hearne displays the conditions that encourage people to revolt but that "nothing happens, and the objectionable social conditions remain tantalisingly unchanged" (44). However, Hearne appears to be proposing that although history has been haunted by revolt, this endemic violence has never significantly changed the objectionable social conditions. This stasis may exist precisely because more of the actors of history are jointly responsible for these conditions than is normally suggested by Caribbean stereotypes. Moreover, the stasis on and around the becalmed ship on which nothing happens (and on and around the frozen psyche of Eliza) highlights the violence of change in several dimensions. The most obvious alteration is the mutiny, but it parallels the wider (global) moral revolution that abolishes the slave trade as well as the technological revolution that effectively ends even the illegal trade. Individual ambitions intersect in the power struggles aboard ship, mirroring the political tensions that lock the fates of three continents in patterns of cause and effect that defy simple chronological narrative.

Hearne's reconstruction of Western history departs from a politically correct stance that valorizes the black, the poor, and the exploited as a single entity. Hearne explores new aspects of marronage by presenting alternatives to verbally affected ideas on class, race, and gender that comprise subsumed propaganda in the modern Caribbean. His discourse undermines the language of slogans, the anesthetic style and bogus rationality that have entrenched in nationalist discourse a romanticized view of race and class traits and their relationship with issues of gender. To grasp the extent to which Hearne deviates from entrenched perspectives, it is necessary to reflect briefly on such current stereotyping.

Nationalist discourse in the Caribbean has been deeply influenced by a rhetoric of negritude, whose sources are as widespread (globally) as the African diaspora itself. In Jamaica, oral discourse on negritude has been further influenced not only by oral traditions of folk culture but also, more recently, by those of black music culture. Jamaica has exported this culture through reggae music and has imported black American equivalents. Elsewhere in the Caribbean, current Jamaican dance-hall music (regularly known as Dansehall) has captivated youth and influenced their language. Parents commonly complain of being unable to understand a word of it, which may well account for its relative lack of restriction.

In valorizing the ghetto, much Dansehall justifies violent resistance to black poverty and exploitation. At the same time, however, the competition between immensely successful performers expresses itself in terms of braggadocio and violent challenge. Oral influences of Dansehall and American rap perpetuate and strengthen stereotypes such as that of the black male as superhuman lover and in so doing entrench attitudes destructive to women. Rhetoric epitomizing the woman as vessel receives little feminist rebuke in the midst of politically correct praise for Afro-Jamaican culture. Dansehall also reinforces the significance of territories dominated by aggressive adventurers. The hero of modern youth culture in Jamaica is the *rudeboy*, the *yardie*, or the *black-I*, who resists those who "oppress I-an-I black bredda" and who are not "inna de struggle." Dansehall entrenches popular stereotypes by uncritical recycling of catchphrases; indeed, the recycling of lyrics is one characteristic feature of the genre. At the same time, Dansehall challenges conventions such as taboos by flooding the airwaves with topics and terms hitherto restricted. Indeed, *explicit lyrics* has itself become a catch phrase in some performances. Radical opposition to imperial discourse is thus, of itself, no longer avant-garde in the Caribbean but popular and even riddled with cliché.

In a sense, Hearne counters such entrenched counterdiscourse by reconstructing a community in which all classes and races are forced into contact as in history. The community reflects, in microcosm, characteristic Jamaican intersections of social boundaries defined by class, race, and gender. Within this construct, Hearne deromanticizes the past and deconstructs even sacred stereotypes of the exploited black victim without denying the reality of that exploitation but recreating it afresh in the horror of the ship's hold. He further explodes the stereotype of the amoral white adventurer without denying immorality but adding depth to perception by creating the outlandishly and gleefully vile Reynolds alongside the guilt-ridden Hogarth. Three women respond to their confinements in widely divergent ways. Hearne introduces, as a new and unpredictable product of the trade, the creole who is ruthless in his determination to survive and profit. Finally, he posits the mulatto man as marooned, echoing stereotypical British discourse even as Britain abandons him: "*I say, sir! You can't leave me like this*" (224).

Hearne places these conflicts of human history parallel to those of natural history, as part of a struggle for survival, an ongoing, amoral test of fitness that is part of the natural world. References to Darwinian theory and its surrounding controversy form some part of the propositions that compose the nineteenth-century setting.

In addition to the alternation between the internal perspectives of individual characters, there is extensive shifting between internal and external perspectives. Indeed, even within external narration (where the narrator remains outside of his characters' minds) shifts occur between closely detailed description and withdrawn, detached record. For example, narration changes to external perspective to describe the movement of the ship and the reactions of the crew. Within this external narration the tone alternates to one of cold detached report to record initiation of the actual mutiny with almost exaggerated objectivity. This perspective backgrounds some of the gruesome details through the use of parentheses (194). A balance in narration between minute observation and global vision ensures a transformation of history that is both meticulous and sweeping.

Through such alternations in perspective, Hearne deconstructs history by redistributing responsibility—which does not mean that he absolves or even diffuses responsibility. He does, however, reassess entrenched assumptions about blame. The ship's name, the *Sure Salvation,* underscores the obvious irony of a morally damnable enterprise whose goal is material salvation, an enterprise that fails, ensuring that its participants are legally condemned. At the same time, the voyage of the *Sure Salvation* concludes with Honeyball's ambiguous assessment of the town on the Abari: "There isn't a damned person in that village they call a town" (220).

Hearne offers alternative perspectives on the facts of the past by approaching history through fiction and specifically through the genre of the sea story. In Fleischman's view, narrative itself constitutes "one of our most basic and powerful hermeneutic constructs for making sense of the data of experience" (314), and in this role Hearne employs that type of fictional narrative most commonly associated with the tall tale as the natural genre for countering imperial history.

The slave ship operates outside of the sanctions of European civilization. The society that has created and profited from it has declared it illegitimate. Its unsavory operations, directed from such loci as the *poop* and the *mess,* focus on its central hole. The final part of the novel, titled "Seizures," presents internal convulsions of power—as Alex wrests command from Hogarth, and Honeyball (temporarily?) from Alex. It also records the convulsion in Eliza's and Hogarth's marital relationship. In addition, the seizures include external interference at the insistence of social change and natural selection. The turning point of the action itself has been the shift from stasis to movement, the seizure of the ship by the wind. References to Darwin's theory underline and make more poignant the theme of competition for survival. The growing dominance of steam power renders obsolete the control of trade by sail and ensures Hogarth's official condemnation and arrest, quite apart from his earlier overthrow by Alex.

The deanchored perspective enables the author to undermine old certainties and invests the sea story with the open-endedness of history. Moral, philosophical, and theological issues entangle in the inevitability of the outcome, infusing the final events of the book with two notions frequently regarded as conflicting. One is a sense of nature's relentless evolutionary change, impelled by the necessity of survival. The other is a sense of the foreknowledge and immanence of divine intention and its strange permission of evil. The ship itself moves both by the "breath of God" and by uncaring elemental force. The tremor that brings it to life and the answering quiver at the core of the seamen marks the link between human voyaging and the external forces of nature that control the ship. These external, momentous forces of change are the context of human effort. Evil (like Reynolds) is an accidental part of such cosmic necessity—"perhaps even God was not concerned with explaining him" (83). Even Reynolds's perspective, the most distorted, can neither permanently warp truth nor fix historical fact incontrovertibly. Indeed, he recognizes, "The sea will not be moulded into our excremental falsehoods. It will not record the shape of any keel. Christ could walk it to the end of time and leave no more mark of his passage than will this floating barracoon we choose to call a ship" (83).

7

Re-membering the
Marooned Consciousness

> But the trouble with the kumbla is the getting out of the kumbla.
> —Erna Brodber, *Jane and Louisa Will Soon Come Home*

FROM THE FIRST Creole narrative in Jamaican fiction, the literary discourse of Jamaica has conveyed power struggles at personal, community, and national levels. Characteristically, the narrator has internalized social conflict and the narrative involves recollection. "My mind has been a-walk back through the years," remembers Vic Reid's old man in *New Day* (369). But such recollection has different premises to external (imperial) histories of the same events. This local view is the first disruption—the breaking of epistemes. Sylvia Wynter has pointed out that as a consequence of George Lamming having placed *The Tempest* within England's creation of empire, the histories of Caliban and Prospero can no longer be understood from outside of that relationship ("Talk about" 135–36), and in *The Pleasures of Exile*, Lamming amply substantiates this claim through his analysis of C. L. R. James's epic rendering of Toussaint. In Jamaican fiction, literary discourse involves an ongoing struggle for control of the idiom of power, which H. Orlando Patterson defines as "the principal way in which power is immediately interpreted in socially and cognitively acceptable terms" (*Slavery and Social Death* 18).

In *New Day*, whatever the flaws of its narrative, Reid initiates the inherently revolutionary thrust of Caribbean writing by rewriting imperial "nonfiction" regarding the Morant Bay Rebellion. The passage of this information between the John Campbells, the eighty-seven-year-old grandfather and the eight-year-old child, is a transmission of oral testimony, unfiltered by colonial judgment. This process brings a new immediacy to history, a new authenticity (of the eyewitness), a new trust (in the kin), a new authority (of the ancestor).

With *The Hills of Hebron*, Wynter ushers in a further epistemic disruption. This novel focuses on a vision of a maroon (not Maroon) community in the mountains, a breakaway community whose core is a millennial vision of a black elect. The leader, Moses, is a deluded prophet of enormously convincing spirituality but, in the end, desperate for material life rather than spiritual achievement. The recognition that kills his spirit comes as he hangs dying on a cross of his own choosing on Easter Sunday. This fatal revelation is that "God is white after all. . . . God is white!" (223). The myth of a black God survives Moses, only to entomb with him the hope of the community. The community fails to realize that freedom entails more than separation and more than a simple inversion of beliefs. It requires a restoration of memory and the ability for indigenous creation. Hope begins when Obadiah connects with his ancestral past and carves a future unmediated by colonial epistemes.

Authorial doctrine intrudes in the novel not only unfortunately but unnecessarily. Without this intrusive voice the narrative powerfully conveys its criticism of repressive worldviews that appear to oppose but, in fact, merely complement each other. The bitter Irish doctor at the asylum is anticolonial but imposes the very ideology he claims to reject, for he regards Moses as his man Friday (132). The local judges and barristers, proud of their independence, are "all black clowns striking postures in a circus of civilization. And both barristers worked out their frustrations on the prisoner, attacking him for being black and stupid and not knowing the white man's ways, not talking like him, not hiding his black madness under a wig and gown as they had done" (128).

In its recognition of a tendency to substitute one form of self-deception for another, the novel presents a grim picture of betrayal within betrayal—betrayal of black by white and black by black, of the individual by the community, of nature by civilization, of humanity by God, of woman by man. However, the novel also begins a movement up and out. The story begins and ends with women rocking children cradled in their arms. At first, the child is illusory, the mother having dissociated herself from unthinkable loss. The conclusion brings a real and perfect living child, reconciliation even after rape, paralleling a movement to rain after drought, to singing after weeping, to building after falling.

In Jamaican fiction a concern for retrieving children has developed in curious relationship to the theme of marronage. Some feminist concerns relate to the treatment of this theme, but the escape of children is an interest common to widely different authors. Jean D'Costa's *Escape to Last Man's Peak* conveys an idyllic yet forbidding grandeur of mountains that draw small fugitives to impenetrable refuges. Conversely, Namba Roy's "sparrows" trek in the opposite direction, only to find themselves devoid of refuge after leaving the mountains (*No Black Sparrows*). Roy's novel of internal conflict in a Maroon society (*Black Albino*) concludes with a fragmentary community of children reunited with the parent community.

The Hills of Hebron conveys marronage at the level of the community, of the individual adult, and of the child by highlighting binary oppositions similarly to Roy's *Black Albino*. However, the setting of *Black Albino* is a literal (though fictional) Maroon community, whereas Hebron is maroonlike but never identified with actual Maroons. Contrast with *Black Albino* throws light on *The Hills of Hebron*, published only a year after Roy's novel.

As a descendent of Maroons and heir to the oral traditions of Accompong village, Roy had direct experience of the Maroon setting, but such realism as naturally follows from this experience contrasts with his presentation, which is highly stylized in language and in textual structure. Edward Kamau Brathwaite unfavorably compares *Black Albino* with novels depicting mixed motives and internal conflict in complex characters. However, Brathwaite also criticizes Wilson Harris's exploration of marronage, ancestry, and filiation in *The Secret Ladder* as misconceiving the Maroon in terms of a cruel abortion of freedom and overemotional negritude (Brathwaite, "African Presence" 88, and cf. Ramchand, *West Indian Novel* 149–53). Maroon legend and history are as fraught with emotionalism as with violence, especially in their ritual celebration of racial loyalty, and Roy's novel acknowledges these powerful forces even while evading extremes of intimate involvement that realism might have evoked. Wynter's tale of a breakaway community in the mountains similarly conveys emotional celebration of racial loyalty.

In *Black Albino*, there is stereotyping through unrelieved binaries of good and evil, straight and deformed, mountain and plain, black and white. However, there are also tensions of withdrawal and exclusion, of expulsion and persecution, and of tribalism and internal fragmentation involving violent resistance that is both outward and inward turned. Among Roy's characters, stark as allegorical figures, is a child whose whiteness is only skin deep. It is a curious tale of marronage within marronage, the village isolated by impenetrable forests and mountain declines, and within this setting the family relegated to its own small dwelling. Then there is the alternative new tribe of children physically separated and within this group the albino—an outcast by virtue of a new problem of skin, the possibility of *cocobay* (Jamaican leprosy).

Roy's novel romanticizes marronage through the stereotype of black as warrior, and in doing so the story sharply delineates moral oppositions yet is not without implied conflicts. Idealism is in fact the downfall of the chief and a flaw in his political acumen. Personal conscience conflicts destructively with the good of the tribe and even with the good of the central family. When the child withdraws to avoid spreading *cocobay* to others of his tribe and they follow and reclaim him, they are themselves found and reclaimed by the great chief. Finding them restores the chief, in turn, from his mental isolation in a past haunted by his dead wife. The novel both celebrates the romanticized past and dissects the vulnerabilities of tribalism and romanticism.

Here, as elsewhere in Jamaican literature, the mountains offer the only real possibility of physical escape, but they also impose claustrophobia, demand endurance, prompt guerrilla-type resistance, and separate heroic characters from the constraints of laws pertaining to the larger society. The rockbound heart of the island also mirrors the toughness of the poor and deprived. In *Black Albino*, however, marronage exacts an endurance that crushes the mother (Kisanka) and resigns her to defeat. Increasingly overcome by isolation and hostility, she withdraws even from the family into growing dissociation. Always her husband's "Little Shadow," she dematerializes completely through death to become a spiritual companion with whom he grows obsessed.

In *The Hills of Hebron*, Wynter creates a feminine character who is isolated even from her separationist community but who is concrete and militant. The breakaway sect is more claustrophobic than Roy's in its rigid regulation of its members' lifestyles. Like Roy's, Wynter's novel focuses on small-scale history—that of family and village chronicle and of rural events rather than that of national and specifically urban history—but it maintains the metaphorical connection between these smaller and larger scales of social evolution. Lemuel Johnson has pointed to feminist reaction against a stereotype of woman as ruined and ruinous fecundity (113), and Wynter's Gatha is an early example of the nontypical traditional woman. Her symbol of independence is an apron, and her hope in the future lies in her child, yet, unlike Roy's Kisanka, she demonstrates her ability to wield power that is essentially political. Her interest in this power is to preserve it for her son, but the fact that her hold on power is essentially a matter of choice empowers her further.

Janice Lee Liddell sees Wynter as dealing with a mother-as-victim syndrome (322), where Gatha's struggle conforms to a cosmic plan, a fanatical commitment to her son's destiny. In Liddell's view, this commitment entraps Gatha in the small enclosure of motherhood and so is a tragic flaw in an otherwise imposing, self-assured Caribbean woman. Isaac's revelation that he "is not coming back" destroys her: "Her mind could not reach beyond this" (256). Liddell's interpretation of this commitment as a tragic flaw rests on her own philosophy that Gatha's fulfillment should not be "inherently connected to the fulfillment of others" (330). However, some women insist that this connection is essential and that to fail to accept this fact is to dismiss all such women of traditional values as little shadows. Because Gatha's other abilities are obvious to all, her commitment to motherhood becomes a matter of choice.

Gatha's political leadership is a coming out from obscurity to recognition and from self-denial to self-affirmation, for "she had been too long shut away in the silence of the defeated not to spread her wings in the rare sunlight of triumph" (48). Unlike Roy's Kisanka, who embraces her status as her husband's "Little Shadow," Wynter's Gatha is one of many black female protagonists who appear to be emancipated by widowhood. (The protagonists of Zora Neale Hurston's *Their Eyes Were Watching God* and Paule Marshall's *Praisesong for the Widow* are obvious examples.) This inference is unpleasant but understandable in the light of her experience of Moses. Moses chooses Gatha in the first place at least partially because of her differences from the other women, but eventually he repeatedly humiliates her with infidelities that she must apologize for suspecting. Her ability to see through him and also past him into a future independent of muddled vision demonstrates her intelligence and locates her tragic flaw as a blind spot, an inability to detect her son's disaffection. Political leadership renders her visible to others, but she has always been there and been real, and her self-assertion is a willed appearance: "But they had taken no more positive notice of her than a man takes of his shadow. Then all at once she was there, enforcing respect" (19). However, Gatha lays hold on their respect to preserve it for her son.

Gatha's vision of the future is essentially pragmatic and recalls *myalist* philosophy. *Myalism* views sin as an offense not so much against God as against society, and in this context resistance (to social injustice) can be seen as the work of God or, at any rate, as contributing to the life of the spirit (Schuler 36, 37, 44). Interestingly, Monica Schuler notes that the postemancipation exodus from plantations throughout the island caused settlements to spring up in the bush and often in inaccessible upland areas. Here "capricious rainfall" caused hardships that triggered *myalist* revival as a response to perverse social conditions (38–40). The prophetic and millennial terms that merge religious activity and social reaction in *The Hills of Hebron* are consistent with a *myalist* claim to be an elect people, setting to right a world in confusion.

Wynter's own critical stance involves a vision of literary history as a series of epistemic shifts. In this view, a Euro-Christian image of God gives way to the human image as a natural organism. This Renaissance vision, which later develops to a scientific explanation for humanity, is still a teleological evolution—its end no longer prescribed by God but still constrained by nature. In Wynter's view, the shift from the religious to the secular (from the values of the spirit to those of the flesh) gives way under colonialism to still newer epistemic binaries whose point of departure is not merely patriarchal but monarchial, a separation of humans (rational) from natives (non-rational). This view is essentially a separation of civilized and centered human from Other, the "vile race" of Caliban, whom Wynter describes as "dys-elected" by nature ("Afterword: Beyond" 361). In *The Hills of Hebron*, a small group of the dys-elected declare themselves elect, declaring a government that is native rather than colonial and rural rather than national and urban. They initially justify themselves in spiritual and patriarchal terms, but Gatha's leadership effectively disrupts their rule by introducing alternative perspectives, human and social rather than spiritual, feminine or androgynous rather than masculine.

Additionally, Gatha's vision is not self-focused but leads to the future through the child. Other perceptions in the novel identify children as extensions of self, but Gatha chooses to retrieve the future for the child rather than for herself. The terrible irony of *The Hills of Hebron* is that the child wants a quite different future. Isaac breaks away from the remote claustrophobic community to build his own life elsewhere. However, it is an escape clouded in moral ambiguity. In putting behind him the rural village, smothering mother, and dead-end existence, he enters an urban maze and confronts, for the first time, the enigmatic and limiting sea. Furthermore, he leaves at the expense of his mother and of the community, with stolen money. His past remains unreconciled and his resistance unfocused. The novel ends on a note of hope for Gatha but not for Isaac.

Several writers react against "strange mad mutations of maternal desire" (cf. Johnson's discussion of Cliff, 138). The recurrent metaphorical association of mother-child relationships with colonialism makes the theme politically significant. In addition, the tendency to frame such discourse as a series or mesh of recollections often produces discontinuity in narrative. *The Hills of Hebron* is not a chronological sequence of recollections by a solitary consciousness but a tale told by an unlimited third-person narrator who shifts between the perspectives of different characters and who is indistinct from the author in intrusive commentary. Unlike Roy, who delivers the events of his saga in chronological order, Wynter rearranges events to an order other than their chronological sequence in which they can illustrate her polemic. Her novel does not require a stylized dialogue to separate her characters from the creole community because she does not portray a community of relatively unbroken African tradition but a local community searching for forgotten roots. Wynter's interference with traditional narrative structure, despite her adherence to English, supports an underlying argument that is, in a sense, a critique of colonial history and an indigenous remembering.

The tendency to convey ideological perspective through fragmented discourse increases in more recent literature. Michelle Cliff's recollection of childhood—specifically feminine childhood—parallels a historical quest for the mother that runs counter to dismembering visions of other writers. Johnson contrasts Cliff's mythos of female wholeness in Jamaica with the landscape that Derek Walcott presents in *The Star-Apple Kingdom*, which will yield sweetness "only . . . upon being ravished" (Johnson 130). Yet Cliff's vision dismembers in other ways, as she retrieves her childhood through remembered pain and attacks epistemes and stereotypes by slashing at the discourse itself.

Cliff looks back through the guilt of light-colored, wavy-haired, middle-class upbringing "to try to see when the background changed places with the foreground. To try and locate the vanishing point where the lines of perspective converge and disappear. Lines of color and class. Lines of history and social context. Lines of denial and rejection. When did *we* (the light-skinned middle-class Jamaicans) take over from *them* as oppressors?" (*The Land of Look Behind* 62). To evaluate conscious efforts to retrieve the past by breaking the lines, it is necessary to have a sense of what these lines represent and how they have defined cultural stereotypes.

Dismembering Stereotypes

In many ways, stereotypes may be regarded as line figures, for they are flat, ready-made out of presupposition, and lacking in perspective. To speak of literary stereotypes is to presuppose a canon, and to identify such stereotypes as emerging in Caribbean literature is to recognize a Caribbean canon. Major lines of demarcation in Caribbean society are those of race, and unsurprisingly, racial stereotypes are most obvious. Kenneth Ramchand's seminal discussion of Caribbean literature selects race as the initial parameter for classification, but he shrugs it off as a "boring socio-literary phenomenon" (178). Less obvious and more interesting are the intersections of race with other dimensions, such as class, gender, and age.

The vision of whites as a group that left nothing but ruin was early entrenched—by whites themselves. As Ramchand points out, Charles Leslie's eighteenth-century account conveys the philistine state of the ruling classes, as do more sympathetic yet equally damning descriptions by Edward Long and Bryan Edwards. Nineteenth-century British novels such as *Marly* and *Montgomery* reinforce the view of corrupt white society, as do early Jamaican fictions such as "Busha's Mistress" and, in this century, Herbert G. De Lisser's *White Witch of Rosehall.* The terrified consciousness that Ramchand has pointed out as linking novels such as Jean Rhys's *Wide Sargasso Sea,* Phyllis Shand Allfrey's *The Orchid House,* and Geoffrey Drayton's *Christopher* has become one aspect of a recognizable type, the white elite compelled by greed but tensed on the verge of black revolt.

The expectation of rebellion itself entrenched a stereotype of the African warrior, and sentimental Caribbean versions of negritude have romanticized the African past and contributed to the vision of blacks as magnificently powerful and inherently warlike. At the same time, denial of African culture and, in particular, African religion, produced the type of the fraudulent and self-serving obeahman whose power is merely deceptive.

What Ramchand has described as the peculiar position of stress in which the coloreds find themselves—rejected by whites and by blacks—has resulted in its own stereotypes. Not only does Ramchand recognize the flaws of novels that fail to develop characterization beyond the unstable mulatto or the colored woman as "socially insecure and sexually over-charged" (45), but he also falls into the trap himself by oversimplifying the motivations of a complex group when he comments that "it was the Coloureds who first began to tread the weary road to Whiteness" (40). Jamaica, unlike Trinidad and Guyana, has no mass of East Indian or aboriginal people and culture, and it is not possible to distinguish its nonwhite voices essentially on the basis of ethnicity. Even within more ethnically complex societies, such distinctions may be misleading. Wilson Harris warns against distilling Caribbean ancestry in search of purity, even as Walcott early voiced the dilemma inherent in Caribbean heritage: "Where shall I turn, divided to the vein?" ("A Far Cry from Africa," *In a Green Night* 18). The Jamaican brown disrupts black-white binarism and complexifies the entanglement of class and race issues.

The intersection of social parameters with racial parameters has naturally associated social protest with the lifestyle of the black urban poor and equated realism with the portrayal of the slum. In general, this phenomenon has excluded coloreds from consideration or predetermined their treatment. Rural settings have less sharply defined class and race stereotypes, although interest has centered almost exclusively on the folk. In rural settings, too, age differences have constituted crucial determinants of character, and links between character evolution and family history have deepened characterization. Yet the country and village setting, like the town, echoes with types— such as the matriarch/grandmother and the left child. Similarly, traditional gender roles have shaped stereotypes recognized and described by numerous critics—stereotypes such as the outcast woman (whore or witch), like woman as undiscovered country to be ravished (see, for example, O'Callaghan 98; Johnson 118). But gender stereotypes have also intersected those of race and class.

Cliff's *Abeng* intertwines personal and national history in a cross-generic re-membering of the feminine body. She mixes history with fiction, autobiography, and ideological exposition not by interweaving the generic types but by laying fragments of their different fabric side by side. *Re-membering* in Cliff's writing is a recollection of childhood for recovery of her self and for the inscription into history of the Maroon warrior, Nanny, as national mother.

The Maroon heritage in Jamaica has always been, in many ways, a subtext to imperial history because marronage begins with departure and separation from the dominant community. In totality, this Maroon heritage elicits a reading of the past that is cumulative and intertextual because the weight of traditional record can neither be rejected nor be blindly accepted but must continue to be rewritten from the alternative perspectives available through the Jamaican experience. This cumulative, folk-oriented, and historically unofficial and uncodified vision has much in common with knowledge available through an oral tradition. Indeed, such traditions remain pivotal in the preservation of culture among Maroons, a group unexposed to formal education. But even beyond this debt to Maroon traditions it is true that, in Jamaica, the nature of current popular understanding of the Maroons preserves this quality of orality, of accumulated snippets of learning and hearsay. What is particularly curious is that even the written corpus comprises a patchwork of records in differing genres and from varying perspectives and that modern counterdiscursive histories project this cumulative and saga-like quality.

Cliff's *Abeng*, a novel, closely mirrors her earlier work, *The Land of Look Behind*, at several points, although the latter is a composite of verse and prose history, social commentary, and autobiography. *Abeng* interweaves oral and scribal traditions into a variety of genres. The novel is heavily ideological, its author's voice freely intruding with overt commentary. Many of these authorial interpolations are historical and can only be validated as part of the novel by reference to the vitality of Maroon history and myth.

The survival of Maroon communities as a sociohistorical phenomenon of Jamaica and the preservation of African traditions within these communities constitute a sort of cultural fossilization. However, the product is not a dry and crumbling remnant but a saga that combines haunting memory and powerful myth with verifiable fact, peopled by characters who defy moral definition. The setting is a past that requires toughness and cunning above all else in its protagonists because the goal of all their efforts is survival and the purpose of struggle is freedom. The Maroon legacy to popular culture thus applauds and romanticizes a particular type of hero—tough, violent, and what Jamaicans describe as *trickify*. The characteristic perspective is of a consciousness at once locked out and locked in. Cliff's ultimate perspective (in *No Telephone to Heaven*) is one of guerrilla resistance and (throughout her work) of resistance to a past that the writer considers fraudulent.

The characters of *Abeng* are stark silhouettes on a past of which they are ignorant. The name of the light-colored child, Clare, does not surprise. Clare's father, who is obsessed with his own whiteness, preserves the family name of Savage—a name fully justified by information regarding his ancestry and by overt commentary. The narrator explains that "the definition of what a Savage was like was fixed by color, class and religion, and over the years a carefully contrived mythology was constructed, which they used to protect their identities" (29). Indeed this inventiveness reaches far beyond the family past, for Mr. Savage fabricates geohistory to account for Jamaica itself. Pale, pealing pictures of the European past, patterned into deteriorating wallpaper, surround the child. Besides, Clare finds herself crowded by the actual consequences of that past—the isolation of maids, the dividing lines between black children and herself. The danger to Clare comes from a background that can "slide so easily into the foreground" (28). The lines are imprisoning, as is her father's conviction that he is one of the elect and that by extension Clare is also: "Her fate was sealed" (45). Her father reinforces the child's increasing separation from her self by referring to her as if she is not present, and she "had heard herself referred to in the third person so often by now, she almost began to think that they were talking about someone else" (147).

Her family effectively isolates Clare from her Other self, her black friend, Zoe, so that their physical and social separation can never be repaired. Images of near-white and black girls bathing and arguing beside a pool on a rural property recur in *Abeng* with intensifying echoes of *Wide Sargasso Sea.* Eventually Clare's entrapment in guilt-riddled memory inverts Antoinette's stricken recollection of how Tia finally betrays and rejects her, for "that night Clare dreamed . . . that she picked up a stone and hit Zoe underneath the eye and a trickle of blood ran down her friend's face and onto the rock where she sat" (165).

For Cliff, this isolation is essentially two dimensional. She presents the problems as those of race and homophobia. The dimension of race subsumes that of class and alienates white (and fair) from black by feelings of revulsion and terror. Cliff inscribes race in uppercase as she records the history of racial attitudes in the white Savage family: "To have a nation of Black freedmen, the justice thought, would be like wearing a garment—he searched his mind for an analogy—a garment dipped in the plague" (45). Blacks too, reject whites with a violence that the text appears to justify. Inez, an ancestral figure, aborts the mixed-up baby that results from *buckra-rape* and that therefore has no soul. In the process she demonstrates her independence of men as the abortion merges into lesbian intercourse, later to be commemorated in the orchid image and scattered references to tongue, orifice, and juice.

Thus, Cliff adopts not only stereotypes of race but of gender, for as men are essentially exploitative in *Abeng,* they are also essentially white. Men in any other forms are essentially emasculated, like Clare's senile and impotent grandfather, whose display of his private parts revolts the child—not because she is embarrassed but because of what she recalls as the sheer ugliness of the organ itself. In this sense, in the process of re-membering woman, Cliff's anti-imperialist rage effects the dismemberment of man, as is epitomized in the shooting of the bull (to give but one instance).

Cliff affirms and welcomes the rage of exiles. In *The Land of Look Behind* she explains, "I came into closer contact with my rage, and a realization that rage could fuel and shape my work. As a light-skinned colonial girlchild, both in Jamaica and in the Jamaican milieu of my family abroad, rage was the last thing expected of me" (15). The end result is that feminine re-membering is frustrated in Cliff, who stands, according to Paula Morgan, "poised here between the greenworld of retreat which transcends history, and the apocalyptic destruction which is at the culmination of the historical process. The issue is what to make of a character who supposedly enters into both" (63).

Inevitable reactions to history, concentrated in such anti-imperialist rage but also apparent in other (related) protest, have produced new totems. One of them is the radical. Another, not entirely unrelated, is the autonomous woman as the logical end of reaction against phallicism. An attack on stereotypes does not necessarily free discourse from stereotyping. Subversive discourse having become the rage, new (or simply reverse) epistemes may supplant the old.

Breaking the Weave: Brodber's Revision of the Dissociated Consciousness

Transgressive discourse as a strategy may be constructive and controlled. In *Jane and Louisa Will Soon Come Home,* Erna Brodber teaches that the directionless radical destroys himself and others, that discourse as camouflage not only protects but entraps, that the spider man's fabrications are a means of survival but that they are also lies from which (without effort) one may never emerge. However, Brodber's surpassing achievement is to re-member woman without dismembering man.

To make this claim is to be forced at once to confront the famous snail. The image of male genitalia independent of man as a person (*Jane and Louisa* 28) is no less dismembering than any other in the literature. However, it is the fragmented recollection of a shattered vision whose reassembly constitutes the action of the novel. Baba as well as Aunt Alice assist Nellie out of her *kumbla*. Aunt Alice makes accessible to Nellie the strength of feminine collectivity (sisterhood), while Baba constitutes male support untainted by expectation of sexual reward. Baba refuses the offer of sex from a body and mind that exist in dissociation from each other and from reality. By cooperating in Nellie's re-memberment, Baba heals woman of the need for retaliative male dismemberment that is a backlash of underevaluating her self. In other words, the slime-dripping snail is a figment of Nellie's own hallucinatory self-revulsion that she must overcome by reassembling her life text:

> You ought to have kicked this man out of your room, coming back on all sorts of transparent pretexts. You ought to have torn up the script and backed out. But he paid the taximan what you knew must have been his week's food, so you let him touch you. Shame. . . . But you can't run! How can you? You want to be a woman; now you have a man you'll be like everybody else. You're normal now! Vomit and bear it.
> Wearing my label called woman.
> Upon my lapel called normal. (28–29)

Nellie cannot confront woman (her self) constructively without confronting man constructively anymore than she can emerge into the present without recognizing the past ("I want to face you," 29).

The dimensions of Nellie's marronage are too numerous and shifting to be thoroughly analyzed within the confines of this work. Race, class, gender, and geography define her distance from other characters, but the complex intersection of these factors in cultural confusion effects her psychological separation. Brodber defines both this psychological separation (imaged in the *kumbla*) and escape from marronage as effected by discourse, and this study will focus on this definition.

The narrator cannot properly see her *kumbla* until therapy has advanced to the point that she is almost ready to leave it. Conversely, she cannot leave it until she has actually seen and described it. Nellie defines her *kumbla* first through analogy, but she also defines it through negation. What the *kumbla* is not is as important as what the *kumbla* is. Positive definition got her in; negative definition may get her out. The definition abounds with negators such as *never, in-, neither, un-, not, no, -less,* and *without,* as in the warning, "Your kumbla will not open unless you rip its seams open. It is a round seamless calabash that protects you without caring" (123). Indeed, the warning reads like a manual accompanying or advertising a product. The definition takes on the discourse patterns of a sales pitch. Short simple sentences and sentence fragments in direct address convey such crisp manufacturer's claims as, "Fed simply by breathing! They usually come in white" (123). The voice of the salesman and fabricator breaks off, and the abrupt interruption is an Annancy story.

Annancy, the master fabricator, weaves his escape from strands that are the expectations of the enemy—an intensely satisfying transgression but one in which it is possible to be entangled forever. Readers are never to forget that the master craftsman is a poacher and a liar, and they must see his weave for what it is. Annancy, who spins the white cocoon, is a "protector of his children," like Great Aunt Tia, who teaches her children to hide in their colonial inheritance. She too spins the cocoons that shelter and entrap them. Annancy's advice to his son reminds readers that escape does not lie in the directionless politics of the radical group in the metropolis. Nellie's lover, Cock Robin, is from among them, and when he burns to death she is stranded in an alien terrain that Annancy's predicament recalls: "Not good for making your way home when you can't row well, when you have no light and when you are nervous because you are poaching on another man's property. It was dark as mud which begins to assume a life of its own, to form glistening malarial rainbows of light, to give birth to fireflies. . . . Don't follow no firefly boy. Look inside of yourself and row. Them will los' you" (124). Annancy escapes by pretending subservience, acknowledging incompetence, surrendering dignity for all posterity in his declaration, "I broke, I los', I bow to you. You is King. I just can't make it, can't mek it at all. I bring the children them. All of them. Take them, eat them, work them, anything" (125–26). Of course the sellout is pretense, credible because his opponent is arrogant and susceptible to such flattery as "You is not like me. You is a big man" (126). The opponent expects and thus believes in Annancy's groveling sentimentality: "Love them you know. Poor children but I have pride (And Nancy cried long eye water)." The opponent believes even in Annancy's affection, expressed in a playful diminutive of King Dryhead's name ("Brother Dries," 127).

To save his child from the king, Annancy must juggle the figures and seem to have more than he has so as to give up enough to satisfy the king's greed without losing all. The child must change color. The father must embarrass the inept accountant into confirming the bogus account so as to camouflage his own incompetence. Annancy escapes not only by juggling figures and by playing on the master's greed but by manipulating the henchman's sense of his own inadequacy.

Annancy also pretends to accept and justify his own ill treatment at the hands of the powerful, and in doing so he justifies his own apparent treachery to his son when he explains that he "has come up on hard times or else he would not be doing you this" (130). He makes excuses to posterity for oppression and reviles his children with their ugliness to allay suspicion. But this is psychological manipulation through discursive strategy; it is a use of language as a mechanism for escape. To begin to believe is to be trapped in the device (130).

There are clear similarities between Brodber's approach to feminine dissociation and that of others in the Caribbean. However, Jamaican fiction also offers sharp contrasts between Nellie's fate and that of Antoinette in *Wide Sargasso Sea*. Brodber's presentation of psychological marronage includes isolation by choice—the isolation of escape and camouflage—as well as isolation imposed by others.

In Jamaican fiction, the transgressor often evades or opposes oppression by devious but necessary means, but it is dangerous to inhabit the web indefinitely. For Annancy, escape lies in dissimulative behavior, but such is not the way out for Nellie. In defining Annancy as the slave who survives by rash actions, without giving in to the master, Patrick Taylor (129) refers to Frantz Fanon's psychiatric and sociopolitical writings. Fanon explores "the mode of behavior of the colonized who constantly resist the system of oppression while appearing to submit." Taylor notes that the colonized may internalize the racist stereotype of the bungling/obedient fool and lose themselves in role play as a strategy for survival (132). Indeed, Taylor adds that Annancy tales are not moralistic; ultimately, this slave/trickster is a rebel, like the gunslinging hero, Rhygin, of Michael Thelwell's *The Harder They Come* (Taylor 143, 148–49) or an amoral survivor like GB in Alvin Bennett's *God the Stonebreaker*. Brodber evokes not the veneration of Annancy but an understanding of subversive and evasive action as a phase of history. Nellie must recognize the distinction between roles and reality, between stereotype and integrity, to re-member her self.

The language of narrative in Nellie's Nancy story and throughout the novel is, for the most part, colloquial English, an informal variety of spoken standard. Brodber code shifts to Creole mainly for dialogue, which she represents through selected features. Why is Nellie's re-membering mostly in English? Where is nation language?

Lloyd King sees Alejo Carpentier as violating a major premise and prescription of West Indian criticism in being "seemingly incapable of using the vernacular, Caribbean nation language to explore Caribbean experience and truth." King goes on to identify Carpentier's work as "a singular and curious challenge to a dominant trend of criticism which links the authentic to the vernacular" (41). No one can accuse Brodber of incapacity to use the vernacular. Her selection of English for much of Nellie's re-membering is quite obviously a matter of choice. Nation language must encompass other codes in addition to the Creole to facilitate the code switching necessary for perspectival shift in the Jamaican consciousness. Indeed, code switching is an essential operation of nation language.

Although it is true that this code switching substitutes orality for traditional literary language and transgresses the canonical discourse of imperial texts, code switching to Creole is not all that renders the discourse transgressive. Here as elsewhere in the literature, discontinuity is a strategy for revising colonial history, and this book has referred in passing to a variety of non-traditional discourse types (such as the sales pitch) embedded in Nellie's stream of consciousness. In addition, it is important that the total text does more than convey Nellie's crisis. The text is the crisis because it is the assembly of the many fragments of her disturbing past, and confrontation with these members of her person will alter the rest of her life. To approach this differently, Nellie's crisis is a text. The script as metaphor for life recurs through the text, and indeed, Nellie's crisis is a textually constructed reality because her fragmentation is the result of intercepting pre-texts, or lines that have been laid down for her in advance to determine her behavior and to prescribe or pre-scribe meaning for her life. Nellie's crisis is conveyed through language but also created by language ("Wearing my label called woman. Upon my lapel called normal," 29).

Full analysis of Nellie's life text should thus ideally concentrate not only on what the language of the novel says but on what language does to Nellie. The text records the effects of prescribed behavior: "It is the liberty of foreign students to be strange so walk through the streets with a mop. The script was writing itself" (27). For the great aunt who wove *kumblas* for her progeny, real life was too messy. Tia fabricated life as an ideal, iconic, decontextualized, and hypostatized artifact of predetermined meaning. Nellie's life text is presented to her as pre-scribed by various authoritative figures. The problem is that these different authorities have different agendas—the pre-text of colonialism and the pre-text of the Caribbean radical abroad, the pre-text of race and class division, the pre-text of the sexually exploitative male and the pre-text of a sexually repressive culture. All lay down lines that weave the stereotype of the helplessly worthless woman with which the novel begins: "Yes now. The chile life spoil. Lord take the case! . . . Oh God. Poor chile. But she must have out her lot. . . . Quiet yourself Nellie. You have nothing to do with it or anything else" (8).

More wonderful than what language does to Nellie is what language does for Nellie. Nellie's text is reassembled not through a single voice but dialogically, through interactive voices that decenter the pre-scribed stereotype. Nellie ceases to conform to the stereotype, to live a life of predetermined meaning, when she recognizes herself as a complex, socially constructed reality, a character in history. This realization happens only when she no longer lives in a formal, abstract, virtual world in which real and actual discourse is marginalized.

Caroline Cooper's discussion of oral culture in Jamaica, *Noises in the Blood,* describes modes of resistance to traditional epistemes and focuses in one chapter on a transgressive discourse that flaunts vulgarity. Such resistance inverts power lines but reinforces the assumption that they must exist. Indeed it entrenches stereotypes of superhuman male sexuality and reverses values of racial dominance rather than exploding such values. In contrast to this aspect of oral popular culture in Dansehall, Brodber departs from stereotype to convey fresh vision. Breaking with literary tradition even as she expertly manipulates it, Brodber employs language that is equally political because she too raises issues of power, but her narrator declares her independence of Annancy (a new totem) and her right to select among the varied voices of her re-membered self.

The perspective is that of the moving camera. Nellie tears her way out of her *kumbla* to face reality with "vision extra-sensitive to the sun and blurred without spectacles" (130). The spying glass can be adopted or discarded "but it magnifies like a pair of two-way bi-focal spectacles. You see and feel everything twice as acutely" (131). The short chapter titled "The Spying Glass" provides an explanation of Aunt Becca's dilemma, but it is a flat explanation, ahistorical. The moving camera of remembered past induces Nellie's re-memberment of self.

"The Moving Camera" places the birth of Nellie's great-grandfather in its sociohistorical context alongside the birth of Queen Victoria. The chapter opens by viewing the colony and its insignificant, "poor-white" baby from a remote and superior locus (134). Then it shifts nearer and views the birth from the stance of the baby's parents. Nearer still, it enters the point of view of the infant preternaturally endowed with wisdom expected in a mature man reliving his past—a wisdom and sensitivity that William does not in fact ever develop, for he is repeatedly described as socially blind. The text presents great-grandfather William in terms of negatives, summed up as *unaware*. Hypersensitively sighted and obsessed with the realities of social and racial boundaries, great-grandmother Tia delivers speeches markedly deontic ("You mustn't say bway, you must say bai. Talk like your father," 138). Through the moving-camera approach to her life text, Nellie rediscovers her past and re-members her self.

Postscript: Long Distance and Authenticity of the Voice

In conveying the separation and distance of pivotal characters, late-twentieth-century Jamaican fiction develops a theme of marronage that throws social and historical issues pertinent to Jamaica into new perspective.

The theme of marronage was foreshadowed even in nineteenth-century novels of Jamaican setting. In these earliest texts, Britain is home and civilization for the observant and lonely stranger in the tropical wilderness. In the same period, the fugitive slave flees the savagery of plantation life in native Jamaica for the home shore of Britain. These perspectives emanate from a value system that is Eurocentric, external to Jamaica and to the rest of the Caribbean. Yet, at this time too, an alternative perspective hints at a black consciousness that is not oriented to Britain as center. One black protagonist, Hamel, tantalizes but cannot fully develop.

The outcast persona is central to the Caribbean canon, and Jean Rhys re-creates the multidimensional alienation of a white creole woman native to Jamaica and transshipped to Britain. This character counters some propositions in the imperial text of *Jane Eyre,* but it also reinforces a trend toward the castaway perspective as definitive of Caribbean experience, in this case represented by the Jamaican woman. The developing persona of the outcast prompts the redefinition of civilization on the one hand and both wilderness and barbarity on the other. This redefinition implies a shifting locus for the concept of home. Thus, Rhys rewrites the European construct of the mad creole, retaining the character's Jamaican setting but showing her homelessness even in this setting. This shift in perspective, together with her underlying departure from temporal sequence, subverts the European episteme (cf. Glissant 145; Gikandi 140) and so replaces European historiography with a Caribbean denial that there is a single perspective on truth.

Some Jamaican authors deal with the theme of arrival by setting this arrival on an alien shore, their characters journeying like Rhys's Antoinette from Jamaica to Britain. In such circumstances, rejection by mother Britain may breed madness. Yet the fascination of *foreign* continues unabated. Violence, lunacy, or both (as a consequence of rejection) increasingly appear in the marooned Jamaican consciousness abroad or at home. Jamaican writers convey this social and psychological distance through strategies of discourse. Gerald Prince distinguishes distance, like voice, from perspective, defining distance as the space (temporal, intellectual, moral, or emotional) between the narrator and the characters, events, situations narrated, and narratee (*Dictionary* 22). Keith Green, however, includes distance with other features of perspective as "highlighting the egocentric nature of deixis (the *origo*) and giving prominence to the major deictic category, reference" (126).

In the literary history of Jamaica, narrative perspective has increasingly conveyed the locked-out yet locked-in narrative vision of the island consciousness. Earlier texts looked in at Jamaica from Britain. Rhys too wrote from Britain but also wrote back to Britain, and she wrote out of a Caribbean past and about a Caribbean past, represented by Jamaica. Jamaican authors have looked from Jamaica to Britain and other metropolitan centers and looked back at Jamaica, although some have tried, alternatively, to re-create the mythical past of African heritage. Others have analyzed the heterogeneity of Jamaica itself, shifting between the perspectives of groups alienated from each other within the island. Individual rather than group isolation may express itself through recollections of personal or family history, and this phenomenon has related metaphorically to national and regional history. An alternative narrative stance looks out and back from the modern Atlantic to global history. In John Hearne's *Sure Salvation*, the Jamaican author re-creates British power in a nineteenth-century seascape—a remarkable counter to the beginnings of this literary discourse, in which British authors placed British adventurer heroes in a Jamaican landscape. Perspectival shifts that produce the Jamaican viewpoint take several forms and have varying effects.

In Jamaican literature, as in other Caribbean writing, code shifting is one method of signaling a perspectival shift, and verbal marronage may reinforce the alienation of a speaker. Both literature from and about Jamaica includes but is not limited to texts in Jamaican Creole. It reflects varieties of both Standard and Creole usage as well as a variety of intermediate forms between both poles. The complex linguistic background of Jamaica is perforce a dimension of the Jamaican setting and of characterization in any fiction that is set in Jamaica. In selecting codes for particular purposes, authors reflect attitudes to language, which have undergone considerable change through time. In the history of literary discourse from and about Jamaica, code shifting has increased in ease, frequency, and acceptability. Changing attitudes have gradually reduced contextual restrictions that might inhibit an author from including Creole; yet these attitudes have always invested the inclusion or exclusion of Creole with meaning.[1] Authors convey variables of language attitude in various ways. The earliest writers, such as Cyrus Perkins, concentrate Creole in comic dialogue, but serious dialogue in Creole is now taken for granted in late-twentieth-century writing.

Early writers may indicate Creole speech by metanarrative comment only or include only limited Creole as a token of otherness. Such tokenism may well be necessary for the non-creole writer, such as the author of *Marly*, and is perhaps adequate in such works where the code functions essentially as an index of distance from normative and familiar behavior. Explicitly and implicitly, incomprehensible surroundings are perceived as wilderness. Part of the hero's alienation from civilization is his exposure to uncodified language. An author such as Michael Scott, who achieves fuller and more genuine representation of Creole speech in the nineteenth century, infuses his romance with color and exoticism.

Within British fiction set in Jamaica, the functions of Creole are rigidly constrained, and in early publications Creole occurs freely only in folktales recorded by curious visitors or residents. The most conservative form of the language known is the idiosyncratic speech of Annancy, the most irrepressible outsider of that oral matrix of songs, tales, and beliefs that precedes the literary experience of most Jamaican children. In this disreputable lect, African features (words such as *nyam*, processes such as reduplication, as in *ragga-ragga*, and so on) occupy the most unacceptable level of expression.

Annancy's language is evasive discourse, the code of the outsider. Not only has Annancy, the weaver of schemes, degenerated from Anànse, the West African deity who weaves the world and the fates of men, but his characteristic speech has suffered a comparable fate of pejoration. To this day, in folktales, the language of Annancy sometimes survives distinct from that of its surrounding Creole narration. Narrators explain this difference as *bungo-talk*—a metanarrative comment that reveals common language attitudes— but his speech is in fact archaic Creole (cf. Lalla and D'Costa, *Language* 66–67). The archaisms are popularly explained as testifying to deformity in the speaker (*him tongue tie, clef' palate*). Language, like anything else that falls under his control, becomes twisted and broken as he persists amorally in achieving his own ends. Indeed, Jamaicans dismiss spoiled or troublesome phenomena with the formula, *Is Annancy mek it*. Similarly, at the end of each tale, narrators of Annancy stories traditionally disclaim responsibility for (and approval of) the hero's actions, distancing themselves through another formula: *Jack Mandora, me no want none*. The historical conditions of slavery, that encouraged the emergence of a hero who survives by any means, unhampered by accepted moral codes, explain the unreliability that excludes tricksters such as Annancy from civilized community.

From its earliest history, the Creole that characterizes Annancy's language has been recorded by writers seized of its remoteness from English. The most serious, such as Robert Charles Dallas, include glosses. The amused and curious, such as Thomas Russell, pause for extensive analysis. Others, such as Capt. Hugh Crow, include Creole to authenticate their own breadth of experience and the comradeship between them and their former cargo. Still others quote Creole to indicate the oddity of its speakers. In response to a request from a slave for a coat to make him look *eerie* (comparable to modern Creole *irie*), Lewis toys with the word, "I assured him that he looked quite *eerie* enough already" (201). The comedy that Creole supplies for the nineteenth-century writers is essentially that of distortion.

This widespread categorization of Creole as humorous by virtue of being strange (hence quaint) entrenches, in earlier literary discourse, constraints regarding its more serious use. Similarly, the association of the black speaker with distortion of personality may associate Creole discourse with deception or insincerity (see Madden 2:103, 105–6; Bernard Senior 227–30). The Eurocentric worldview associated with literacy naturally excluded the worldview of Jamaican oracy as a distorted perspective.

Only at the turn of the century does Thomas MacDermot represent the Creole as the speech of characters with whom he is in sympathy and whom he is treating seriously. More and more, current writers include Creole even outside of dialogue to convey thoughts that are part of narrative, and some move to Creole as a medium of narrative for large portions of the discourse. In describing Roger Mais's sensitivity but imperfect control of his own medium, Jean D'Costa points out the challenge occasioned by the wealth of styles available to the Caribbean writer (*Roger Mais* 60).

The choice always implies an attitude. The writer who avoids alternatives to Creole where such alternatives traditionally suggest themselves also conveys a language attitude—perhaps a sort of subtractive bilingualism or refusal to use a code that may seem to conflict with language loyalty. Jamaican discourse takes various forms. Cliff's eclectic fragmented discourse actively and consciously resists normativity in a markedly radical style without extensive Creole narration. The selection of Creole is a successful strategy only if appropriate, and a writer's unswerving adherence to written Standard English may be wholly appropriate even in the most modern literary discourse of Jamaica. After all, Jamaican language includes the formal Standard as well as an informal Standard (laced with semantic nuances that are inescapably Jamaican), the Creole (rural or urban), and intermediate forms. Hearne's linguistic choices are as sociohistorically correct as Winkler's or Brodber's, and they are no less Jamaican.

Yet the definition of standard language in Jamaica requires care. Official status is associated with education and written language, but Creole is no longer exclusively oral versus the codified Standard. With changing attitudes, Creole is now textualized to varying extents from the pole of totally Creole narrative to the pole of token Creole dialogue. Jamaican literary discourse now interweaves oral and literary strategies in what is increasingly recognized as an oral/scribal continuum (cf. Rohlehr, "Literature and the Folk" 68, and Cooper 4).

Even where the Standard excludes obvious localisms, literary language in Jamaica is to some extent culture specific. Shared Caribbean experience and coreference may imply similar points of departure, and shared social knowledge renders the discourse more legible. In addition, words rendered in English orthography may have separate meanings in English and Creole. Thus, interpretation may vary according to the extent of the reader's exposure to Creole.

All of these dimensions throw into new perspective current Caribbean perceptions of *nation language,* a phrase which in regional usage appears to refer almost exclusively to a code that is obviously Creole. However, *nation language* must in an unprejudiced view be more inclusive, covering (for example) lexical items that are deceptively identical in form to those of an English base but conveying other meanings in Creole, especially where the Creole speaker mentally pronounces the word so differently from its international counterpart as to render it unintelligible to the uninitiated. Thus, the literary discourse subverts the imperial code to convey not only the written Standard but oral Creole. Indeed, part of *nation language* must surely be this secret encoding of Creole epistemes under guise of conformity (and with all the advantages of international "legibility")—the most subtle of the linguistic transgressions that constitute the verbal dimension of marronage.

Jamaican literary discourse is heterogeneous not only because it has come to permit and at times to demand Creole but because it continues to maintain Standard English. Writers of Jamaican fiction avoid total alienation of a critical mass of readers by never recording at length an exact representation of Creole. The purpose is to achieve the "faithful record" effect of direct speech in the Creole rather than to replicate speech exactly. In discussing the faithful-record effect, Michael Toolan emphasizes the importance of "a collective and conventional perception of significant differences" as the basis of existence of both a language and a dialect of a language (31). Authors represent Creole in writing by placing a selection of widely recognized features alongside those from the international code, features so familiar in writing as to be unnoticeable to the general reader. In addition, significant mixing of Creole and Standard also occurs through shifts, but this mixing is neither random nor unchecked. Such combination would eventually result in an undifferentiated medium, which would suit no one, as it would merely deplete the total richness of a discourse with so much potential for sensitive manipulation of codes. Hubert Devonish has described the maintenance of autonomy together with rule-governed mixing in Jamaican oral language. Between the options available, writers also make creative but rule-governed choices, which are linked to such factors as setting but also constrained by external factors such as the writer's dependence on international readership.

Literary discourse in Jamaica is mold breaking because it writes back to resist imperial epistemes and because it refuses to do so uncritically, to be bound by rhetoric that has frozen into anti-imperialist or other obsessions. Thus, Hearne inverts imperial history by manipulating its own terms and traditional genres in *The Sure Salvation*. The traditional and the outrageous interweave in *The Lunatic*. In this way Brodber also makes visible, through Standard English intercepted by Creole, the shells that the creole consciousness may weave, shells that are protective but uncaring and from which one must break out to be whole. Annancy's discourse of transgression provides a camouflage for escape and has become comfortable, but it is essential to resist entrapment and to see through deceptive devices that may enforce fixed patterns: "Devious one, don't I know crushed snail when I see it?" (34).

Not all writers select and maintain a point of departure that their readers are likely to share. Some authors construct an unfamiliar and unpredictable perspective, such as that of a lunatic, or select a point of departure generally anathemized, such as that of a slave trader. Others juxtapose conflicting points of departure in their creole characters. Olive Senior, for example, conveys rifts in communication through drift in lexical meaning to reveal intracultural gaps in a fragmenting society.

Current Jamaican writers, such as Hearne, alter generic distinctions between fiction and nonfiction. Such alteration affects perspective because it interferes with attitudes of certainty or uncertainty about events and so challenges assumptions that identify nonfiction with truth. Nonfiction has traditionally textualized the past, but an important development in the Caribbean has been the recharting of the past in fiction, the reconstruction of truth from a Caribbean perspective. Works written to counter imperial discourse tend to fragment narrative by disrupting a temporal line of events to highlight causal connections in a Caribbean view of history. This disturbed linearity denies a holistic vision and presents truth as multifaceted and cumulative. However, a Caribbean vision can itself be subverted. Some Jamaican literary discourse offers alternative (even mutually exclusive) meanings, some of which devalorize assumptions entrenched in Caribbean fiction as a whole and so deconstruct the regional given. In different ways, for example, both Hearne and Brodber debunk stereotypes of exploitation and victimization. Brodber in particular offers constructive alternatives to mutual violation.

Definitive features of Jamaican language separate its literary discourse from other literature in English, despite the constant interchange between Creole and Standard English associated with intertextuality. Such intercepting codes facilitate the expression of alternative worldviews such as those revealed through Aloysius's interchange with the flame-heart tree in *The Lunatic* or those glimpsed in the farm creatures of *Myal*. This juxtaposition of conflicting worldviews suggests that reliability in a narrative consciousness may be relative, fostering multiplicity of meaning. Jamaican discourse demonstrates the intertextuality of Caribbean and imperial texts, the shared knowledge system inevitable in the postcolonial Caribbean that undermines presuppositions of established British texts, and a local independence of entrenched (regional) counterdiscourse. The literary discourse of Jamaican fiction is characteristically dialogic to facilitate adjustment of perspective for accessing different facets of truth. The association of code shifting with perspectival shifts involved in writing back raises the issue of how far intertextuality can be viewed as a (scribal) aspect of Caribbean language contact.

Jamaican literature is distinctive in both its epistemic and its systemic constraints. Its epistemic constraints foster characters that are ex-centric—physically, ideologically, and at times psychologically sundered from normative communities, protagonists claustrophobically confined and stubbornly resistant. What Wilson Harris and Edward Kamau Brathwaite have recognized as geopsychic correlates in Caribbean literature tend to link characters in Jamaican fiction with remote or bounded settings that underscore toughness. In literature where the physical dimensions of marronage are not literally those of a Maroon community, the psychological dimensions of marronage are nevertheless intensely conveyed in the recurrent explorations of the experiences of leaving and being left.

Marronage (physical or psychological) involves a perspective that looks out from a situation that may be temporarily stable but barely so. The present results from discontinuity and dislocation, implies uncertainty, and demands watchfulness. If the locus is temporarily stable, it is often merely a position at which to turn and fight. Although Maroon activity occurred elsewhere in the Caribbean, Jamaica is particularly marked by a history of frequent slave rebellion and two extended Maroon wars. Throughout this history of resistance, rebels survived by becoming one with the mountains, and although early literature set in Jamaica most clearly conveys features of the maroon persona in the folk hero of oral fiction, features of this persona subtextually disrupt imperial themes, even within the British tradition, as in *Hamel*.

The unifying impression of the Maroon experience is one of incredible endurance within a rock-bound interior that is at once a hiding place and a vantage point. The dialectic of withdrawal and rejection complicated by mutual violent pursuit imposes intense emotional reactions. For the maroon persona, negritude produces both stigma and pride and fosters a celebration of tragic history. The physical withdrawal from oppression to an internal fastness lends itself to comparison with an inner landscape of the consciousness that inhabits this setting—to a psychological terrain. The wilderness is of the interior versus that of the civilization beyond. Similarly, the island itself contrasts as wilderness physically constrained and remote from civilizations that are metropolitan and foreign. The maroon and the castaway present different faces of the same phenomenon, except that the maroon is yet more isolated in the mountain wilderness that is itself within the island wilderness.

The physical and psychological fastness is the site for return to ancestral traditions. The theme of marronage in Jamaican literature exposes the ambivalent historicity associated with marooned personae, for the flight of the maroon is prompted by more than an anxiety to escape. Caribbean negritude sought first to return, as Edouard Glissant points out (153). Revalorizing Africa in the Caribbean imagination was to an important extent a reaction against "exacerbated Eurocentricism" as Aimé Césaire explains (Rowell 55, and Gikandi, discussing this reaction, 11). Marronage thus characteristically involves the journey of an elusive, searching, and at times vagrant type, tension-fraught refuge, and persistent effort to return to some submerged and other heritage. The variability of linguistic codes in Jamaica enables marginality to be directly reflected through code choice and shift. The characteristic discontinuity of postcolonial textual structure facilitates subtexts that convey in the selected code alternative, conflicting, or outlandish visions.

Marronage defines not only epistemic but also systemic constraints on Jamaican discourse. In creating a character, a writer may suggest nonconformity or madness and convey uncertainty regarding a speaker's reliability. Loneliness and homelessness are additional facets of exclusion and rejection, so that setting too is isolated, sometimes through the anonymity imposed by the ghetto but quite often by a literal wilderness setting. Point of view, conveyed by deixis and other features of discourse, reinforces insularity and alienation in setting and characterization. Plot tends to highlight causal rather than temporal relations between consecutively presented events, fragmenting the chronological flow of events, disconnecting situations, and reinforcing the speaker's dislocation.

Of these systemic dimensions, marronage most sharply defines characterization, especially as defined by point of view. For example, marronage defines child characters isolated by combined circumstances, which include accidents of skin color. Vic Reid's Toto, the mixed son of the Mau Mau hunter, belongs nowhere. "Wonder whose kid he was," muses the British soldier who discovers his body (*The Leopard* 108). Namba Roy's Tambo is black but albino, rejected by the Maroons, who cling to their African heritage (*Black Albino*). Jean D'Costa's Wuss Wuss, another albino, has a brighter career, leading the other children to safety in the mountains, to an isolated cave that is his home (*Escape to Last Man's Peak*). Most isolated children are less happy because they are products of abandonment—such as Olive Senior's Jacko and Elean Thomas's Putus and Icylane. These characters often turn out to be the adult maroons of the literature, rebellious, spaced-out, even criminal. But some, such as Brodber's Nellie, tear their way out of isolation back into sunlight. Forging a discourse for re-membering involves not only retrieval and reassembly but reconciliation. Polyphonic narrative in Jamaican fiction includes intercepting voices not only of different personae but also of the fragmented individual consciousness that reaches back to the past through a variety of lects. Brodber's re-membering involves an integration of voices.

The relationship between setting and context is crucial in Caribbean discourse and inseparable from characterization. Both setting and the context of fiction associated with Jamaica involve relationships between Jamaica and *foreign* (where *foreign* is northern and metropolitan) and between cultures within Jamaica rather than between Jamaica and the rest of the Caribbean. Spatial relations orient characters to their setting so as to cause these characters to distinguish Jamaica from elsewhere or to distinguish Jamaica as elsewhere. On the whole, both setting and context for this literature lack a sense of Caribbean community. The relationship has been one of parallelism in experience rather than a linkage through interchange.

To explore characterization in Jamaican literature is to assess the orientation of that individual to a community or the distance of the alienated self from the community. Speakers who are unanchored in their spatial or temporal frameworks (strangers, visitors, ghosts, zombies, lunatics, rejects, fugitives) vary in their reliability, leaving room for alternative readings of the events they report. Alternating perspectives, which may be conveyed through intercepting codes, imply a fluidity of truth and produce hierarchy in meaning rather than simple presence or absence of semantic features.

Increasingly, the alienation of Jamaican characters in the literature is so extreme as to constitute dissociation or lunacy. The setting of *The Lunatic* contrasts with the abnormal calm and horror of Hearne's voyage. *The Sure Salvation* is a journey into hell; the island setting of *The Lunatic* is ostensibly a tourist paradise masking madness. Still, in *The Sure Salvation* also, society, surrounded by water and rigidly stratified, reflects a pathological landscape, mind-bending alienation, and disintegration. Rifts between perception and reality appear in the distorted worldviews of individuals as well as in the sociopolitical context of the novel, and deviance is both stylistic as well as thematic, the confrontation of versions presenting textual crises.

The degree of alienation in the marooned persona is thus proportional to physical, ideological, and psychological distance from civilization. Thus, characterization relates closely to setting. The components of meaning that link character with setting appear at first to be binary, for example civilization versus wilderness/savagery, home versus vagrancy, inside versus outside, conformity versus deviance, order/sanity versus disorder/insanity, rule-ordered existence versus anarchy/chaos, and life versus death. Some components actually exist in an implicational hierarchy, which means that the relationships between the components of meaning for a particular term are such that individual possession of one property from the hierarchy entails the possession of others below that property in the hierarchy. Characters in Jamaican settings confront traditional views of civilization in which lack of home tends to imply lack of material possessions, and lack of material possessions tends to entail lack of personal value, worthlessness.

In fact, Jamaican fiction provides characters who lack sets of features that traditionally define civilization. Indeed, varieties of the marooned persona can be identified by sets of such deficits. Even visitors such as Montgomery are distant from a home community and lack permanence in the setting of the novel. Strangers such as Marly are similarly distant from their home community and sensitive to the unfamiliarity of their surroundings. Tricksters such as Roland or Annancy are avoided as unreliable and devoid of truth. Early Eurocentric vision conceives of black characters outside of subservient roles in the social hierarchy as savages, external to refined community, threatening security, lacking history, and lacking a codified language. In the current literature, vagrant lunatics, such as Aloysius, are homeless, derelict, devoid of reason, incapable of acceptable speech, and unable to conform to an ordered lifestyle. Narrators who float in states of dissociation tend to alternate between retrospectivity and prospectivity and so exist outside of the normal passage of time. In extreme cases they approximate zombies, haunting the margins of life and outside of the natural order of existence. These and other varieties of marooned personae, as social rejects, share an overwhelming sense of loss and undergo identity crises.

Jamaican texts induce redefinition of entrenched values by linking setting and characterization to produce new perspectives. The ex-centric character is defined essentially by perspectival features that highlight spatiotemporal, ideological, or psychological orientation or distance. Discourse strategies for such characterization may involve manipulation of deixis and interference with temporal structure, subversions of canonical prescriptions, semantic drift and anomaly, flouting of pragmatic rules, highlighting of thematic role reversals, or shifts between codes.

The coexistence of Jamaican Creole and Jamaican Standard English and the rule-governed variation within and between these distinct codes are as characteristic of modern Jamaican literary discourse as of the oral language. *Nation language*, as far as Jamaica is concerned, is not one extremity of the system but the system as a whole, thus enabling Jamaican discourse to subvert simultaneously both imperial discourse and counterhegemonic discourse that is itself entrenched in a growing Caribbean canon. Code choice in Jamaican literary discourse is linked to plurality of meaning, possible because the presence of new or hitherto unsuspected truths can be conveyed by shifts in discourse to convey the perspective of a dislocated consciousness, the maroon persona. One dimension of this alienated even dissociated consciousness is a verbal marronage in which a quality of separation and resistance is effected by linguistic or narrative strategies.

Mary Louise Pratt argues for a linguistics of contact that will examine structured relations between dominated and dominant rather than utopian models of imagined communities. Such communities, she argues, are based on differences resulting from separation between community and subcommunity ("Linguistic Utopias" 48–56). Yet the orientation of the marooned speaker in Jamaican literature is one of separation, distance, and fragmenting relationship, one of insistent Otherness. The effect of Creole representation, involving as it does a shift from the normativity of universally accepted conventions, is a distancing effect (compare Toolan on reader alienation and lostness in confrontation with dialect, 35–38). Even readers who share the code do so essentially as a medium of speech rather than writing. In the midst of recognition and familiarity, they too may experience the dislocation of a shift from scribal conventions and share with the non-Creole reader at least momentarily the experience of the Other.

The Other (in marronage) is both self and a subcommunity whose code conveys distances rather than affinities. At surface, the struggle of the self takes precedence over that of the subcommunity. The selection of Creole still conveys the distance of its speakers from a dominant community besides emphasizing the speakers' identities within their own groups. At the same time, the self implies the subgroup in conveying features that can be defined areally—by gender, class, or race. The network of fissures within the shipboard community of the *Sure Salvation* and the underlying insanity of local civilization in *The Lunatic* indicate that the dialectic is not between individuality and homogenous normativity but between self (or subgroup) and a community riddled with its own fissures and contradictions, a community that is not itself stereotypical.

In its isolation and confinement the creole consciousness may perceive civilization from a state of mental crisis such as Brodber symbolizes in the *kumbla*, which is semantically related to several familiar images: the room/attic/cabin, the womb/vessel/hold, and the tomb/hole/trap. The facility with which these may be metaphorically applied to the island or the mind intensifies the association of marronage with psychosis.

Similarly, the discourse conveys linkages among greed, lust, exploitation, and commerce and among guilt, stain, and filth. Gendered oppression is one dimension of this dialectic of containment and escape, of exclusion and resistance. But it is also often a metaphor for the struggle of colonized against colonizer and is related to the metaphor of family fragmentation for postcolonial or neocolonial politics. Thus, the discourse redefines civilization (and, by implication, savagery) to reveal the fluidity of truth about power, reason, and responsibility. In so doing the discourse replaces stereotypes of past victimization and exploitation with an indigenous vision of essential humanity in a present for which all are responsible and of an untried shore to which it is possible to bring only native abilities. Even the most guilt-ridden consciousness "stares at the star-drenched, receding horizon as the occasionally adjusted rudder leaves a scarcely curving wake astern under a deeply ploughing stern. All the journeys of his life, the criss-crossing of the globe to which he has beaten with his cargo of invested ambitions, are now forging at twelve knots out of an ever-growing circle to a shore on which he will land with nothing" (*Sure Salvation* 198).

By manipulating perspective, Jamaican literary discourse goes beyond rewriting exploitation and even beyond stripping adventurers to the vulnerability of the human flesh that is their cargo and currency. Jamaican writers force entry into global history, for by the same strategy of alternating perspective, the discourse of the dissociated consciousness disrupts both traditional silences and newer, catchy rhetoric with piercing confrontation between historical periods, far-flung shores, ethnicities, genders and fragmented identities: "But such pain! And I so unprepared for it! . . . I heard a woman screaming until the whole world seemed disturbed" (*The Sure Salvation* 181).

In some fiction, a moving camera perspective reveals the links and gaps between the self and the local community, past and present. In such cases, the balance between the individual's connection with the community and independence of the community may move marronage beyond alienation toward integrity. Through code shifting, Jamaican literary discourse conveys this altered perspective of a marooned consciousness with the strength and resilience for re-membering the self: "Mass Nega mine yourself. Mi smell you dinner but mi no want none. We walk not by your leave or in your shade but with your blessing" (*Jane and Louisa* 147).

Notes

1. The Dimensions of Marronage in Jamaica

1. As noted in the acknowledgments, I am indebted to MELUS, the Society for the Study of Multi-Ethnic Literature of the United States, for permission to draw substantially on "Dungeons of the Soul" for material in the next few paragraphs.

2. This general definition, acceptable to R. A. Hudson (202), differs from W. Labov's restricted use of the term for conscious connections between linguistic and nonlinguistic characterizations. In most instances, observers make these connections quite unconsciously (see Labov 248).

3. P. Werth parodies structuralist obsession with binary oppositions (33–34). Structuralist attempts to arrive at abstract descriptions of an idealized world (*langue*) is taken in this study to be of limited help in analyzing the multicultural language actually used (*parole*) in Caribbean literature.

4. Spatiotemporal perspective is essentially perceptual, equivalent, as Fowler points out, to viewing position in the visual arts, an angle from which the object of representation is seen. Ideological perspective involves a mental rather than physical stance, an attitude to the object represented, and Paul Simpson focuses on this plane of perspective, specifically as it is conveyed by deixis, modality, or transitivity.

2. An Assembly of Strangers: Isolation and British Romanticism in Jamaican Settings of the Nineteenth Century

1. As in chapter 1 (note 1) I am indebted to MELUS for permission to draw on "Dungeons of the Soul" in the following pages.

2. Chapter 7 discusses the relevance of code shifting to perspective and the changes in language attitude reflected in the literary history of Jamaica. The relevance of Creole to social identity in early Jamaica requires investigation. It is clear that Creole was, even then, not rigidly constrained by race or social rank, and variation within racial and social groups is attested (Lalla and D'Costa 98). Consequently, Mufwene argues that decreolization, as structural attrition, is insupportable on the basis of diachronic evidence. The literature indicates the early coexistence of and variation between Creole and Standard English as well as the understanding of Creole by all social classes. Yet uncertain is the degree to which the Creole differed from territory to territory in the anglophone Caribbean in this early period (Lalla and D'Costa 109ff.).

3. Letter from John Aarons to the author, National Library of Jamaica, 1991.

4. Hamel's voicelessness appears to be meaningful in view of the numerous representations of Creole documented for this period. Lalla and D'Costa reconstruct the form of the Creole spoken in Jamaica in the eighteenth and nineteenth centuries and describe attitudes conveyed by observers of that time.

3. The Jamaican Outsider in the Caribbean Canon

1. Analepsis is an anachony that evokes events past, as distinct from prolepsis, which flashes forward to the future. Both are gap-filling devices for recall or anticipation of ellipsis (see Prince, *Dictionary* 5, 77).

4. Leavings

1. Paula Morgan's sensitive and timely exploration of feminine development in Caribbean, African, and black American novels focuses on the black consciousness and so does not linger on *Wide Sargasso Sea*. Morgan's cross-cultural examination orients her to affinities and differences between regions rather than between territories within regions, and her approach and mine are thus, in a sense, complementary.

2. The difficulty of growing up, especially for girls, is an increasingly important theme in Caribbean literature. Several Caribbean writers convey such conflicting pictures of the mental world in their child protagonists, who are at home in the Britain of their fantasies. Gikandi describes Zee Edgell's Beka as "in a state of limbo between an emerging national culture and the colonial situation" (221) and Merle Hodge's Tee as unable to identify with any of the "fetishized voices" of the colonial culture (*Crick, Crack Monkey* 204).

3. An interesting contrast to Maydeen is Grace, the American Quaker heroine of Evan Jones's *Stone Haven*. Grace is conceived of in traditional roles—teacher, wife/sexual partner, mother. Betrayal by her husband isolates her in a wilderness that began as a site for adventure but becomes a trap ("There was no way back. Jamaica that had been her personal proving ground of faith had become a prison," 195).

4. The material in this section of chapter 4 is based largely on a paper titled "Intercultural Communication in 'Country of the One-Eye God,' " first presented at the Conference on West Indian Literature, the University of Guyana, 1992, and used here with permission of *Carib: Journal of the West Indian Association of Commonwealth Literature and Language Studies*.

5. Earlier Jamaican literature celebrated the quests of innumerable small waifs and strays. Left untended following the ravages of an epidemic and fearful of being sent to a labor camp, Jean D'Costa's children of *Escape to Last Man's Peak* search for a locus at which to establish an alternative free community in the mountains. Namba Roy's "sparrows" find that they have exchanged the physical marronage in the mountains where they were born for marronage that is social and psychological (*No Black Sparrows*).

5. Naked into the Storm: Winkler and the Wilderness Within

1. Earl R. Mac Cormac explains metaphor as an evolutionary knowledge process in which new associations generate "expressions that disturb the status quo of ordinary language," and these conceptual alterations often bring about changes in the way the speakers act in the world (149).

2. Two types of multiple meaning can be traced in *The Painted Canoe*. Both distinct senses of homonyms and a generativity of related senses occur. The latter form of multiple meaning includes both literal polysemy, by which the word meaning is modified over a period of language history, and metaphorical meaning. Kittay distinguishes types (121–22), but it is not always easy to identify one form of polysemy from another. Indeed, the point of overlap may be most important, as in *The Painted Canoe*, where the boundary blurs between different meanings of *dark, mad*, and other crucial terms.

3. Much of current Dansehall music celebrates the values of the *gunarch* and the *gundeliero*, including grisly threats of physical cruelty between rival singers. Songs include challenges to "just cross de border" (in "Dominate," by Cutty Ranks) and promises of murder or mutilation, for example, to chop your liver out (in "Cutter," also by Cutty Ranks). Some censorship controls the level of overt violence or explicit sexuality on Jamaican airwaves. Perhaps because of reduced understanding as a result of differences between Creoles of different territories, other areas that import this music are more liberal. In Trinidad, a wide range of explicitly violent music is more freely accessible by radio. In any case, such tapes can be purchased over the counter (sold to any age group) and, until recent legislative steps to control this practice, blared routinely over the sound systems of maxi-taxis that transport children to and from school.

4. Much of the material in this section is taken from "Unmasking Deviance: Theme and Language in Jamaican Fiction" and appears with the permission of the *Journal of West Indian Literature.*

7. Re-Membering the Marooned Consciousness

1. John R. Rickford and Elizabeth Closs-Traugott note the increasing use of Creole in writing to convey genuineness in the voice (252–61), quite apart from faithfulness of the record.

Bibliography

Alleyne, Mike. " 'Blacked Out': Post-Colonial Alienation in Recent Black British Novels." Paper presented at the twelfth annual conference on West Indian literature, University of the West Indies, Mona, Jamaica, 12–14 April 1993.

Allfrey, Phyllis Shand. *The Orchid House*. London: Constable, 1953.

Anderson, Paula Grace. "Jean Rhys' *Wide Sargasso Sea:* The Other Side/'Both Sides Now.' " *Caribbean Quarterly* 28 (1982): 57–65.

Ashcroft, Bill, Gareth Griffiths, and Helen Tiffin. *The Empire Writes Back: Theory and Practice in Post-Colonial Literature*. New York: Routledge, 1989.

Atwood, Margaret. *Surfacing*. London: Virago, 1979.

Baugh, Edward, ed. *Critics on Caribbean Literature*. London: Allen and Unwin, 1978.

Baugh, Edward, and Mervyn Morris, eds. *Progressions: West Indian Literature in the 1970s*. Kingston, Jamaica: Department of English, University of the West Indies, Mona, 1990.

Bennett, Alvin. *God the Stonebreaker*. Caribbean Writers Series, no. 7. London: Heinemann, 1973.

Bennett, Louise. *Annancy and Miss Lou*. Kingston, Jamaica: Sangsters, 1979.

Birbalsingh, Frank. *Passion and Exile: Essays on Caribbean Literature*. London: Hansib, 1988.

Birch, David. *Language, Literature, and Critical Practice: Ways of Analysing Text*. London: Routledge, 1989.

Bolton, W. F., ed. *An Old English Anthology*. London: Arnold, 1963.

Brathwaite, Edward Kamau. "The African Presence in Caribbean Literature." *Daedalus* 103 (Spring 1974): 73–109.

———. "Caribbean Man in Time and Space." *Savacou* 11–12 (1975). Also in *Carifesta Forum: An Anthology of Twenty Caribbean Voices*, ed. John Hearne, 199–208. Kingston: Institute of Jamaica, 1976.

———. "Creative Literature of the British West Indies during the Period of Slavery." *Savacou* 1 (June 1970): 46–73.

Brodber, Erna. *Jane and Louisa Will Soon Come Home*. London: New Beacon Books, 1980.

———. *Myal*. London: New Beacon Books, 1988.

Brontë, Charlotte. *Jane Eyre*. Ed. Q. D. Levis. Harmondsworth, Middlesex: Penguin Books, 1966.

Cameron, Deborah, ed. *The Feminist Critique of Language*. London: Routledge, 1990.

Campbell, Mavis C. *The Maroons of Jamaica, 1655–1796*. Trenton, N.J.: Africa World Press, 1990.

Carew, Jan. "The Caribbean Writer and Exile." *Journal of Black Studies* 8 (1978): 453–75. Also in *Fulcrums of Change: Origins of Racism in the Americas and Other Essays* (Trenton, N.J.: Africa World Press, 1988), 91–114.

Carpentier, Alejo. *The Kingdom of this World*. New York: Alfred A. Knopf, 1957.

———. *The Last Steps*. Trans. Harriet de Onis. New York: Avon Books, 1979.

Cassidy, Frederic G., and Robert LePage. *Dictionary of Jamaican English*. 2d ed. Cambridge: Cambridge University Press, 1980.

Clark, Leslie. "Social Knowledge and Inference Processing in Text Comprehension." In *Inferences in Text Processing*, ed. Gert Rickheit and Hans Strohner, 95–114. Amsterdam: Elsevier, 1985.

Cliff, Michelle. *Abeng*. Trumansburg, N.Y.: Crossing Press, 1984.

———.*The Land of Look Behind*. Ithaca, N.Y.: Firebrand Books, 1985.

———.*No Telephone to Heaven*. New York: Dutton, 1987.

Cobham-Sander, C. Rhonda. "The Creative Writer and West Indian Society." Ph.D. diss., University of St. Andrews, 1981.

———. "Women in Jamaican Literature, 1900–1950." In *Out of the Kumbla: Caribbean Woman and Literature*, ed. C. B. Davies and E. S. Fido, 195–222. Trenton, N.J.: Africa World Press, 1990.

Cooper, Carolyn. *Noises in the Blood: Orality, Gender, and the 'Vulgar' Body of Jamaican Popular Culture*. Warwick University Caribbean Studies. London: Macmillan, 1993.

Crow, Capt. Hugh. *Memoirs*. London: 1830.

Crystal, David. *A Dictionary of Linguistics and Phonetics*. 2d ed. Oxford: Blackwell, 1985.

Cudjoe, Selwyn. *Resistance and Caribbean Literature*. Athens: Ohio University Press, 1980.

Dallas, Robert Charles. *The History of the Maroons*. 2 vols. London: Longman and Rees, 1803.

Dance, Daryl Cumber. *Fifty Caribbean Writers: A Bio-Bibliographical Critical Sourcebook*. Westport, Conn.: Greenwood Press, 1986.

Davies, Carol Boyce, and Elaine Savory Fido, eds. *Out of the Kumbla: Caribbean Woman and Literature*. Trenton, N.J.: Africa World Press, 1990.

Dawes, Neville. *The Last Enchantment*. London: MacGibbon and Kee, 1960.

D'Costa, Jean. *Escape to Last Man's Peak*. London: Longman, 1975.

———. *Roger Mais: The Hills Were Joyful Together and Brother Man*. Critical Studies of Caribbean Writers, ed. Mervyn Morris. London: Longman, 1978.

D'Costa, Jean, and Barbara Lalla, eds. *Voices in Exile: Jamaican Texts of the Eighteenth and Nineteenth Centuries*. Tuscaloosa: University of Alabama Press, 1989.

de Certeau, Michel. *The Writing of History*. Trans. Tom Conley. New York: Columbia University Press, 1988.

De Lisser, Herbert G. *Jane's Career: A Story of Jamaica*. London: Methuen, 1914. Reprint. London: Heinemann, 1972.

Devonish, Hubert. "On the Existence of Autonomous Language Varieties in 'Creole Continuum Situations.' " Paper presented at the biennial conference of the Society for Caribbean Linguistics, Cave Hill, Barbados, 1992.

Drayton, Geoffrey. *Christopher*. London: Collins, 1959.

Eagleton, Terry. *Literary Theory: An Introduction*. London: Blackwell, 1983.

Edgell, Zee. *Beka Lamb*. London: Heinemann, 1982.

Edwards, Bryan. *The History, Civil and Commercial, of the British Colonies in the West Indies*. 2d ed. 2 vols. London: Stockdale, 1794.

Elam, Keir. *The Semiotics of Theatre and Drama*. London: Routledge, 1980.

Fanon, Frantz. *The Wretched of the Earth*. Trans. Constance Farrington. New York: Grove Press, 1968.

Fine, Gary Alan. "Rumours and Gossiping." In *Handbook of Discourse Analysis*, ed. Teun van Dijk 3:223–37. London: Academic Press, 1985.

Fishman, J. A. "Domains and the Relationship between Micro and Macro-Sociolinguistics." In *Directions in Sociolinguistics: The Ethnography of Communication*, ed. J. J. Gumperz and D. H. Hymes, 435–53. New York: Holt, Rinehart, and Winston, 1972.

Fleischman, Suzanne. *Tense and Narrativity: From Medieval Performance to Modern Fiction*. Austin: University of Texas Press, 1990.

Fowler, Roger. *Linguistic Criticism*. Oxford: Oxford University Press, 1986.

———. *Linguistics and the Novel*. London: Methuen, 1977.

———. "Power." In *Handbook of Discourse Analysis*, ed. Teun van Dijk, 4:61–82. London: Academic Press, 1985.

Furst, Lillian. *The Contours of European Romanticism*. London: Macmillan, 1979.

Frye, Northrop, *Anatomy of Criticism: Four Essays*. Princeton, N.J.: Princeton University Press, 1957.

Gass, William H. "The Vicissitudes of the Avant-Garde." In *Criticism in the Twilight Zone: Perspectives on Literature and Politics*, ed. Danuta Zadworna-Fjellestad, 87–100. Stockholm: Almgvist and Wiksell International, 1990.

Gikandi, Simon. *Writing in Limbo: Modernism and Caribbean Literature*. Ithaca, N.Y.: Cornell University Press, 1992.

Gilbert, Sandra M., and Susan Gubar. "Sexual Linguistics: Gender, Language, Sexuality." *New Literary History* 16 (1984–85): 515–43.

———. *The Madwoman in the Attic: The Woman Writer and the Nineteenth-Century Literary Imagination*. New Haven, Conn.: Yale University Press, 1979.

Glissant, Edouard. *Caribbean Discourse: Selected Essays*. Trans. J. Michael Dash. Charlottesville: University Press of Virginia, 1989.

Grant, Jane W. "The Literature of Exile." M.Phil. diss., University of Essex, 1979.

Green, Keith. "Deixis and the Poetic Persona." *Language and Literature* 1 (1992): 121–34.

Greenfield, Stanley B., and Daniel G. Calder. *A New Critical History of Old English Literature*. New York: New York University Press, 1986.

Grice, H. P. "Logic and Conversation." In *Syntax and Semantics 3: Speech Acts*, ed. P. Cole and J. Morgan, 41–58. London: Academic Press, 1975.

Griffiths, Gareth. *A Double Exile: African and West Indian Writing between Two Cultures*. London: Marion Boyars, 1978.

Hall, Joan H., Nick Doane, and Dick Ringler, eds. *Old English and New: Studies in Language and Linguistics in Honor of Frederic G. Cassidy*. New York: Garland, 1992.

Hamel, the Obeah Man. 2 vols. London: Hunt and Clarke, 1827.

Hamley, Col. William G. *Captain Clutterbuck's Champagne: A West Indian Reminiscence*. Edinburgh and London: Blackwood, 1862.

Harris, Leonie. "Myths in West Indian Consciousness." In *Progressions: West Indian Literature in the 1970s*, ed. Edward Baugh and Mervyn Morris, 207–15. Kingston, Jamaica: Department of English, University of the West Indies, Mona, 1990.

Harris, Wilson. *The Secret Ladder*. London: Faber and Faber, 1963.

———. *The Womb of Space: The Cross-Cultural Imagination.* Westport, Conn.: Greenwood Press, 1983.

Harrison, Nancy R. *Jean Rhys and the Novel as Woman's Text.* Chapel Hill: University of North Carolina Press, 1988.

Hassan, Ihab. "Ideology, Theory, and the Self: Toward an Independent Criticism." In *Criticism in the Twilight Zone,* ed. Danuta Zadworna-Fjellestad, 1–15. Stockholm: Almgvist and Wiksell International, 1990.

Hawkes, Terence. *Structuralism and Semiotics.* London: Methuen, 1977.

Hearne, John, ed. *Carifesta Forum: An Anthology of Twenty Caribbean Voices.* Kingston: Institute of Jamaica, 1976.

———. *The Sure Salvation.* London: Faber and Faber, 1981.

Hemmerechts, Kristien. *A Plausible Story and Plausible Way of Telling It: A Structuralist Analysis of Jean Rhys's Novels.* New York: Peter Lang, 1987.

Henkel, Jacqueline. "Linguistic Models and Recent Criticism: Transformational Generative Grammar as Literary Metaphor." *PMLA* 105 (1990): 448–63.

Hodge, Merle. *Crick, Crack Monkey.* 1970. Reprint. Oxford: Heinemann, 1981.

———. *For the Life of Laetitia.* New York: Farrar Straus Giroux, 1993.

Hoffman, Ludger. "Intercultural Writing: A Pragmatic Analysis of Style." In *The Taming of the Text,* ed. Willie Pan Peer, 152–75. London: Routledge, 1988.

Hudson, R. A. *Sociolinguistics.* Cambridge: Cambridge University Press, 1980.

Hurston, Zora Neale. *Their Eyes Were Watching God.* 1937. Reprint. New York: Harper and Row, 1990.

James, C. L. R. *Beyond a Boundary.* New York: Pantheon, 1983.

James, Wilson. *The Romantic Heroic Ideal.* Baton Rouge: Louisiana State University Press, 1982.

Johnson, Lemuel A. "A-beng: (Re)calling the Body in(to) Question." In *Out of the Kumbla: Caribbean Woman and Literature,* ed. C. B. Davies and E. S. Fido, 111–42. Trenton, N.J.: Africa World Press, 1990.

Jones, Evan. *Stone Haven.* Kingston: Institute of Jamaica Publications Ltd., 1993.

King, Lloyd. *Toward a Caribbean Literary Tradition.* St. Augustine, Trinidad: Multi-Media Production Centre, University of the West Indies, 1993.

Kittay, Eva Feder. *Metaphor: Its Cognitive Force and Linguistic Structure.* Oxford: Clarendon Press, 1987.

Kloepfer, Deborah Kelly. *The Unspeakable Mother: Forbidden Discourse in Jean Rhys and H. D.* Ithaca, N.Y.: Cornell University Press, 1989.

The Koromantyn Slave: or West India Sketches. London: Hatchard, 1823.

Kristeva, Julia. *Desire in Language: A Semiotic Approach to Literature and Art.* Trans. Alice Jardine, Thomas Gora, and Léon Roudiez, ed. Léon S. Roudiez. Oxford: Blackwell, 1980.

———. "Women's Time." *Signs* 7 (1981): 13–35.

Labov, W. *Sociolinguistic Patterns.* Philadelphia: University of Pennsylvania Press, 1972.

Lalla, Barbara. "Black Laughter: Foundations of Irony in the Earliest Jamaican Literature." *Journal of Black Studies* 20 (1990): 414–25.

———. "Discourse of Dispossession: Ex-centric Journeys of the Un-living in *Wide Sargasso Sea* and the Old English *Wife's Lament.*" *Review of International English Literature* 24 (1993): 55–72.

———. "Dungeons of the Soul: Frustrated Romanticism in Eighteenth to Nineteenth Century Literature of Jamaica." *Multi-Ethnic Literature of the United States*. Forthcoming.

———. "Fe Tek Bad Ting Mek Juok." Review of Caroline Cooper, *Noises in the Blood: Orality, Gender, and the 'Vulgar' Body of Jamaican Popular Culture. Journal of Caribbean History*. Forthcoming.

———. "Intercultural Communication in 'Country of the One-Eye God.' " *Carib: Journal of the West Indian Association for Commonwealth Literature and Language Studies*. Forthcoming.

———. "A Sociolinguistic Approach to Critical Analysis in the Caribbean." Paper presented at the ninth biennial conference of the Society for Caribbean Linguistics, University of the West Indies, Cave Hill, Barbados, August 1992.

———. "Unmasking Deviance: Theme and Language in Jamaican Fiction." *Journal of West Indian Literature*. Forthcoming.

———. "Word-Mesh: Dimensions of Change in the Formation of a Creole Lexicon." In *Old English and New: Studies in Language and Linguistics in Honor of Frederick G. Cassidy*, ed. Joan H. Hall, Nick Doane, and Dick Ringler, 127–42. New York: Garland, 1992.

Lalla, Barbara, and Jean D'Costa. *Language in Exile: Three Hundred Years of Jamaican Creole*. Tuscaloosa: University of Alabama Press, 1990.

Lamming, George. *The Emigrants*. London: Michael Joseph, 1954.

———. *In the Castle of My Skin*. New York: Schocken, 1983.

———. *Natives of My Person*. New York: Holt, Rinehart, and Winston, 1972.

———. *The Pleasures of Exile*. London: Allison and Busby, 1984.

———. *Season of Adventure*. London: Allison and Busby, 1979.

———. *Water with Berries*. London: Longman Caribbean, 1971.

Lanser, Susan Snider. *The Narrative Act: Point of View in Fiction*. Princeton, N.J.: Princeton University Press, 1981.

Lench, Elinor. "The Wife's Lament: A Poem of the Living Dead." *Comitatus* 1 (December 1970): 3–23.

LePage, Robert, and Andrée Tabouret-Keller. *Acts of Identity: Creole-Based Approaches to Language and Ethnicity*. Cambridge: Cambridge University Press, 1985.

Leslie, Charles. *A New History of Jamaica*. Dublin: Nelson, 1791.

Levin, Richard. "The Poetics and Politics of Bardicide." *PMLA* 105 (May 1990): 491–504.

Lewis, Gordon K. *Main Currents in Caribbean Thought: The Historical Evolution of Caribbean Society in Its Ideological Aspects, 1492–1900*. Baltimore: Johns Hopkins University Press, 1983.

Lewis, Matthew G. *Journal of a West India Proprietor*. London: Murray, 1834.

Liddell, Janice Lee. "The Narrow Enclosure of Motherdom/Martyrdom: A Study of Gatha Randall Barton in Sylvia Wynter's *The Hills of Hebron*." In *Out of the Kumbla: Caribbean Woman and Literature*, ed. C. B. Davies and E. S. Fido, 321–30. Trenton, N.J.: Africa World Press, 1990.

Long, Edward. *The History of Jamaica*. 3 vols. London: Lowndes, 1774.

Lubbock, Percy. *The Craft of Fiction*. London: Jonathan Cape, 1965.

Mac Cormac, Earl R. *A Cognitive Theory of Metaphor*. Cambridge, Mass.: MIT Press, 1985.

MacDermot, Thomas. *Becka's Buckra Baby*. Kingston: Gleaner Co., 1930.

McKay, Claude. *Banana Bottom*. New York: Harper and Brothers, 1933.

Madden, Richard Robert. *A Twelvemonth Residence in the West Indies*. 2 vols. London: James Cochrane, 1835.

Mais, Roger. *Black Lightning*. London: Jonathan Cape, 1955.

———. *Brother Man*. London: Heinemann, 1974.

Marly, or, The Life of a Planter in Jamaica. 2d ed. Glasgow: Printed for R. Griffin, 1828.

Marshall, Paule. *Praisesong for the Widow*. New York: Putnam's, 1983.

———. *Selected Poems*. New York: Bookman, 1953.

Milne-Home, Pamela. *Mamma's Black Nurse Stories: West Indian Folklore*. Edinburgh: Blackwood, 1890.

Milroy, Leslie. *Language and Social Networks*. Oxford: Basil Blackwell, 1980.

Milroy, Leslie, and S. Margrain. "Vernacular Language Loyalty and Social Networks." *Belfast Working Papers in Language and Linguistics* 3 (1978): 1–58.

Moi, Toril. "Feminist Literary Criticism." In *Modern Literary Theory*, 2d ed., ed. Ann Jeferson and David Robey, 204–21. London: Batsford, 1986.

———. *Sexual/Textual Politics: Feminist Literary Theory*. London: Methuen, 1985.

Montgomery; or, the West Indian Adventure. A Novel by a Gentleman Resident in the West Indies. 3 vols. Kingston: *Kingston Chronicle*, 1812–13.

Moore, Gerald. *The Chosen Tongue: English Writing in the Tropical World*. London: Longmans, 1969.

Moreton, J. B. *West India Customs and Manners*. 2d ed. London: Parsons, 1793.

Morgan, Paula. "A Cross-Cultural Study of the Black Female Authored Novel of Development." Ph.D. diss., University of the West Indies, 1994.

Nebeker, Helen. *Jean Rhys, Woman in Passage: A Critical Study of the Novels of Jean Rhys*. Montreal: Eden Press Woman's Publications, 1981.

Nelson-McDermott, Catherine. "Myal-ing Criticism: Beyond Colonising Dialectics." *Review of International English Literature* 24 (October 1993): 53–67.

Nemoianu, Virgil. *The Taming of Romanticism: European Literature and the Age of Biedermeier*. Cambridge, Mass.: Harvard University Press, 1984.

Nugent, Lady Maria. *Lady Nugent's Journal of Her Residence in Jamaica from 1801 to 1805*. Ed. Philip Wright. Kingston: Institute of Jamaica, 1966.

O'Callaghan, Evelyn. "Interior Schisms Dramatised: The Treatment of the 'Mad' Woman in the Work of Some Female Caribbean Novelists." In *Out of the Kumbla: Caribbean Woman and Literature*, ed. C. B. Davies and E. S. Fido, 89–109. Trenton, N.J.: Africa World Press, 1990.

O'Gorman, Pamela. "An Eighteenth-Century Jamaican Oratorio." *Jamaica Journal* 22 (November 1989–January 1990): 41–45; 23 (February–April 1990): 14–19.

Orwell, George. *Animal Farm*. 1951. Reprint. London: Longman, 1964.

Paquet, Pouchet. *The Novels of George Lamming*. London: Heinemann, 1982.

Patterson, H. Orlando. *An Absence of Ruins*. London: Hutchinson, 1967.

———. *Children of Sisyphus*. London: New Authors, 1964.

———. *Slavery and Social Death: A Comparative Study*. Cambridge: Cambridge University Press, 1982.

———. *The Sociology of Slavery: An Analysis of the Origins, Development, and Structure of Negro Slave Society in Jamaica*. London: Granada, reprinted for Sangster's Book Stores Ltd., Jamaica, 1973.

Perkins, Cyrus. "Busha's Mistress; or, Catherine the Fugitive." *Daily Telegraph and Guardian*, 28 and 29 September 1911. On file, National Library of Jamaica.

Pollard, Velma. *Considering Woman*. London: Women's Press, 1989.

Pratt, Mary Louise. "Linguistic Utopias." In *The Linguistics of Writing*, ed. N. Fabb, et al., 48–66. New York: Methuen, 1987.

———. *Toward a Speech Act Theory of Literary Discourse*. Bloomington: Indiana University Press, 1977.

Price, Richard. *Maroon Societies: Rebel Communities in the Americas*. New York: Anchor, 1973.

Prince, Gerald. *Dictionary of Narratology*. Lincoln and London: University of Nebraska Press, 1987.

———. *Narratology: The Form and Functioning of Discourse*. Berlin: Mouton, 1982.

Puri, Shalini. "An 'Other' Realism: Erna Brodber's *Myal*." *Review of International English Literature* 24 (1993): 95–115.

Ramchand, Kenneth. *The West Indian Novel and Its Background*. London: Faber and Faber, 1970.

Reid, Capt. Mayne. *The Maroon*. 3 vols. London: Hurst and Blackett, 1862.

Reid, Vic. *The Leopard*. Caribbean Writers Series 18. London: Heinemann, 1980.

———. *New Day*. 1949. Reprint. Caribbean Writers Series 4. London: Heinemann, 1973.

Rhys, Jean. *Wide Sargasso Sea*. Harmondsworth, Middlesex: Penguin, 1968.

Rickford, John R. *Dimensions of a Creole Continuum: History, Texts, and Linguistic Analysis of Guyanese Creole*. Stanford, Calif.: Stanford University Press, 1987.

Rickford, John R., and Elizabeth Closs-Traugott. "Symbol of Powerlessness and Degeneracy, or Symbol of Solidarity and Truth? Paradoxical Attitudes towards Pidgins and Creoles." In *The English Language Today*, ed. S. Greenbaum, 252–61. Oxford: Pergamon Press, 1985.

Riley, Joan. *The Unbelonging*. London: Women's Press, 1985.

Robinson, Carey. *The Fighting Maroons of Jamaica*. Kingston, Jamaica: Collins and Sangster, 1969.

———. *The Iron Thorn*. Kingston, Jamaica: Kingston Publishers, 1993.

Rohlehr, Gordon. "Articulating a Caribbean Aesthetic: The Revolution in Self-Perception." In *My Strangled City and Other Essays*, 1–16. Port of Spain, Trinidad: Longman, 1992.

———. "The Folk in Caribbean Literature." *Tapia Literary Supplement*, December 17, 1972, 7–9, 13–14.

———. "Literature and the Folk." In *My Strangled City and Other Essays*, 52–85. Port of Spain, Trinidad: Longman, 1992.

Ross, Frederick Stead, and Thomas Holderness. *A Glossary of Words Used in Holderness and in the East-Riding of Yorkshire*. 1877. Reprint. English Dialect Society Series C, no. 16. Vaduz: Kraus, 1965.

Ross, George. Diary. The Library of Fourah Bay College, Free Town, Sierra Leone.

Rowell, Charles. "It Is through Poetry That One Copes with Solitude: An Interview with Aimé Césaire." *Callaloo* 12 (Winter 1989): 48–67.

Roy, Namba. *Black Albino*. London: Longman, 1961.

———. *No Black Sparrows*. London: Heinemann, 1989.

Russell, Thomas. *The Etymology of Jamaican Grammar, by a Young Gentleman*. Kingston, Jamaica: M. DeCordova, MacDougall, 1868.

Salkey, Andrew. *Come Home Malcolm Heartland*. London: Hutchinson, 1976.

———. *A Quality of Violence*. 1959. Reprint. London: New Beacon Books, 1978.

——. *Return to An Autumn Pavement*. London: Hutchinson, 1960.
Saunders, David. "Copyright, Obscenity, and Literary History." *English Literary History* 57 (1990): 431–44.
Schuler, Monica. *"Alas, Alas, Kongo": A Social History of Indentured African Immigration into Jamaica, 1841–1865*. Baltimore: Johns Hopkins University Press, 1980.
Scott, Michael. *Tom Cringle's Log*. 2 vols. 1833. Reprint. London: Gibbings, 1894.
Searle, J. R. *Expression and Meaning*. Cambridge: Cambridge University Press, 1979.
Senior, [Bernard Martin]. *Jamaica as It Was, as It Is and as It May Be*. London: T. Hurst, 1835.
Senior, Olive. *Arrival of the Snake Woman and Other Stories*. London: Longman Caribbean, 1989.
——. *Summer Lightning*. London: Longman Caribbean, 1986.
Shakespeare, William. *King Lear*. In the Arden Shakespeare. London: Methuen, 1964.
A Short Journey in the West Indies. 2 vols. London: Murray and Forbes, 1790.
Simpson, Paul. *Language, Ideology, and Point of View*. London: Routledge, 1993.
SISTREN. *Lionheart Gal*, ed. Honor Ford Smith. London: Woman's Press, 1986.
Slemon, Stephen. "Modernism's Last Post." *Review of International English Literature* 20 (1989): 3–17.
Staley, Thomas. *Jean Rhys: A Critical Study*. London: Macmillan, 1979.
Stevens, John, and Ruth Waterhouse. *Literature, Language, and Change: From Chaucer to the Present*. Interface Series. London: Routledge, 1990.
Taylor, Patrick. *The Narrative of Liberation: Perspectives on Afro-Caribbean Literature, Popular Culture, and Politics*. Ithaca, N.Y.: Cornell University Press, 1989.
Thelwell, Michael. *The Harder They Come*. London: Pluto, 1980.
Thomas, Elean. *The Last Room*. London: Virago Press, 1992.
Thorpe, Marjorie. "Beyond the Sargasso: The Significance of the Presentation of the Woman in the West Indian Novel." Ph.D. diss., Queen's University, Kingston, Ont., 1975.
Toolan, Michael. "The Signification of Representing Dialect in Writing." *Language and Literature* 1 (1992): 29–46.
Trowbridge, Ada Wilson. "Negro Customs and Folk Stories of Jamaica." *Journal of American Folklore* 9 (1896): 279–87.
Udal, J. A. "Obeah in the West Indies." *Folklore* 26 (1827): 253–95.
van Dijk, Teun, ed. *Handbook of Discourse Analysis*. 4 vols. London: Academic Press, 1985.
Walcott, Derek. *In a Green Night*. London: Jonathan Cape, 1962.
——. "The Muse of History." In *Carifesta Forum: An Anthology of Twenty Caribbean Voices*, ed. John Hearne, 111–28. Kingston: Institute of Jamaica, 1976.
——. *The Star-Apple Kingdom*. New York: Farrar Straus Giroux, 1979.
Walker-Johnson, Joyce. "*Myal*: Text and Context." *Journal of West Indian Literature* 5 (1992): 48–64.
Warner-Lewis, Maureen. "Language Use in West Indian Literature." In *History of Caribbean Literatures*. Amsterdam: International Comparative Literature Association, forthcoming.
——. "Mask of the Devil: Perverse Artistic Energy in Caribbean Literature."

Paper presented at the tenth annual conference on West Indian Literature, University of the West Indies, St. Augustine, Trinidad, 1991.

Watts, Margaret, ed. *Washer Woman Hangs Her Poems in the Sun*. Port of Spain, Trinidad: Watts, 1990.

Werth, P. "Roman Jacobson's Verbal Analysis of Poetry." *Journal of Linguistics* 12 (1976): 21–74.

Wilson, Elizabeth. " 'Le voyage et l'espace close': Island and Journey as Metaphor: Aspects of Women's Experiences in the Works of Francophone Caribbean Woman Novelists." In *Out of the Kumbla: Caribbean Woman and Literature*, ed. C. B. Davies and E. S. Fido, 45–57. Trenton, N.J.: Africa World Press, 1990.

Winkler, Anthony. *The Great Yacht Race*. Kingston, Jamaica: Kingston Publishers, 1992.

———. *The Lunatic*. Kingston, Jamaica: Kingston Publishers, 1987.

———. *The Painted Canoe*. Kingston, Jamaica: Kingston Publishers, 1983.

Wyke, Clement H. *Sam Selvon's Dialectal Style and Fictional Strategy*. Vancouver: University of British Columbia, 1991.

Wynter, Sylvia. "Afterword—Beyond Miranda's Meanings: Un/silencing the 'Demonic Ground' of Caliban's Woman." In *Out of the Kumbla: Caribbean Woman and Literature*, ed. C. B. Davies and E. S. Fido, 355–72. Trenton, N.J.: Africa World Press, 1990.

———. *The Hills of Hebron*. London: Jonathan Cape, 1962.

———. "Talk about a Little Culture." In *Carifesta Forum: An Anthology of Twenty Caribbean Voices*, ed. John Hearne, 129–37. Kingston: Institute of Jamaica, 1976.

Zak, William F. *Sovereign Shame: A Study of King Lear*. Lewisburg, Pa.: Bucknell University Press, 1984.

Index

About the Author

Barbara Lalla is a senior lecturer in the Department of Language and Linguistics at the University of the West Indies. She received her B.A. and her Ph.D. from the University of the West Indies.